D0927936

WITHDRAWN

Still Following Percy

Still Following Percy

Lewis A. Lawson

University Press of Mississippi
Jackson

Library of Congress Cataloging-in-Publication Data

Lawson, Lewis A.
    Still following Percy / Lewis A. Lawson.
        p.   cm.
    Includes bibliographical references and index
    ISBN 0-87805-826-5 (cloth : alk. paper)
    1. Percy, Walker, 1916–   —Criticism and interpretation.
    2. Percy, Walker, 1916–   —Knowledge—Psychology.   Regression
    (Psychology) in literature.   4. Loss (Psychology) in literature.
    5. Psychoanalysis and literature.   I. Title.
    PS3566.E6912Z743   1995
    813'.54—dc20   95-16820
                                                                     CIP

British Library Cataloging-in-Publication data available

CONTENTS

Contents

PREFACE

I first began following Percy when I read *The Moviegoer* (1961) the year after it was published. The next few years, I'd read a few pages now and then, as a break from grading freshman themes. This paragraph was a favorite:

> Evening is the best time in Gentilly. There are not so many trees and the buildings are low and the world is all sky. The sky is a deep bright ocean full of light and life. A mare's tail of cirrus cloud stands in high from the Gulf. High above the Lake a broken vee of ibises points for the marshes; they go suddenly white as they fly into the tilting salient of sunlight. Swifts find a windy middle reach of sky and come twittering down so fast I think at first gnats have crossed my eyelids. In the last sector of apple green a Lockheed Connie lowers from Mobile, her running lights blinking in the dusk. Station wagons and Greyhounds and diesel rigs rumble toward the Gulf Coast, their fabulous tail-lights glowing like rubies in the darkening east (*M* 73).[1]

That snapshot of the Lockheed Connie always got me, for I had worked on the flight line in a Connie squadron in the Navy, watching each dusk for months as one of our Connies back from Japan landed against a background even more exotic than New Orleans, *mauka* Oahu. Yet I had never been struck by her avian gracefulness until

---

1. Walker Percy, *The Moviegoer*. New York: Noonday, 1967. References for the five subsequent novels are in each case to the Farrar trade edition. References to the novels will be incorporated into the text as: *The Moviegoer, M; The Last Gentleman, LG; Love in the Ruins, LR; Lancelot, L; The Second Coming, SC; The Thanatos Syndrome, TS.*

Preface

Walker Percy hung her in the sky—as a Constellation ought to be—
with the ibises and swifts. When *The Last Gentleman* (1966) was published, I realized that I was like Will Barrett in front of the Velázquez
at the Metropolitan Museum: I needed someone—who else but?—
to see for me and teach me the word.

In time I got no respite from freshman themes even by such a
snapshot as this one of Sharon Kincaid, in which Percy mixes metaphysical conceit with mock-medical description: "An amber droplet
of Coca-Cola meanders along her thigh, touches a blond hair, distributes itself around the tiny fossa" (*M* 95). If Donne could have his flea,
couldn't Percy have his droplet? When *Love in the Ruins* (1971) was
published, I used these snapshots of Moira Schaffner as an increased
dosage against instructor's ennui:

> The golden down on her forearm is surprisingly thick. I turn her arm
> over and kiss the sweet salty fossa where the blood beats like a thrush's
> throat. (*LR* 252) I suck the cold-warm flesh of her forearm covered by
> long whorled down. The fine hair rises to my mouth and makes a skein
> like the tiny ropes that bound Gulliver. (*LR* 256) Her golden deltoid curves
> in a single strong arc, a whorl of down marking its insertion. Now she
> turns a page and supinates her forearm to hold the spine of the magazine:
> down plunges the tendon into the fossa at her elbow. Sweet fossa. I kiss it.
> (*LR* 346)

In desperation I started hiding myself from those freshman themes
in the reference section of the library. To give myself a look of seri-
ousness I would appear to study a bibliography, not the *PMLA* bibliography—which has a certain Augean aroma—but a bibliography as
far afield as I was able to comprehend. There was a limit to my
known world; the Alcove of Science and Technology represented my
Pillars of Hercules: I never sailed through them.

Everytime I looked in a bibliography I had the feeling that Percy
was following me. Citations of his essays lurked in the Philosophy,
Religion, and Psychology Alcove, haunted the Arts and Humanities
Alcove, and even occasionally whistled around the Aeolian Alcove,
Social Sciences. Now I had always regarded a library as a numinous
place in which serendipity might someday descend upon me. So
when two or three of these citations had so winsomely revealed

themselves, I suspected that Clotho Fate, whom all the boys wanted to date (prominent local family), was winking at me, ready to spin my thread. I looked for other Percy essays and read the ones I had already found. I started reading the books necessary for any kind of adequate response to Percy's essays, to discover that I had encountered another of Hercules' labors. No sooner would I read one book than, Hydra-like, two more would appear in its place.

Soon after, I received another fateful gift, literally tossed at my feet like a golden apple, so that I had to pick it up or fall over it, off the front stoop. The *Washington Post Book Week* of December 25, 1966, contained Percy's brief article "From Facts to Fiction," which confirmed my intuition that his essays and his fiction were but different ways of telling the same story. The article made him sound approachable, so I wrote to ask if I had found all his essays. He told me of two that I had missed (their citations were probably in the ultima Thule Alcove). I started thinking about what became "Walker Percy's Indirect Communications," not published until 1969, delayed so that I could also discuss *The Last Gentleman,* which had by then been published.

Succeeding at that essay fated me to dedicate my theme-free time to Walker Percy's writing. In short, I developed an obsession, which was diagnosed later by a reviewer of a grant proposal invited by NEH: "This man is not a critic but a cultist." The doctors at NEH offered me no hope—and no grant. My hopeless condition hasn't changed; neither has theirs. Succeeding at that essay also enticed me to look at the personality behind and within the writing in a certain way for quite a long time. Knowing that Percy was a fifty-year-old physician with a leaning toward pathology and psychiatry and having struggled with modest success to grasp his articles about existentialism, semiotics, psychiatry, and some subjects that defied easy labeling, I had a very definite picture of the man. When he read the manuscript of "Walker Percy's Indirect Communications," the subject remarked: "While I am thinking of it, Percy in the article sounds better than Dr. Percy—who sounds a bit like the kindly Dr. Christian who took time off from medicine to edify his fellow humans." In medical school the moviegoing Percy probably saw too many Dr. Christian movies, for even Jean Hersholt, the actor who played the doctor-edifier, was the victim of his spleen. But my picture of him was far more august: his habitation would be a room walled with books, probably atop a tower, like Jung's, at Bollingen. In time I came to appreciate the fact that he had resided in the South before he ascended the tower, so that he was not impervious to a cultural past—which I accordingly had to regard—but I had no sense of a man struggling with a personal past or buttressed by family and friends.

For fifteen years I wrote essays that began with the premise that Percy was a novelist of ideas. Those essays dealt with his response to such major isms as existentialism, scientism, stoicism, medical materialism, and gnosticism and to his Christian faith. *Following Percy* (1988) collects those essays.

About ten years ago, I had a new idea. (One new idea every ten years is about all I can handle, for it demands serious and respectful attention.) By then I was old enough to realize that the popular distinction between the intellect and the emotions (precedence to the intellect, of course) is specious. No matter how we trick out our adult ideas, they always have an emotional core, which means that they almost always have a core originating in the experience of infancy or early childhood. That core depends upon the relationship that the individual experienced with his mother and his father.

My awareness grew that, collectively, mothers and fathers in Percy's novels are, dead, missing, peripheral, or at best, vague or ineffectual. Binx Bolling's father is dead, his mother—remarried with a second family so large that she might live in a shoe—is distant. Will Barrett's father is dead, his mother absent and unaccounted for. Tom More's father is dead, his mother a caricature businesswoman. In *The Thanatos Syndrome* (1987) Percy betrays his indifference to such a stick figure: Marva is said to be Tom's *wife's* mother (*TS* 354). In *Lancelot* (1977) Lance Lamar's father is dead, his mother lately also.

I began to think that these individual mothers and fathers collectively function as index characters, pointing to the internal image of mother and father, respectively, created in Percy's consciousness by his experience with his actual mother and father and freed through regression in service of the ego to the pages of his fiction. This line of thinking led me to psychological theory, a tool that I had used early in writing essays on Wilkie Collins and William Faulkner.

Given the prominence in *The Last Gentleman* and *The Second Coming*

(1980) of the father who committed suicide and the fact that Percy's father committed suicide, the impact of the father on the son in Percy's thought seemed the more fruitful idea to consider. What Percy told Wyatt Prunty (Tolson 396), "I guess the central mystery of my life will always be why my father killed himself," suggests that he himself gave that pain pre-eminence. Percy's exposure to Freudian theory in his analysis would have inclined him to that emphasis, even though the analysis gave him little relief, if any.

I certainly would not deny that Percy's fiction reveals that he was haunted by his father's death, and I admire Jay Tolson's delicate treatment of the father theme in his excellent biography. All the same, I have continued to think that Percy suffered earlier and more harshly from maternal deprivation than from paternal loss and, subsequently, maternal loss. The death of his father occurred when Percy was thirteen; his psychic system was sufficiently mature by then that he could apprehend his father as a concrete individual possessed of an autonomy. Recalling him in his fiction Percy could visualize his father in his particularity, his loving qualities shadowed by his untreatable depression. In the human psyche the experience of maternal deprivation may start in the womb, certainly may start immediately at birth. (There is a possibility that Percy's tendency to regression began with his difficult birth.) At such time the psychic system lacks the maturity to respond to the maternal figure as an individual but rather experiences her as a symbol, a feature of environment—a park-like landscape, a movie theater, a tower, for instance—or as an archetype, the Great Mother, later split into the Terrible Mother and the Good Mother. Despite Percy's general skepticism about Jung's thought—and there is a lot that is very speculative—Jung's concept of the archetype was the origin of my search for the maternal figure in Percy's fiction. From there I went on to study object-relations psychologists, in particular, and other thinkers who believe that the need for the security of maternal love is the cradle of all human character formation. With their help I have written the essays that appear here, in preparation for a biography that I hope to complete in the next two or three years, if I can just escape those themes hung on me by Megaera Fury (another prominent local family, said to be related to the Fates).

Preface

A word about the individual essays. "Neurobiology and Psycho-analysis is the Work of Walker Percy" was first given at the convention of the American Association for the Advancement of Science; facing an unfamiliar audience, I argued that doing science and doing fiction, while studying different phenomena and having different criteria for validity, are basically alike in seeking to create a narrative. "Walker Percy's South(s)" was given at the convention of the European Southern Studies Association; to an audience not confused by proximity to the South and disposed to see it only as a social construct I described the several psychological responses that it evoked in Walker Percy's imagination.

The three essays on *The Moviegoer* treat different aspects of the role of regression in the novel. First of all, the argument has been popularized by Ernst Kris that all artistic creation depends upon a controlled regression, a loosening of rational restraints that allows access to the unconscious. The novel thus owes its existence to the very phenomenon with which it is concerned. Second, the novel is about Binx Bolling's nearly disabling fantasy of returning to an intrauterine existence, of living in the movie theater-womb. "The Moviegoer Dates the Love Goddess" shows how carefully Walker Percy uses Aphrodite lore to analyze Binx Bolling's Don Juan behavior, as he searches for the woman-movie star to replace the woman he lost, first to his father and then to Roy (interesting name, that, since it was the name of both Walker Percy's father and next brother). In the third essay, I use Michael Washburn's *The Ego and the Dynamic Ground* to connect Binx's reconciliation with the mother archetype and with God, a double reconciliation that frees him to marry a mortal and to tell his story.

There are four essays on *The Last Gentleman*, proof of the powerful hold that the novel has had on me. It seems to me the most confessional of the novels; perhaps it is for that reason that it seems his most deceptive and allusive novel. Or is its mystery partly a matter of Walker Percy's confusion, not to mention my own? At any rate, I have returned again and again to search for the psychological imperatives that underlie Will Barrett's seemingly inappropriate response to individuals and to places, imperatives that are as hidden to Will Barrett as they are to me. What all four essays share is the general theme that Will Barrett is haunted, not by some particular, identifiable presence, but by a pervasive absence, "the secret and somehow shameful heart of childhood itself" (*LG* 11).

The last two essays treat *Love in the Ruins* and *Lancelot,* respectively. The Tom More of *Love in the Ruins* seems to be Walker Percy's image of himself as he might have been, had he not lost his contentment with the scientific view. Tom is not nearly so haunted as Binx and Will, not nearly so driven by psychological imperatives, but tempted to think that behavior can be adjusted by chemistry and electricity. But he is not totally free of the past. Certainly his quest for a Utopia could be traced back to a fantasy of intrauterine bliss, and his "Nobel Prize Complex," dealt with here, could be a response to the sense of fallen glory for which a compensation must be found. Lance Lamar may be Walker Percy's image of himself as he might have been, had he not come to grips with the family sense of honor and pride that Bertram Wyatt-Brown treats so masterfully in *The House of Percy.* Although Lance never reveals his motivation for mining his house, his intent must have been suicidal, for only chance makes him the sole survivor. Just as he desires the destruction of the house with himself in it, so he labors to destroy the reputation of his mother, who is represented by the image of the house. Overwhelmed by his fantasy of intrauterine bliss, he is so obsessed with genitality with substitute Margot that when he learns that he does not have sole possession of her genitals, he regresses to that early point when he had been shocked to learn that he was not the sole possessor of his mother's genitals. Thus the story of "Uncle Harry," which Lance may simply have manufactured, to provide the necessary villain, in order to shield from himself his Oedipal animosity. *Lancelot* is a brilliant novel, a searing revelation of the destructiveness that may have its origin in frustrations of infancy.

Come to think of it, I was not entirely off the mark to regard Percy as a man isolated in a tower of thought. My early mistake was to think that he was the master of intellectual thought, rather than the hostage of emotional thought. It is possible that Percy came to see himself as a man in a tower. Consider Percy's bitterest story: Lance Lamar in his pigeonnier, a man who must enter the uterine Bel Isle—apparently an Eden, but actually a Sodom, and so destined for destruction in a gaseous explosion—in pursuit of Margot the Terrible Mother to the womb-room—whom he had first imagined as the Good Mother of his infantile oral fantasy, good enough to eat (*L* 171)—a man at the end of his story in a tower-like room, who has the choice of looking at the City of the Dead and a movie theater showing dirty movies or hearing the Good News from Father John. Consider Percy's romance of reconciliation: Will Barrett, a man who had spent his working life living in a Manhattan tower overlooking Central Park, who must enter a uterine cave, a "theater" (*SC* 209, 224), there to climb a "chimney" (210) into a tower-like space in which he will die unless a miracle occurs, a man who is given his miracle and is reborn through love and faith, so that he gains both a psychological Good Mother and a spiritual Good Mother. Consider Percy's comedy of love and faith triumphant, *The Thanatos Syndrome:* Tom More, returning from prison, must confront the secularist forces represented by the cooling towers by ascending the fire-tower occupied by Father Rinaldo Smith, at the same time that he must forgive his wife for her innocent sexual behavior with another man and himself for his not-so-innocent dalliance with a woman who reminds him of his mother.

At that point Percy's fiction stops: Tom climbs down from the tower, escapes the temptress cousin Lucy, returns to his "little Cajun cottage of the weathered board-and-batten and a rusty tin roof" (*TS* 12–13), there to help his patient by talking with her and listening to her: "She falls silent, but her eyes are softer, livelier, are searching mine as if I were the mirror of her very self" (*TS* 372). What Tom has learned is that many a person needs to be reconstructed, needs to return to the original situation, in which mother is the mirror, as Winnicott puts it (111–18), giving the child a self through love and language.

Is it just my imagination or is Tom More's story very like Walker Percy's? Having fought through his terrors with Divine help, Tom seems ready to help others with the wisdom that he has gained. Percy's successful fight is chronicled in his fiction, culminating in *The Second Coming,* in which there is a recognition of the need of God and a realization that only a willed effort to love a loving, breathing woman can defeat the haunting memory of that earliest woman. For me, there is a decline of personal involvement and hence of creative inspiration in *The Thanatos Syndrome*—Percy is too intent upon an agenda. (There: I am *not* a cultist.) I would not regret it that, if he had lived, he had never again written fiction. For he still had his dream of showing even those who will not see that language is a mystery, a miracle effected by Divine love and through human love. Come to think of it, that's the miracle that shines through his novels, in both content and craft. Why else would I follow them so many years?

I want to acknowledge the help of four remarkable women, Barbara, who is that collection of persons that a wife of nearly forty years must be; Mrs. Walker Percy, whose presence was essential, I feel, for Walker Percy to tell his story; Seetha Srinivasan, who insisted that I tell my story properly; and my mother, to whom the book is dedicated, whose love kept me from becoming an awful novelist.

Lewis Lawson
Thanksgiving Day 1994

ACKNOWLEDGMENTS

With the exception of "Regression in the Service of Transcendence in *The Moviegoer*" and "Will Barrett's Psychoanalysis," which have not been previously published, each of the following essays originally appeared in a scholarly journal or collection of essays and appears here after revision through the kind permission of the editors.

"Microbiology and Psychoanalysis in the Work of Walker Percy," *RANAM* [Recherches Anglaises et Nord-Américaines], 24 (1991), 1–8.

"Walker Percy's South(s)," in *Rewriting the South: History and Fiction*, eds. Lothar Hönnighausen and Valeria Gennaro (Tuebingen: A. Francke, 1993), pp. 359–70.

"The Dream Screen in *The Moviegoer*," *Papers on Language and Literature*, 30 (Winter 1994), 25–56.

"The Moviegoer Dates the Love Goddess," *Southern Quarterly*, 33 (Fall 1994), 6–25.

"Will Barrett under the Telescope," *Southern Literary Journal*, 20 (Spring 1988), 16–42.

"'The Parent in the Percept' in *The Last Gentleman*," *Mississippi Quarterly*, 46 (Winter 1992–93), 39–59.

"Will Barrett and 'the fat rosy temple of Juno'," *Southern Literary Journal*, 26 (Spring 1994), 58–76.

"Tom More's 'Nobel Prize Complex'," *Renascence*, 44 (Spring 1992), 175–82.

"Moviemaking in *Lancelot*," *South Central Bulletin*, 3 (Winter 1986), 78–94.

Still Following Percy

Neurobiology and Psychoanalysis in the Work of Walker Percy

The two subjects, neurobiology and psychoanalysis, are ordinarily thought to be poles apart: neurobiology must be one of the hardest of the sciences, while psychoanalysis is one of the arts, albeit one of the *medical* arts. Most people would no doubt suppose that not even Crazy Glue could bond these incompatibilities together.

But neurobiology can be reconsidered as being a somewhat more tentative knowledge than its reputation claims. One of the leaders of the discipline, William H. Calvin, in his remarkable book *The River That Flows Uphill,* acknowledges that what is not yet known is far more interesting than what is known: "We neurophysiologists can now even conceive mental images about the inner workings of the human brain itself—and even construct scenarios for how the brain makes up scenarios" (5). That, he says, is what the "scientific method" is all about, creating a scenario, a likely narrative for the scrutiny of others. At the same time, just a bit more "hardness" can be claimed for psychoanalysis. In *Sincerity and Authenticity* Lionel Trilling offers a description of psychoanalysis which many people would accept: psychoanalysis is a therapy "based upon narration, upon telling" (140). Indeed, many would argue the case much more strongly, by asserting that the purpose of psychoanalysis is to enable the individual analysand to create a likely narrative of his life, an act that will inevitably incorporate him into humanity by informing him of the universality of his experience. In *Re-Visioning Psychology*, James Hillman argues that psychological discovery of "the process of seeing through" must contain the act of narratization: "Third, the present event, the phenomenon before us, is given a *narrative*. A tale is told of it in the metaphors of history, or physical causality, or logic. We tell ourselves something in the language of 'because'. The immediate is elaborated by fantasy, so that a metamorphosis occurs as the immediate becomes part of an account" (141).

Narrative, then, becomes the central concern of our thinking about both our brains and our minds, indeed it becomes the universal concern of life, even though its universality is still so ignored that the two fields to whom its centrality is so important are still regarded as being completely disparate. All of us are privileged to be spectators of the competition between the dual scenarios of neurobiology and psychoanalysis, the former having to do with the racial *drives* and the latter having to do with the individual *desires*. They are both thought to be primarily interested in what goes on in the head, and they should therefore have a very close connection with one another, but they seem destined, like the lines of linear perspective, to meet only at infinity. Many of us are privileged not to get too greatly distressed by either scenario, suffering neither physical tumor nor psychological trauma; there are those absolutists who profess faith in the primacy of one or the other, but most of us seem equally indifferent to both, for they remain distant and abstract concepts, even though our indifference exists in the same nearby place as the concepts, the head, in other words *no* place that we can visualize. Once in a while, though, an individual is privileged to exist between the two scenarios, which, it turns out, are not distant from one another at all, but close enough to grind against each other like millstones. Such a privileged person was Walker Percy (1916–1990).

A few aspects of Walker Percy's life before he committed himself to writing. He was born the first child of a wealthy family, in Birmingham, Alabama. When he was thirteen, his lawyer father killed himself with a shotgun, just as *his* father had done, twelve years before. Indeed, as recent study has revealed, suicide has been a frequent response to life among the male members of the Percy family over a long period of time (Wyatt-Brown). When Percy was fifteen, his mother died in an automobile wreck that she may have deliberately caused. Despite these losses, Percy—sustained by his adoptive father, his father's first cousin—graduated from the University of North Carolina at the age of twenty-one. Seemingly, his faith in "medical materialism" (James 29) had not been shaken, for he then entered the College of Physicians and Surgeons at Columbia University. But at the same time he submitted himself to a psychoanalyst for an hour a day five days a week. After three years (the first two with Janet Rioch, the last with Gotthard Booth), he withdrew from analysis, without resolution.

Graduating from medical school in 1941, he began his internship at Bellevue Hospital in New York City. Within five months his adoptive father died of a stroke; three months later Percy had to suspend his internship because he had contracted tuberculosis in the pathology laboratory. During a three-year convalescence, he began to think of writing, about the gaps in the description of humankind provided by the reigning view of objective-empiricism. Given his history of family breakdown, parental breakdown, psychological breakdown, and psychosomatic breakdown—all of which are not finally disparate, but inextricably connected phenomena—is there any way that his life's subject could not be neurobiology and psychoanalysis, the twin narratives that contextualize life and so give it meaning?

When Percy began to construct his life as narrative, he saw himself as "the castaway." An early critic suggests that Karl Jaspers' "shipwrecked man" and Martin Heidegger's image of *Geworfenheit* contributed to Percy's choice of his iconic personal image (Luschei 39). But Jose Ortega y Gasset's *The Revolt of the Masses* also deserves credit: "The man with the clear head is the man who . . . looks life in the face, realizes that everything is problematic, and feels himself lost. . . . Instinctively, as do the shipwrecked, he will look around for something to which to cling, and that tragic, ruthless glance, absolutely

5

sincere, because it is a question of his salvation, will cause him to bring order into the chaos of his life. These are the only genuine ideas, the ideas of the shipwrecked" (115–16). The great popularization of the image of "the castaway," as the excellent *Images of Crisis: Literary Iconology, 1750 to the Present* points out, is Robinson Crusoe (Landow 16–18), to whom Percy refers or alludes in nearly everything that he wrote. The 1959 essay "The Message in the Bottle" contains the most significant employment of the image, beginning as it does with "Suppose a man is a castaway on an island," and ending with Percy's identification of Ortega's "question of salvation": ". . . what if a man receives the commission to bring news across the seas to the castaway and does so in perfect sobriety and with good faith and perseverance to the point of martyrdom? And what if the news the newsbearer bears is the very news the castaway had been waiting for, news of where he came from and who he is and what he must do? Well then, the castaway will, by the grace of God believe him" (Percy *MB* 119, 149). Such was Percy's need to put himself under narrative scrutiny.

In his chapter on "The Divided Self, and the Process of Its Unification," William James distinguishes between the "healthy-mind," who needs to be born only once, and the "sick soul," who needs to be twice-born. This is because "the world is a doubled-storied mystery" for the "sick soul," a lower story for the natural and a higher story for the spiritual. By "story" James means a floor of a building, and I accept his cheery pragmatic architectural model; but, seizing upon the pun, I will say that life as a narrative is also double-storied. Both Walker Percy's biography and his veiled autobiography in writing argue that, in his thirtieth year, recognizing his soul sickness, he took decisive actions to be reborn. First he married, as a renewed attempt toward psychoanalytical healthiness; then he became a Catholic, in defiance of the neurobiological scenario that his father and grandfather had accepted. As he began to write, he explored the consequences of both his decisions, using fiction primarily, but not exclusively, to explore the psychoanalytical mystery that was one story of his life and non-fiction primarily, but not exclusively, to explore the neurobiological mystery that was the other story of his life.

The fiction tended toward (veiled) confession (not only of religious dilemmas), while the non-fiction tempted him toward (veiled) evangelization, so that he had to practice deception in both narratives. One obvious deception was to use the French secularists Albert Camus and Jean-Paul Sartre as his immediate stylistic models for *The Moviegoer.* Perhaps he balanced his conscience in his early metaphysical essays, for they depend on French Roman Catholics, Jacques Maritain, on symbolization, and Gabriel Marcel, on intersubjectivity.

In the 1950's Percy wrote at least two novels, *The Charterhouse* and *The Gramercy Winner,* which have not been published, perhaps because they were not sufficiently confessional and because they were too openly evangelical. In his essay in *Walker Percy: Novelist and Philosopher,* Gary M. Ciuba, as yet the only analyst of *The Gramercy Winner,* generally supports my supposition (Ciuba 13–23). Although Jay Tolson, Percy's first biographer, has an intuition that *The Charterhouse* exists, its whereabouts is unknown: I fear for its existence, for in response to my request to see it, Percy wrote once that he was taking it out to throw into the bayou that very day (WP Letter to LL 5/16/67). During the same years Percy was successful in non-fiction, publishing the bulk of the essays that constitute *The Message in the Bottle* (1975). Each of those essays is successful as an independent whole, but it must be admitted that *The Message in the Bottle* depends upon two later essays, "The Delta Factor," and "A Theory of Language," respectively the first and the last, to assert Percy's scenario of the origin of knowledge through hearing (which requires a predecessor Other). His scenario is, of course, an attempt to refute Descartes' scenario of the origin of knowledge through isolated meditation upon what is seen. By the time he published *The Message in the Bottle* he was ready to assert—in a rather veiled way—that the capacity to symbolize evolved perhaps a million years ago by a means not explained by non-theistic treatments of language. The eruption of language he designates "the Delta factor," which he positions somewhere between Alpha and Omega. The individual recapitulation of this evolutionary event he designates "the Helen Keller phenomenon," following the tradition established by Ernst Cassirer, Jacques Maritain, and Susanne Langer, of using Helen Keller's autobiographical

7

account of her leap from the stimulus-response, dyadic world of the signal to the conceptual, triadic world of the symbol (Lawson "The Cross").

Granted that the use of Helen Keller's description is hallowed by tradition, that it is certainly vivid, and that it is accessible because of its popularization in the stage and movie productions of *The Miracle Worker*. But Keller's autobiography—or its dramatization—cannot emphasize the reality of the lengthiness, the intricacy, and the intimacy of the birth of consciousness through symbolization. In all those qualities the birth of conceptualization resembles the earlier, physical birth, and—as post-Freudian psychoanalysts are more and more demonstrating—requires the same predecessor Other present, the mother (or almost invariably somewhat inadequately, a surrogate). Although Percy was aware of a few of the analysts who were beginning to create a scenario that linked language development with object relations, he does not use the mother-child model for illustration, but borrows Charles Sanders Peirce's father-child model. It may be that Percy was still at this time too dependent upon Freud, who does not dwell upon the maternal relationship, because of his investment in his discovery of the Oedipal relationship. But there is also reason to think that Percy's inability to acknowledge the mother-child relationship resulted from the inadequacy of his own mother-child relationship.

In *Madness and Modernity* C. R. Badcock quotes Anna Freud's description of the basic psychoanalytical presupposition: "We take it for granted that the amount of insight possessed by an unanalyzed person is minimal, and that this is due to the protective barrier between the id and the ego, erected to shield the latter from any excessive awareness of mental discomfort, pain, anxiety, narcissistic hurt, etc." Then Badcock continues: ". . . the ego can obtain extensive indirect knowledge of its id—not to mention the unconscious part of its superego—by undergoing a competently carried out psychoanalysis, or, in rather rare cases, through the possession of poetic or artistic gifts or an unusual capacity for candid self-knowledge" (152). Since Percy had withdrawn from analysis, had been unwilling to complete his narrative there, he was in effect betting that he possessed a poetic gift or an unusual capacity for self-knowledge. Whether one or the other—probably both—he found *it*, the inspiration to create his narrative. He preferred to speak of his inspiration as his "knack," which he speculated, was the result of inheritance or of "a rotten childhood" (Percy "Questions" 403–04). That is to say, his depression may have been neurobiologically or psychologically induced—probably both. The "knack," he confessed, had "theological, demonic, and sexual components." But he said no more, forcing us to look to the fiction, penetrating through the surface—distorted by repression—to the depths, the home of "the theological, demonic, and sexual components." What seems safe in saying, before we approach the fiction, is that his sense of displacement demanded that he narratize his experience. In *The Origins of Love and Hate,* Ian D. Suttie thus expresses the same idea: ". . . in all his social activities—Art, Science and Religion included—man is seeking a restoration of or substitute for that *love of mother* which was lost in infancy" (71).

Because of the limitations of space, I cannot trace out in detail Percy's life narrative through all six of his novels. Obviously each narrative surface is particularized by its social context of different characters, different settings, and different plots. But beneath the surface of the present moment, before the registering eye of a remarkably consistent first-person narrator (who is, at least through *Lancelot*, offering a narrative which is a reconstruction of the past), there is a stream of consistent significant imagery. I use the word *significant* in its original meaning: *signifying,* that is, acting as a symbol, a visible object that stands in place of an idea not visually present.

This protagonist (Binx Bolling [*The Moviegoer*], Will Barrett [*The Last Gentleman* and *The Second Coming*], Lance Lamar [*Lancelot*], and Tom More [*Love in the Ruins* and *The Thanatos Syndrome*]) is "born," comes to himself, awakens, finds himself in a world that is characterized only by spatial reference. The other dimension, time, is either objectified as a unit of commerce or abstractified as a unit of scientific measurement: thus the protagonist observes other people either busying themselves acquiring and consuming bottles of Perrier time or busying themselves capturing phenomena to put into boxes of Greenwich Mean Time, the materialists or the scientific idealists, respectively. Rejecting both such measurements, the protagonist remains mystified by the enduringness of time, which stretches from

9

beginning to end. He does not yet understand or—if understanding—accept St. Augustine's assertion, in Book XI of *The Confessions*, that it is the human's awareness of the enduringness of time that establishes the human as a souled creature.

Paradoxically the protagonist arms himself with a signature visual instrument or object that will, presumably, link him, connect him, to ever receding exteriority, the expanding universe: the motion picture apparatus (*The Moviegoer*), the telescope (*The Last Gentleman*), the lapsometer (*Love in the Ruins*), the motion picture and the television apparatuses (*Lancelot*), the gun sight (*The Second Coming*), and the computer screen and the azimuth (*The Thanatos Syndrome*). His intention is to fix the bounds of the universe so that he can fix *his* point on the celestial graph paper. But the universe continues to expand, so he continues to shrink.

Yet the protagonist's apparent effort to go outward may hide an unrecognized intuition that the answer will be found by going inward. In *Re-Visioning Psychology* James Hillman offers a clue to the Percy protagonist's most pronounced recurrent activity:

> To psychologize we need to "get closer" or even to "back off" for a different perspective; or to look at things from a new angle. Other motifs are: turning lights on or off, entering, descending, climbing up or fleeing to gain distance, translating, reading or speaking another tongue, eyes and optical instruments, being in another land or another period of history, becoming insane or sick or drunk—all of which are concrete images for shifting one's attitude to events, scenes, and persons. Watching images on a screen or making images with a camera also present modes of psychologizing. But best of all is glass. Glass in dreams, as windows, panes, mirrors, presents the paradox of a solid transparency; its very purpose is to present seeing through. Glass is the metaphor par excellence for psychic reality: it is itself not visible, appearing only to be its contents, and the contents of the psyche, by being placed within or behind glass, having been moved from palpable reality to metaphorical reality, out of life and into image. Only when the alchemist could put his soul substances in a glass vessel and keep them there did his psychologizing work effectively commence. Glass is the concrete image for seeing through. (141–42)

All of Percy's novels, then, are efforts at "psychologizing," "seeing through." Yet the first four must be read as failures of the protagonist to "see through," for the instruments in those novels reveal that the viewer cannot simply observe remote indifferent exteriority: whether seen or not the reflection of the viewer's eye on the glass of the eyepiece asserts that the presence of the viewer inevitably influences the world that is being viewed.

All the while, then, each of the first four novels shows the reader, if not the protagonist, that the ocular piece of a visual instrument is not a satisfactory literal model of human consciousness. Human vision is not merely a present event, unaffected by past or future; the brain may be the locus of the visual sensation, but the elusive mind, wherever it is, is the locus of mentation, the assignment of existential value to sensation, the incorporation of space-time events into the life narrative. The Percy protagonist visually records the environment's multitude of objects, but does not symbolize them, discover what they stand for. At least not consciously; unconsciously he does. We readers can see how the protagonist, who wants only to live in the present, is drawn back constantly to the past (both his personal past and his racial past). We see such images as parks (Central Park especially), globes, the yin-yang, breasts, caressing, thumb-sucking, eating, caves and Charles Foster Kane (alluded to in *The Moviegoer*) and Philip Marlowe (referred to in *Lancelot*), two of the cinema's most flagrant seekers of the original object. These images attempt to escape the id to surface in the ego, as they reveal the Percy protagonist's personal yearning for a restoration to the lost mother figure and his racial yearning for the restoration to the Garden of Eden. The Paradise-Apocalypse myth is never far distant from the theme of a Percy novel.

Only in *The Second Coming* and *The Thanatos Syndrome* is the optical instrument or object an indication of successful "seeing through." In *The Second Coming* Will Barrett has reached the point in his life that he sees the world by sighting it with his Luger, revealing a death wish that is neurobiologic in origin. Then he sees a young woman who lives in a greenhouse (such as the one in *Eden* Park, Cincinnati, in which he had worked as a youth), who will (as the personification of his lost mother object) restore his vigor: upon meeting him, she presents him with two golf balls that he had lost. Thus Percy can intimate that he has finally "seen through" to the condition of loss that

11

had distressed him all of his life. Since the young woman's name is Allie Huger (alleluia, praise the Lord), she and Will appropriately make love under a stained glass window used as a patch for the greenhouse roof. If learning language from the original object occurs through divine agency, so too does sharing language with the one with whom one shares life/love, the richest experience of intersubjectivity.[1] The mother-figure having been regained in *The Second Coming*, she becomes in *The Thanatos Syndrome* a Beatrice figure (there is also another figure blatantly named "Vergil"), who enables Tom More to "see through" a computer screen, in order to understand the hellish conspiracy concocted by two secular humanists, one a scientist and the other a physician, who would remove the capacity to conceptualize from the masses—and incidentally remove also the capacity for language. At the same time, a priest is finally able to get Tom More to understand full consciousness, which is cointentional. The very etymology of *conscious*, as Percy pointed out, is "knowing with" (Percy "Symbol" 274). Cartesian consciousness is therefore a derivative, deprived consciousness. Full consciousness requires "triangulation"[2]: a speaker and a hearer, each using an azimuth, "the way," as it were, to locate an object stereoptically, so that it *exists*, "stands out" from exteriority. Appropriately, this narrative—a comedy in the sense that Dante's narrative is a comedy—concludes with Tom More the psychiatrist, having observed a priest using an azimuth, helping a patient to construct (reconstruct) her narrative.

Many readers of Walker Percy remark upon the intense effect that his fiction has upon them. Perhaps that effect results, at least in part, from two phenomena that I have been discussing. Perhaps he reawakens in us those dim, forgotten, repressed images of childhood terror and nostalgia, home-sickness, feelings paradoxical but all the same lodged in our memory. Since this memory is universal, we experience that presentation of solidarity that Conrad, in his Preface to *The Nigger of the "Narcissus,"* announces as the paramount responsibility of the artist.[3] And perhaps knowing *more* than the Percy protagonist knows about his own situation, we identify intensely with him, yearning to help him and lamenting his failed opportunities to sense the symbolic significance of an ordinary object: a smudge of darkness on an insurance salesman's forehead (*The Moviegoer*), a

Holsum bread truck passing in the night (*The Last Gentleman*), a big unidentified fish on a trotline (*Love in the Ruins*), a silent friend willing, Christlike, to listen to a murderer's ravings (*Lancelot*), a shy girl looking for a father to teach her to name things, who has the gumption to use a bread truck for her escape (*The Second Coming*), an eccentric old priest who believes that Satan is now the Great Depriver of language, hence ultimately of consciousness and community (*The Thanatos Syndrome*). We sympathize and we tremble, for we wonder if we have the grace to see the symbol that will reintegrate our life, making it into a narrative. One thing is for sure: we know that we are more likely to see the symbol because we have read Walker Percy's struggle to finish *his* narrative, thus to escape the fatal grasp of neurobiology and psychology.

13

Walker Percy's South(s)

Walker Percy was rather ambivalent about whether or not he was a *southern* novelist. As a good existentialist, he may have been afraid that if he accepted the title his work would be measured only by the general criteria of the genre *southern novel,* which means, ultimately, being judged by the specific criteria of the work of William Faulkner. As Percy's friend Flannery O'Connor put it, "Nobody wants his mule and wagon stalled on the same tracks the Dixie Limited is roaring down" (276).

That was why Percy stayed in the car while his friend Shelby Foote spent two hours with Faulkner when they stopped by Oxford on their way from Greenville, Mississippi, to the University of North Carolina in 1933; he was afraid that he would be reinfected with the fatal Faulknerian style (Chandler 96).[1] The year before, having just read *The Sound and the Fury,* Percy wrote his freshman English placement essay *à la Faulkner,* "one long paragraph without punctuation." These criteria landed Percy in "a retarded English class" (Brown 10). Such was the terror of his early experience with Faulkner that Percy must have decided that he would wear his colors as a southern novelist only with a difference, for he told an interviewer: "Faulkner and all the rest of them were always going on about this tragic sense of history, and we're supposed to sit on our porches talking about it all the time. I never did that, My South was always the New South. My first memories are of the country club, of people playing golf" (Atlas 186). Perhaps Percy here exaggerates to set himself apart from the Faulkner tradition. For Percy's South was not always the New South; on other occasions he acknowledged a personal indebtedness to the Old South as well, as when he said, ". . . I miss the South if I am gone too long. I prefer to live in the South but on my own terms. It takes some doing to insert oneself in such a way as to not succumb to the ghosts of the Old South or the happy hustlers of the new Sunbelt South" (Percy "Why" 4).

In fact, his experience of the South was so varied that he obviously had a conception of the South containing more than these two domains so well known to anyone familiar with southern history. Percy lived all of his nearly seventy-four years in the South, except for his four years in medical school at Columbia University, New York City, three years of convalescence from tuberculosis at sanitariums in New York state and Connecticut, and his short stay in New Mexico during continued convalescence. During his life in the South, he lived in Birmingham, Alabama, as a child; in Athens, Georgia, as a child-adolescent; in Greenville, Mississippi, as an adolescent-young man; in Chapel Hill, North Carolina, as a college student, with occasional stays in Sewanee, Tennessee. The last thirty-three years of his life he lived in Louisiana, the first three in New Orleans and the last thirty in Covington, across Lake Pontchartrain from New Orleans. He said that he chose Covington as his permanent residence not because it was a pleasant place but rather because it was a pleasant nonplace (Percy "Why" 4).

Percy's itinerary—in all its numbing itemization—is offered to make a point: with hindsight it can be seen that Percy's life-journey traveled through a succession of "Souths" from which he was fundamentally alienated toward a South which had no ghosts to haunt him. The physical journey was mirrored, after his conversion to Roman Catholicism in 1947, by his Augustinian journey through the City of Man toward the City of God, a journey which promised a culmination of absolute and blissful reconciliation. For all his brave talk here about living in the South on his own terms, it is quite clear

15

from his fiction that he did not. Response to place is not a Cartesian transaction in which the perceiver somehow perceives the perceived without image ever becoming imagination. On the contrary, response to place is always "moodish," as Heidegger would say (173): indeed he would reverse the flow of emphasis to argue that mood precedes perception of place to reveal to *Dasein* the amount of "thrownness" it must bear. The "moodish" response surely becomes greater when the response is a memory of a past place, which, we may be reminded by Proust, is the raw material of the act of fiction. Neither in his response to the present[2] nor in his memory of the past did Percy live in the South on his own terms. On the contrary, the recurrent evocation of certain places in his fiction reveals that he was haunted not by one South, but by a virtual stream of "Souths."

Recall Percy's statement previously quoted: ". . . I miss the South if I am gone too long. I prefer to live in the South but on my own terms. It takes some doing to insert oneself. . . ." That verb *insert* or some equivalent verb must also be used to describe human sexual intercourse, the insertion of one body into another body. Percy was a body, not a thing; therefore, if his statement has any vital significance it means that originally and most deeply the South was a body for him.

In his discussion of the "tendency to fill the hole" as being "one of the most fundamental tendencies of human reality," Jean-Paul Sartre, in *Being and Nothingness,* offers several useful insights, most particularly the insight that it is only from the standpoint of the tendency to fill the hole that any discussion of sexuality can begin (613), that is, that any discussion of sexual activity must recognize that the act is a manifestation not of a mechanistic drive, but of an existential need. But Sartre attributes this need to the hopeless human project of filling the *en soi,* the empty universe, truly a "useless passion" (615).

Rather, I prefer to accept the explanation offered as early as Plato's *Symposium* and as recently as Sandor Ferenczi's *Thalassa* and the writings of such "object-relations" psychoanalysts as Robert Bak: that sexual activity is an effort to effect fusion, ultimately the original fusion with the original object—mother (1–7). If sexual activity is a mechanical drive, then how to account for post-coital depression?

Mechanistically speaking, orgasm as the release of tension should be the culmination of the drive. But after orgasm flesh fails, fusion is lost. If object-loss causes sexual activity, then it is possible to say that a human being could suffer all its life from post-coital depression, given a severe sense of object-loss and the consequent rejection of any surrogate object as subject. The fiction of Walker Percy suggests that the original and deepest South was the mother whose loss he mourned.

The overt mother-figure in Percy's novels is remarkable for her un-remarkableness. Mrs. Anna Castagne Bolling Smith wants no close relationship with Binx. Mrs. Lucy Hunicutt Barrett had died when Will was a very young boy. The real dirt on Mrs. Marva More is that she is a real estate agent. Mrs. Lily Lamar died before Lance tells his story. By the time he wrote *The Thanatos Syndrome*, Percy apparently had so little interest in Tom More's mother that he mistakenly identified Marva as the mother of Ellen, Tom's wife (*TS* 354). All the mothers are virtually or actually absent—but, on second thought, that is what is significant. The only technique for writing about absence is *not* to write about it.

Or, at least, not to write about it directly. There is a haunting and insistent mother-theme in Percy's novels evoked by a particular Alabama landscape, the country club golf course next to his childhood home. Percy may have implied to an interviewer that the country club connoted the New South to him, but in his fiction the golf course appears as Eden, home of Eve, so named by Adam because the word means "the mother of all living" (*RSV*, Genesis, 3:20). Of course Eden was lost the minute that Eve told Adam that he was buck naked. Here the Bible offers excellent phenomenology: we become conscious when we become self-conscious through the utterance of another. According to both Bible and object relations theory, we gain consciousness of self from the words of another, usually the mother, but in so doing we lose our sense of original fusion with mother and thus become alienated (Lawson "Cross" 3–12). The infant loses the sense of being enclosed in the uroboros, or yin-yang.

Paradise is thus lost, but not forgotten. Mythically the topography of paradise does not greatly differ from the original meaning of the Old Iranian word, a walled and treed garden or park or oasis in the desert (Jacoby 22). Thus we collectively mythologize and individually fantasize about park-like landscapes. It was a happy accident that Freud "compared fantasy to a natural preserve like Yellowstone Park—a bit of the pristine wilderness preserved within the confines of civilization" (Arlow 142). For Percy the fantasy park which symbolizes paradisal mother is New York City's Central Park: that is why Binx Bolling has the two Currier and Ives prints of skating lovers in Central Park over his bed and that is why Will Barrett loiters in Central Park and uses it as the place of his semi-seduction of Kitty Vaught.

At other times Percy just goes ahead to use a country club golf course as the symbol for a country club golf course, as in *The Last Gentleman* and *The Second Coming* (although in the latter Will still remembers Central Park—with *nostalgie noir,* a fallen place to which he took his wife's dog for its nocturnal naughty). In *Love in the Ruins,* the paradisal promise of the country club golf course is underlined by the name of the development in which it is situated, *Paradise Estates.* In *Lancelot* the name of the Lamar estate, *Belle Isle,* announces its primordial character.[3]

Whatever the appearance of this southern Eden, the fact is that it does not deliver whatever it is alleged to possess. It is a landscape of the mind, a fantasy; it activates physical behavior toward a surrogate object. Essentially it is a fantasy of the body which encloses; therefore, it should come as no surprise that the Percy protagonist is highly genitalized (though literal readers complain that Percy is a prude): the Percy protagonist dreams of inserting his body back into the original unity, "basic unity" as Little calls it. Binx must think he is almost in heaven with his Aphrodite: "Sharon cleaves to me as if, in staying close, she might not see me" (*M* 136). Tom and Ellen More wind up "twined about each other as the ivy twineth" (*LR* 403). In *The Second Coming* Will Barrett announces the culmination of the mother-theme with absolute clarity when he describes inserting himself into Allie Huger: "There was an angle but it did not make trouble. Entering her was like turning a corner and coming home" (*SC* 339). It is the enclosing activity of Margot Reilly's leg that awakens Lance Lamar's desire for her as body, after she has shucked her rig-up as a Southern belle, for he immediately regresses to infancy before getting physical with her; first he uses his mouth on her (*L* 71). In a description of a second copulation, Lance makes his action unequivocal: "She was like a feast. She was a feast. I wanted to eat her. I ate her" (*L* 171).

All too often the female personifying the southern Edenic mother is the most meretricious of images. Kitty Vaught may ride with Will in the camper *Ulysses*—which is aptly named since that eponymous epic poem celebrates a homecoming to the original object (Bergmann 25, 241)—but she becomes just another ditzy sorority girl when they reach her country club home in Alabama. Lola Rhoades may live in Tara but it is a replica built by a member of the Mafia; she may whistle "Going Home" through her teeth while she plays Tom like a 'cello between her knees, but the fact is that he nearly suffocates *in flagrante delicto*. And Margot Reilly may be dressed as a belle before Lance enters her parts (*L* 81), but she displaces him with first Merlin and then Janos Jacoby, all the while unconsciously mocking Lance's southern myth by bank-rolling and bit-acting in the goofiest southern movie ever reported. Thus is Eden quickly lost, with the consequence that a second southern landscape more often shows up in Percy's imagined world. This landscape is of the contemporary South.

All of Percy's protagonists have the sensibility of a consciousness which has been formed by the scientific school that originated with Rene Descartes and Isaac Newton. As Cartesians, they build their epistemology upon the distance which separates subject from object, *res cogitans* from *res extensa*. Thus they turn to optical instruments which purport to draw far things near: with self-conscious irony Binx Bolling acts as if there is a movie screen in his mind upon which there is projected the distant world in which he cannot really participate; Will Barrett abandons psychoanalysis ("the talking cure") to buy a telescope that exposes the true grittiness of things; Tom More invents the lapsometer, which penetrates appearance to focus upon the place where human drives originate—in the chemico-electrical firing of the individual brain cells; and Lance Lamar fantasizes that he is a scientist discovering irrefutable proof with his microscope, then uses a television camera to monitor people as if they were rats in a maze. As Newtonians all, the Percy protagonists have a proclivity

19

to see their word atomistically, to be bombarded by noxious particles or other minutia.

The combined habitual actions of the Percy protagonist—framing a limited visual field by technology and then focusing upon the smallest discernible phenomenon—are of course highly venerable phases of the scientific process. But in the case of each Percy protagonist his signature "scientific" activity may be traced to an origin in a psychic structure that was severely damaged in the past. Binx's haunting of movie houses may be a search for the "dream screen" that psychoanalyst Bertram Lewin identifies as a symbol for the lactating breast that so many of his patients have lost (Lewin *Image*). Will Barrett's reliance upon a telescope to connect him to the external world may recall Freud's citation of the telescope to symbolize the gappy, selective character of disturbed consciousness in his seminal work *The Interpretation of Dreams*. Tom More's interest in the lapsometer developed after the death of his daughter and his wife Doris, whose identification as the Apple Queen of the Shenandoah Valley qualifies her as an Eve figure. Lance Lamar's frenzied pursuit of the ocular proof of Margot's infidelity becomes more and more obviously an attempt to enter the past to confront the mother from whom he felt alienated. Approaching the bed in which Jacoby and Margot are coming to climax, Lance, sucking his thumb, climbs in, too. Then he dismembers Jacoby, disconnects Jacoby from Margot as if disconnecting a rival brother from the mother's breast.

Thus, the action so prominent in a Percy protagonist—the use of a scientific instrument to gain clarity of perception—simply obscures the fact of how distorted his original vision of things is and has been. The Percy protagonist is by no means alone in his reliance upon a hyper-rational methodology that is really a hyper-irrational response to the world, an interpretation of the world that features severance, which leads to schizophrenia, rather than an interpretation which features connection, which leads to intersubjectivity. In his recent study *Culture and Consciousness*, Mel Faber grounds the development of the modern Western alienated consciousness in the relationship between the infant and the maternal object that Western culture has allowed to deteriorate.[4] Faber's assertion would have been even stronger if he had indicated, as other writers have, that the very originators of the modern scientific view were themselves victims of object loss. It has been argued that Rene Descartes forged his philosophy of severance to combat the depression that resulted from his experience, at age one, of his mother's death (Stern 91). Similarly, there is an assertion that Isaac Newton's turn outward to exteriority resulted from his mother's apparent abandonment of him (Manuel 23–25). Thus our most prevalent contemporary epistemological system—that is to say, the according of reality to material phenomena—was the child of two men who, because of their respective sense of early loss of object and consequent personal devaluation, were impelled to construct a system that worshipped objective objects, but ignored the possibility of the incorporation of the subject in the object.

It could have been a psychology that Walker Percy shared with Descartes and Newton that made him choose scientific empiricism leading to medical empiricism as his career (Percy "From Facts"). If the world of things could be studied with enough intensity, the world of feelings might be repressed, feelings about the father who killed himself when Percy was thirteen and about the mother who may have killed herself when he was not yet sixteen.[5] At the same time he was pursuing his medical training, though, he felt the need of three years of five-day-a-week psychoanalysis, which was terminated without resolution. Shortly thereafter, he contracted tuberculosis, which forced him into two years of convalescence. Only then did he begin to read the existentialists and other thinkers who had critiqued Western scientism. In time he began to write essays in which he too pointed out the limitations of that system, but he makes no confession of his reason for having been so infatuated with it in the first place. In his fiction, however, the scientific world is a southern landscape, the same as the idyllic southern landscape, except that it is populated by a protagonist who has fallen—just as, in *The Second Coming*, Will Barrett, suffering from Hausmann's syndrome, which includes a symptom termed *wahnsinnige Sehnsucht*, translated "inappropriate longing" by the narrator (*SC* 302), literally keeps falling down on the country club golf course. Once he falls in love with Allie, though, he can walk across the course "like a businessman walking home across the Great Meadow in Central Park on

21

a fine fall day" (*SC* 326), and we know then, that for the first time a Percy protagonist will return to the motherland.

Just as there are two southern landscapes representing contrasting versions of the mother figure—one, the idyllic mother; two, the mother deteriorated into matter—so there are two other southern landscapes, each representing a version of the father figure. Generally speaking, these father figures represent the value systems conventionally known as Old South and New South, respectively. Usually the Old South is represented by a Mississippi or rural Louisiana landscape, while the New South is represented by an Alabama or a Georgia landscape, but there are so many exceptions to this generalization that it will be more fruitful to discuss each novel individually than to impose an inadequate generalization upon them all. What can be said with assurance is that the New South's landscape is dominated by LeRoy Percy, Walker Percy's father, in Birmingham, and that the Old South's landscape is dominated by William Alexander Percy, LeRoy's first cousin and adoptive father of Walker and his brothers, whose home was in Greenville, Mississippi, the site of Walker's mother's drowning.

In *The Moviegoer*, Binx Bolling lives in the contemporary South of New Orleans. Although he lives on Elysian Fields, which "was planned to be, like its namesake, the grandest boulevard of the city, something went amiss, and it runs an undistinguished course . . ." (*M* 9). While he dreams of Central Park, he has no real defense against his environment except disguise: he pretends that he is a happy hustler of the Sunbelt South. His father gave him no code or model for inspiration, but instead fled his own alienation to find death in World War II. His Aunt Emily has become his surrogate father; she personifies the best of the Old South, southern stoicism, whose patron is Robert E. Lee. But she lives by the law, not love, and thus does not understand Binx, thinks that he wants only "to go to the movies and dally with every girl that comes along" (*M* 226), which is true, psychoanalytically speaking: internally seeking his mother's breast, Binx externally gropes Woman's breasts, displays the Don Juan syndrome toward each romantic object. At the same time, there is something fundamentally odd about Aunt Emily: although she waves a sword, she wears a skirt—this may be an acknowledge-

22

ment that William Alexander Percy, despite his chivalric temperament, was not known for his heterosexual interest. At the conclusion, then, Binx marries Aunt Emily's stepdaughter, Kate—who may also suffer from separation anxiety—in effect acknowledging his own condition, while he also implies a new-found faith in a Heavenly Father, as he takes his siblings to Audubon Park, thus subduing his *wahnsinnige Sehnsucht* for Central Park.

In *The Last Gentleman* Percy conflates the two father-figures to show Will Barrett suffering so traumatically from mother loss that he cannot even remember her. Rather, his consciousness is clotted by eruptions of New and Old South memories which imply that neither of those value systems offers him any defense against his loss of the idyllic South and consequent exile in the contemporary South. Without knowing why, he embarks upon fugues to Civil War battlefields and Cincinnati's Eden Park and reads Freeman's *R. E. Lee*, hoping that this time, miraculously, the South will not lose; in other words, he acts out a *wansinnige Sehnsucht* for the original, "un-lost" landscape: his almost assignation with Kitty Vaught—the "great epithelial-warm pelvic-upcurving-melon-immediate Maja" (*LG* 288) in the Gettysburgian "sniper's den" in Central Park unifies all the major motifs of his quest. When his search is frustrated—he gets hit in the head at a Confederate monument by a contemporary southern mob (*LG* 288)—he follows a false father-figure, Sutter Vaught, a creature of the contemporary South who reveals his scorn for the idyllic mother South by engaging in a "nooner" in a "lewd wood" next to the number seven hole of the country club golf course (*LG* 349). In desperation, Will follows Sutter, who has taken his dying brother to New Mexico. There Will meets a true father, a Roman Catholic priest, but fails to grasp the priest's miraculous use of words to restore the dying boy to eternal paradise. The novel concludes with Will removed from the South to the Southwest, but with no notion of what difference the change in geography makes.

In *Love in the Ruins*, the external southern landscape is contemporary Louisiana. Although Tom More has his home in Paradise Estates and his consciousness is almost always affected by Early Times bourbon, his larger world is dominated by the Fedville Complex, in which scientists of various disciplines study the technology by which human beings may be treated as machines. When Tom loses first his daughter and then his mother-substitute wife Doris, he decides to beat the scientists at their own game by creating a unified field theory and then the implementing technology to create Utopia, the restitution of original unity. The father-figures whom he must surpass are Descartes, Newton, Freud, and Einstein: his transcending achievement will be to treat consciousness as an object. Thus he creates his "lapsometer"—an influencing machine, psychoanalysis would call it—which will absolutely tranquilize consciousness. He will, in other words, so act upon the landscape of matter that he will return the human race to the landscape of mother. Happily, this Faustian endeavor fails, but Tom is forgiven his grandiose dream. At the conclusion, a new mother-figure, Ellen Oglethorp, of Georgia—Percy's mother's home state—marries him, and a Roman Catholic priest, Father Simon Smith, offers him communion on Christmas Eve, transforming matter not with a machine but with words.

If Percy had somewhat slighted his southern theme in *Love in the Ruins,* he returns to it with a vengeance in *Lancelot.* As I earlier indicated, Lance Lamar stretches his image of the original object over the figure of Margot Reilly, his second wife. She is to replace his dead first wife, Lucy Cobb, also of Georgia, who had been an ideal mother substitute. All goes well while Margot restores Belle Isle to its original brilliance, acting like the rich woman who rescued post-bellum Jefferson Davis by installing him in Beauvoir (*L* 78). Then Margot is detected in her unfaithfulness, even at the same time that she has brought the film crew into Belle Isle to desecrate that original place by recreating it as the contemporary South.

Nothing short of blowing up the degraded contemporary South will satisfy Lance: in true gnostic fashion, if he cannot possess the ideal, he will totally destroy the real. (This same psychology governs his recreation of his actual mother's behavior.) The explosion kills Margot and two of her cinema colleagues—Lance had already personally dispatched Jacoby, "a mother's boy" (*L* 241)—and lands Lance in a hospital for the criminally insane. There he feels compelled to tell the story of his fall from Eden to Father John, a long lost friend who had shared his paradisal childhood. Father John had apparently fallen, too, but had sought reconciliation through the Word.

24

As Lance tells of the recent past, he gradually begins to include material from more remote levels of the past. At first these levels of "pastness" involve himself; but then they relate stories that he has received of the family past; and eventually, they reach the mythic, universal past. Gradually the connection becomes clear: the psycho-analytical story of the individual loss of the mother is the recapitulation of the religious story of the universal loss of the Garden of Eden. Lance had been faced with a choice of responses to make to the loss of his substitute. He speaks often of his Old South father, a poet and worshipper of Robert E. Lee, but, according to Lance, a man who was a weakling, a bribe-taker, and a conspirator to his own cuckoldry. Lance, therefore, has no choice but to follow another father-figure, a great-great-grandfather who, when his mother's name was maligned, killed the maligner, beheaded him, dismembered him, and fed the fragments to the catfish (*L* 154–55). Lance follows the path of family violence, the dark underside of the tradition of lofty honor, a proclivity for violence such that if it has no external outlet would turn against itself. But Lance's violence does not restore him to original unity; rather he feels nothing but isolation, as he looks out at the contemporary landscape of New Orleans, a porno movie house and a graveyard. He is finally left with Father John, who can say the words that will reconstitute Lance's world, if Lance will ask.

The Second Coming resumes the life of Will Barrett, who had not remained in New Mexico, but returned to New York to become a man of the law like his father. He had married the rich and fat Marion Peabody, whose first and family name and physical appearance indicate that she was not an adequate mother-substitute. Besides, she was a Yankee. Will had practiced corporation law for thirty years, living at 76th and Broadway in high style and low spirits. Now he has taken early retirement to play golf daily on a North Carolina country club course. All is not perfect, though: he keeps falling down and slicing out of bounds. Sometimes he dreams of Ethel Rosenblum, a high school classmate, a whiz in algebra who could factor out equations better than anyone else in class: "a/a = 1.1 = 1! Unity!" (*SC* 7). Thus she is the very spirit, the *ethyl* of primary unity. Her family name recalls "rosebud," the clue to Citizen Kane's *wahnsinnige Sehn-*

sucht (Carringer), to which the moviegoer Percy had alluded in *The Moviegoer*. But at the same time, Will is haunted by the ghost of his father, an "old mole" (*SC* 162) who destroys golf courses and who urges him to commit suicide, as he had. The "old mole" allusion recalls another man who, according to Freud, was very much disturbed by his longing for his mother. These contradictory longings suggest the dilemma posed by Freud in "Mourning and Melancholia": "In the most opposed situations of being most intensely in love and of suicide, the ego is overwhelmed by the object, though in totally different ways" (quoted in Bak 1).

One day, on the course—the landscape of the mother—Will has a graphic glimpse of his sexual/psychological fantasy of original unity and of the dilemma which its loss has forced him to face: "Suddenly he knew why he remembered the triangular patch of woods near the railroad tracks where he wanted to make love to Ethel Rosenblum. It was the very sort of place, a nondescript weedy triangular public pubic sort of place, to make a sort of love or to die a sort of death" (*SC* 162). If we cannot find love (provided by the adequate substitute of the object lost) that will make public life pubic, that will make our nondescript contemporary life idyllic, then we are dead and might as well be. It must be Eros or Thanatos. Enter Allie Huger, who gives Will back his golf balls (*SC* 74) and shows him the way back home. But love is such a gift that it must be a sign of the Giver; therefore, Will, at the end, gratefully seeks God's love as well.

The Thanatos Syndrome (1987), true to its title, does not deal much with Eros, therefore has very little of a southern theme. The Louisiana setting is contemporary South, but Tom More has no seething revulsion for it, indeed he fights the social engineers Comeaux and Van Dorn out of a desire to restore humanity to its frailty long before he is lectured by Father Smith to understand the local plot as a part of the Devil's cosmic game plan. This new-found tolerance in the Percy protagonist can be understood by examining what happens—and does not happen—between Tom More and his distant cousin Lucy Lipscomb.

That she is a significant object to Tom is revealed by the fact that on three occasions her presence induces *déjà vu*, the first (*TS* 102–

106) and the second (*TS* 135), an overwhelming of the ego because of the anticipation of sexual pleasure, and the third (*TS* 156), of the anticipation of bad news, both of the ways that Freud thought the ego could be overcome by the object. Her presence also induces Tom to impute motherly behavior to her: he thinks, ". . . I am old enough to be her father, yet she's more like a mother, might any moment spit on her thumb and smooth my eyebrows" (*SC* 105). Tom's intuition is borne out, soon enough (*SC* 161). She also picks lint off his jacket (*SC* 143). Such licking and picking are sufficient reasons for his decision not to get involved with her (*SC* 348)—as many people have discovered, to their regret. She also offers herself for copulation, but Tom may be so drunk and distracted that little if anything occurs.

Lucy is probably offering herself as a mother-substitute, which is a bit awkward since Tom's mother Marva is said to be still flourishing in local real estate. Lucy does not, however, evoke visions of golf courses or other paradisal locales in Tom. On the contrary, when Lucy and Tom talk family, at her run-down, unrestored estate, they trace their lineage back to the original New World More who (like the original New World Percy) married an American wife and fathered children by her only to have his English wife and her child show up at Pantherburn (also the name of a Percy estate). The original More's solution (like the original Percy) was to take a great notion to jump in the river and drown. It seems that Percy is saying that it is time for him to recognize that the past was never ideal and that present persons should not be measured against past images. Tom will, therefore, stay with his wife Ellen, even though she seems to have gotten a bad case of the middle-age crazies: she unwittingly becomes addicted to drugs and is infected with genital herpes by her bridge partner. Ellen thus makes an excellent personification of the contemporary South, which Tom can finally accept because he has escaped the spell of the idyllic South.

With the South restored to its single state of fallenness—the City of Man—it may then be contrasted with the City of God. Percy seems to have come to the realization when he was in New Mexico in 1946 that he would love or die, that he would have to choose between Eros and Thanatos. The choice to love is not so simple as it might seem,

27

for the decision to marry a wife meant that he would have to reject his fantasy of the perfect original object and the family tradition of solving everything by suicide (both static concepts and therefore under the dominion of Thanatos). A choice of this kind is not a one-time act—it must be reaffirmed daily. This is the truth so profoundly revealed in Walker Percy's southern world.

THREE

The Dream Screen in *The Moviegoer*

It is not often noted, but the narrative proper of Walker Percy's *The Moviegoer,* while it offers a very seductive "virtual present," is actually a re-presenting of selected events from an eight-day period that occurred at some point over a year in the past.[1] The Epilogue establishes the fact that Binx has been re-presenting to himself the feelings that he had earlier experienced, but had not been able to articulate; Percy's technique is illuminated by Charles Sanders Peirce's model of consciousness: the self-which-is silently converses with the self-which-is-just-coming-to-be. Percy implies such a strategy:

> When I sat down to write *The Moviegoer,* I was very much aware of discarding the conventional notions of a plot and a set of characters, discarded because the traditional concept of plot-and-character itself reflects a view of reality which has been called into question. Rather would I begin with a *man* who finds himself in a *world,* a very concrete man who is located in a very concrete place and time. Such a man might be represented as *coming to himself* . . . (Percy "From" 9)

The man coming to himself is the Binx who has selected and arranged a group of images so that their form conveys, represents, names his feelings to himself. These images—and, indeed, the form they take—would have been formed from and influenced by dreams, so that it is appropriate that dreams and dreaming are inescapably prominent in the content of the narrative. The boy Binx who got "excited" about "Freud's *Interpretation of Dreams*" (*M* 138), but was rebuffed by his mother's lack of interest, is—in the "virtual present" of the narrative power—the thirty-year old Binx who is unconsciously driven by dreams caused by the rebuffing mother to "act out," and is in the Epilogue the Binx who, by virtue of his marriage and his conversion to Christianity (both restitutions of the lost object), can now understand and name his past condition for himself.

During the eight days of his life that he recollects, Binx goes to the movies four times and refers to twelve identified and several unidentified movies. There is some truth to the diagnosis of Binx provided by a film critic:

> One encounters chronic moviemania in rigid, inhibited types who feel exquisitely uncomfortable when forced into close interpersonal contact. Safe only in well-defined social situations, intolerably anxious if called upon to improvise, these people sleepwalk through the day's routine and only come alive at second hand, as proxy participants in the adventures of their screen idols. (Walker Percy's elegant novel *The Moviegoer* describes such a case. (Greenberg 4)

But there is not enough to Greenberg's analysis. Binx shows no interest in cinematographic technique, nor indeed does he say much about acting technique; he comments on a film narrative or a character's action only if it re-presents in some way some aspect of his life. The movie screen is his dream screen, in the sense that Robert T. Eberwein describes the connection between the two screens in *Film and the Dream Screen*.

Throughout Binx's recollection it is the image of the movie theater, rather than the memory of a specific movie, which offers the more evocative impression. The theater has been interpreted as a dream symbol: "This is the place where the typical stories of man's life are shown, that is, the mythogems are presented to consciousness" (Harding 171). When Binx describes his "neighborhood theater in Gentilly" (*M* 7)—the evocative *gen* the source of so many birth-related words—he emphasizes its form, not its function of presenting constantly changing attractions: the theater "has permanent lettering on the front of the marquee reading: Where Happiness Costs So Little" (*M* 7). He adds, "[t]he fact is I am quite happy in a movie, even a bad movie," his choice of preposition suggesting the primacy of the experience of enclosure in his moviegoing. It is not too much to suggest that he experiences "*nyctophilia*," defined by Bertram Lewin as "an erotic pleasure in darkness, which enters as a wish-fulfillment element in fantasies of being in the 'womb,' or more properly, as the German word *Mutterleib* suggests, of being in the mother's body" (*The Image* 40). In short, Binx has a need, whether by dreaming or by moviegoing, to regress to "the first incestuous objects of the libido," as Freud puts it (*Interpretation* 350).

When Binx begins his recollection, he indicates that he had been awakened to the possibility of a search by a dream of his wounding in the Korean War, an event to which he will refer several times in his narrative. That event was no doubt traumatic, yet the imagery which Binx uses to describe it suggests that that memory "screens" a memory of a more primal wounding: "I remembered the first time the search occurred to me. I came to myself under a chindolea bush. . . . My shoulder didn't hurt but it was pressed hard against the ground as if somebody sat on me" (*M* 10–11). "Only once in my life was the grip of everydayness broken: when I lay bleeding in a ditch" (*M* 145). The first citation is made meaningful by J. C. Flugel's comment about anxiety, during his discussion of "birth fantasies." Tracing the word *anxiety* back to the Sanskrit *anhus*, meaning "narrowness or constriction," he argues that anxiety "bears witness to the fundamental association of fear with pressure and shortness of breath, which—the former owing to the passage through the narrow vagina, the latter to the interruption of the foetal circulation—constitute the most menacing and terrifying aspects of the birth process" (70). The second citation is a rather vivid description of the moment of birth.

If Binx's memory of his war wound is a re-presentation of his birth trauma, it is significantly appropriate that he thinks of the wound in

31

connection with all three women who play psychosexual roles in his life. As a result of the car collision on their way to the Gulf Coast, Sharon has to cut away Binx's T-shirt: "I was shot through the shoulder—a decent wound, as decent as any ever inflicted on Rory Calhoun or Tony Curtis. After all it could have been in the buttocks or genitals—or nose. Decent except that the fragment nicked the apex of my pleura and got me a collapsed lung and a big roaring empyema" (*M* 126). It is noteworthy that Binx's wounding results in a lung condition, for there is a long tradition of suspecting nostalgia as a cause of some lung conditions (Rosen 448–50). When Sharon, the mother substitute, sees the scar, she obligingly becomes maternal: "Come on now, son, where did you get that?" (*M* 26). Binx is jubilant, must think that his seduction is as good as done. Later, at the fishing camp, Binx uses the episode of his wounding to try to get his mother to understand how he has felt about his entire life: "What I am trying to tell you is that nothing seemed worth doing except something I couldn't even remember" (*M* 158). In other words, through the screening process he represses any recognition of the primal wound and therefore regresses in fantasy and in acted-out Don Juan behavior. And, finally, when he realizes in Chicago that he is falling in love with Kate, he says: "There I see her plain, see plain for the first time since I lay wounded in a ditch and watched an Oriental finch scratching around in the leaves . . ." (*M* 206). Binx implies that his mental visualization is finally free of "the parent in the percept."[2] His ability to choose an appropriate mate enables him to transcend his yearning for the mother who will not nurture.

The first movie that Binx mentions is not one that he actually attends during the time being recollected; this strategy gives Binx the opportunity to imply from the outset that his moviegoing is *a la recherche du temps perdu*—almost all of the movies to which he refers are re-releases. Since it is unidentified by title—thus losing its individuality, becoming a generic movie—the movie he mentions is just one that he "saw last month out by Lake Pontchartrain" (*M* 4) with his then-sweetheart Linda. What he says about the theater, little as it is, says much about his psychosexual regression: "[a] strong wind whipped the waves against the seawall; even inside you could hear the racket" (*M* 4), and "the theater was almost empty, which was

32

pleasant for me" (*M* 5). For Binx the theater replicates his intrauter-ine residence, which he would of course not like to share.

In this regard, it is significant that the theater is "out by Lake Pont-chartrain" and Binx has a date with him. Binx is acting out Sandor Ferenczi's contention that man has a drive to water as it symbolizes his phylogenetic history both as a fish and as a foetus. Such a drive activates the fantasy of copulating with the mother; since this activity is forbidden, the actual copulation must occur with a substitute ob-ject, which is what Binx's succession of secretaries represents, all of whom he takes to the Gulf Coast. Ferenczi's "situation of the penis in the vagina, the foetus in the uterus, and the fish in the water" (*Thalassa* 45) will surface again.

In his state of regression from the reality-principle, as Freud called it, Binx would have watched this movie closely:

> The movie was about a man who lost his memory in an accident and as a result lost everything: his family, his friends, his money. He found himself a stranger in a strange city. Here he had to make a fresh start, find a new place to live, a new job, a new girl. It was supposed to be a tragedy, his losing all this, and he seemed to suffer a great deal. On the other hand, things were not so bad after all. In no time he found a very picturesque place to live, a houseboat on the river, and a very handsome girl, the local librarian. (*M* 4–5)

The Thalassan content of the movie thus replicates the meaning that the theater has for Binx.

The theme of the movie is "[a]mnesia[,] . . . the perfect device of rotation."[3] Binx very carefully neglects the ending, stopping his re-capitulation at the point of rotational triumph, at which point the ego-hero has reached Eden, "a very picturesque houseboat on the river," and an ideal mother-substitute, "the local librarian." For if rotation climaxes, post-coital depression is inevitable; rotation's "only term is suicide or self loss." (Percy, "The Man" 95). Just a few minutes later, Binx admits his premature withdrawal from the plot: "The movies are onto the search, but they screw it up. The search always ends in despair. They like to show a fellow coming to himself in a strange place—but what does he do? He takes up with the local librarian, sets about proving to the local children what a nice fellow

33

he is, and settled down with a vengeance. In two weeks time he is so sunk in everydayness that he might just as well be dead" (*M* 13). Binx has already admitted that his rotation with Linda is over.

There is one final comment to be made about this first description of moviegoing. Binx always places himself in a movie theater, his fantasy substitute for the maternal womb, when he illustrates, either by implication or by explication, the various aspects of his theory of psychology (certification, alienation, rotation, and aesthetic repetition). He very closely situates his intellect within a matrix of mother-loss.

Thus, early on Wednesday morning, before Binx ventures into his objective-empirical world (as a young bachelor stockbroker in New Orleans, scion of a very old Louisiana family), he has already—by using Mrs. Langer's analogy, "[c]inema is 'like' dream"—described his *felt life*. For all the apparent specificity and solidity of Binx's world, Gentilly is "very spacious and airy and seems to stretch out like a field under the sky" (*M* 10); if such a description does not convey enough *unheimlichkeit*, then Binx's response to the homes near the Lake should be noted: "at this hour of dawn they are forlorn. A sadness settles over them like a fog from the lake" (*M* 84). This white mist—to be exposed before the week is out, at Binx's mother's fishing camp—is now just "a fog of uneasiness, a thin gas of malaise" (*M* 18): "What is the malaise? you ask. The malaise is the pain of loss. The world is lost to you, the world and the people in it, and there remains only you and the world and you no more able to be in the world than Banquo's ghost" (*M* 120).

On Wednesday night, Binx does go to a movie, *Panic in the Streets*, with his Aunt Emily's stepdaughter Kate. In the movie Richard Widmark plays a public health inspector who discovers "that a culture of cholera bacilli has gotten loose in the city. . . . There is a scene which shows the very neighborhood of the theater" (*M* 63). Such a movie, focusing upon the objective-empirical world, emphasizes the values of its worldview. Thus, for people indoctrinated with that worldview, to see the familiar re-presented by a visual apparatus is to see heightened reality. Such a movie would seem to hold no promise for Binx, but there is that phenomenon of "the triumphant reversal of alienation through its re-presenting" (Percy "The Man" 93). Binx calls

34

this "phenomenon of moviegoing . . . certification" (*M* 63): "Nowadays when a person lives somewhere, in a neighborhood, the place is not certified for him. More than likely he will live there sadly and the emptiness which is inside him will expand until it evacuates the entire neighborhood. But if he sees a movie which shows his very neighborhood, it becomes possible for him to live, for a time at least, as a person who is Somewhere and not Anywhere" (*M* 63). As a curative for emptiness—malaise, "the pain of loss"—such a reversal is, however, a Band-Aid. Alienation endures.

And since it does, Binx must look for a rotatory deliverance: on Thursday morning he embarks upon the seduction of his new secretary, Sharon. Already he has begun to fantasize her as Aphrodite, seeing her as a golden creature (*M* 95). Binx admits: "[d]esire for her is like a sorrow in my heart" (*M* 68). His description of his desire is no more exaggerated than is to be expected of a healthy twenty-nine year old man in the Big Easy, but the psychosexual ramifications of his desire are better appreciated with the aid of Robert Romanyshyn's phenomenology of desire, too long to be repeated here, except for its summary:

> If desire is the story of a homecoming, then it is the story of a home which is present *before* one's *consideration* of the heavens but paradoxically also absent until *after* this *consideration*. It is a home which does not exist but paradoxically always is, a home which is not a fact but more like a promise. It is a nostalgic home, this home of desire. It is the home out of which dreams of paradise and tales of the gardens of Eden are born. It is the home we have never had but have always lived. (51–2)

Sharon, then, is the latest object to excite Binx's fantasy of the mother-land. As he secretively reads *Arabia Deserta* (*M* 68), a title which describes his life in Gentilly, he dreams of Sharon, the oasis, the place where the water is.

Charles M. Doughty's long trek to Mecca—as a disguised Christian among the Muslims—reminds Binx of how he came to undertake his "horizontal search." He had pursued a "vertical search"—an intellectual quest founded on Plato, currently manifested by objective-empiricism[4]—until he discovered that it left him "left over" (*M* 70), his adaptation of Sartre's *de trop,* the individual who is superfluous in any scientistic worldview. It happened in a hotel in Birmingham (the same city in which Walker Percy discovered alienation); Binx read *The Chemistry of Life,* which explained everything but himself, which is not chemical; he closed the book, to go see *It Happened One Night,* which is offered, in "The Man on the Train," as an illustration of this movement: "Zone crossing is of such great moment to the alienated I because the latter is thereby able to explore the It while at the same time retaining his option of noncommitment" (88). Then, therefore, Binx adopted the "horizontal search," the alienated way, with its specious deliverances of short-term reversal, rotation and aesthetic repetition. Disguised as successfully as Charles Doughty, Binx displays his noncommitment most apparently as he explores the *en soi* of his succession of secretaries.

On his way home on Thursday afternoon, Binx stops off at the Tivoli Theater. Since the theater as a form is the locus of Binx's womb fantasy, which often reveals itself in his hankering after such Eden-like places as oases and parks, the Tivoli, named after the famous Italian gardens, would have special appeal for him. The manager practically forces Binx to take a "sample look" (*M* 73) at a Jane Powell musical, but the cheerful outgoingness of the actress is enough to drive him to despair.

Yet one happy movie does not an alien make. Binx has to admit, "it was here in the Tivoli that I first discovered place and time, tasted it like okra" (*M* 75), during a re-release of *Red River* a couple of years before. It is Binx's recollection of the experience as a gustatory event which demands close attention; in *Film and the Dream Screen* Robert Eberwein bases the following paragraph on the thought of Julia Kristeva:

> The infant's relationship to its mother after birth can be described as a kind of "semiotic" *chora.* ". . . In its vocalizations and cries (these actions themselves revivals of more primitive activities engaged in within the womb), the infant tries to survive by calling for food. The mother responds to these anaclises by offering herself." Notice the similarity of the terms used by Kristeva to describe the mother and the kind of language one might use to describe the viewing situation in a theater. The mother sustains the infant by "providing . . . an axis, a projection screen, a limit, a support for the infant's invocation . . ." The union of infant and mother in the semiotic

chora fixes a "space": "Orality," audition, vision: archaic modalities upon which the most precocious discretion emerges. The breast given and withdrawn; lamp light capturing the gaze; the intermittent sound of voices or music—these great anaclisis, . . . hold it, and thus inhibit and absorb it in such a way that it is discharged and calmed through them. . . . Therefore, the breast, light, sound become a *there;* place, point, marker. . . . The mark of an archaic point, the initiation into "space," the "chora." . . . There is not yet an outside. (32)

In the Tivoli Binx had, to say it another way, become energized by a dream of repetition, by a desire to go back to the time of symbiosis, before breast was lost as language was gained. Thus he became the moviegoer.

Binx's recollection of the Tivoli experience reminds him of another movie: "Once as I was travelling through the Midwest ten years ago I had a layover of three hours in Cincinnati. There was time to go see Joseph Cotton in *Holiday* at a neighborhood theater called the Altamont—but not before I had struck up an acquaintance with the ticket seller, a lady named Mrs. Clara James, and learned that she had seven grandchildren all living in Cincinnati" (*M* 75). Binx mentions the ticket seller because he had just previously explained his dependence upon meditation: "If I did not talk to the theater owner or the ticket seller, I should be lost, cut loose metaphysically speaking. I should be seeing one copy of a film which might be shown anywhere and at any time. It is possible to become a ghost and not know whether one is in downtown Loews in Denver or suburban Bijou in Jacksonville." The film experience, he realizes could be a metaphor for the objective-empirical method: Cartesian reality is universal and eternal, with the human being reduced to being a spectator. But now that he is alienated from the objective-empirical, Binx knows that salvation—if there is to be any—will be local and immediate, spoken to his person by another person.

The Cincinnati movie occurs to Binx for several reasons having to do with a sense of place. For one thing, Cincinnati is the home of the famous Eden Park. The theater's name, Altamont, would remind him of the hometown of Thomas Wolfe (celebrated in "The Man on the Train" [95] as a practitioner of the repetitional movement in literature). Clara James might suggest Laura James, the mother-substitute for Eugene Gant in *Look Homeward, Angel*. The movie title, *Holiday*, suggests that Binx, in recalling the Tivoli, has been tempted to yearn for the *Urkinohaus*, the *Mutterleib*. The setting of the movie has an idyllic, Thalassan name, Lake Placid, especially in contrast to Saranac Lake, five miles down the road, where Walker Percy had to deal with both tuberculosis and alienation. The movie thematizes the contrast between objective-empirical values, contained in the marble-walled Seaton mansion, and object-relation values, contained in the playroom. Johnny Case arrives to become engaged to Julia Seaton, but when he meets sister Linda, they fall in love. According to Timothy W. Johnson, the playroom "is Linda's refuge—a warm, intimate room filled with dreams, childhood mementos, . . . and a portrait of their [dead] mother over the fireplace" (759). The only trouble with Binx's recollection? The lead male actor was Cary Grant, not Joseph Cotten: like Binx's memory, all aesthetic repetitions are unreliable.

Escaping from Jane Powell, Binx reaches his apartment, in the basement of the house of Mrs. Schexnaydre (pronounced locally "SCHEX nay der," but Gallo-psychoanalytically as "*chez* NAY dir"). However her name is pronounced, she is the "bad mother" for the ego-hero; Mrs. Schexnaydre's house is built on this mythological substrate:

> When [the hero] arrives at the nadir of the mythological round, he undergoes a supreme ordeal and gains his reward. The triumph may be represented as the hero's sexual union with the goddess-mother of the world (sacred marriage), his recognition by the father-creator (father atonement), his own divinization (apotheosis) . . . : intrinsically it is an expansion of consciousness and therewith of being (illumination, transfiguration, freedom). The final work is that of the return. . . . (Campbell 246)

Mrs. Schexnaydre has three dogs—a fractionate Cerberus—but Binx most despises the one that he has nicknamed "Rosebud," in honor of its "large convoluted anus" (*M* 77). As a student of moviegoing, Binx must know that *Citizen Kane* hinges on an object named Rosebud, which is the key to understanding that Charles Foster Kane's destiny was determined by the loss of his mother (Mayne 116–19). Once Binx can get past "Rosebud," he can get to his bed, over which "hang two Currier and Ives prints of ice-skaters in Central Park. How sad the little figures seem, skimming along in step! How sad the city seems!" (*M* 78) Early on Wednesday Binx had said: "I . . . once met a girl in Central Park, but it is not much to remember" (*M* 7). Thus he implies that while he can try to repress his thoughts during the day he cannot control the dreams that hang over his bed at night. With his mind still very much in the mood awakened by his memory of *Holiday*, he goes to a movie on Thursday night. Nor should the type of movie he selects come as a surprise:

> Tonight, Thursday night, I carry out a successful experiment in repetition.
>
> Fourteen years ago, when I was a sophomore, I saw a western at the movie-house on Freret Street, a place frequented by students and known to them as the Armpit. The movie was *The Oxbow Incident* and it was quite good. . . . Yesterday evening I noticed in the *Picayune* that another western was playing in the same theater. (*M* 79)

When he and Kate come out of the movie, Binx says, "A successful repetition": "What is a repetition? A repetition is the reenactment of past experience toward the end of isolating the time segment which has lapsed in order that it, the lapsed time, can be savored of itself and without the usual adulteration of events that clog time like peanuts in brittle" (*M* 79–80). Binx's analogy between aesthetic repetition and peanut brittle (*sans* goobers) is like Ethel Spector Person's analogy between aesthetic repetition and the "lover's reel" in stressing that memory is selective (128). But Binx's analogy is additionally appropriate in stressing that the experience, in his case, is gustatory:

> How, then, tasted my own fourteen years since *The Oxbow Incident?*
> As usual it eluded me. (*M* 80)

Binx's frustration is predicted by "The Man on the Train":

> Unlike rotation, [repetition] is of two kinds, the aesthetic and the existential, which literature accordingly polarizes. The aesthetic repetition captures the savor of repetition without surrendering the self as a locus of experience and possibility. When Proust tastes the piece of cake or Captain Ryder finds himself at Brideshead, the incident may serve as an occasion for either kind: an excursion into the interesting, a savoring of the

past as experience; or two, the passionate quest in which the incident serves as a thread in the labyrinth to be followed at any cost. This latter, however, no matter how serious, cannot fail to be polarized by art, transmitting as the interesting. The question what does it mean to stand before the house of one's childhood? is thus received in two different ways—one as an occasion for the connoisseur sampling of a rare emotion, the other literally and seriously: what does it really mean? (*Man* 95–6)

Since Binx is still engaged in rotation and aesthetic repetition, he has not surrendered "the self as a locus of experience and possibility" in order to pursue "the passionate quest." Thus he can only "savor" the past—Percy is consistent from genre to genre in attributing gustation to aesthetic repetition. But only in the novel, in that genre's covert way, will he ever admit that the gustatory response is ultimately *lactophilia*.

As if to demonstrate his refusal to surrender to the passionate quest, Binx dedicates Friday and Saturday to the great rotation of seducing Sharon. He is so engrossed in his plan that he does not need to go to a movie on Friday night, just watches a little television. Then, by noon on Saturday, he has persuaded Sharon to go to the beach with him. Once in his MG, she seems to intuit her role as a mother-substitute, for she begins to address him as "son" (*M* 124) or "boy" (*M* 132). Through a fortunate accident, Binx is able to impersonate "Rory Calhoun or Tony Curtis" (*M* 126), even "Bill Holden" (*M* 127), as one of them would appear if he was playing a wounded war hero; Sharon is so captivated and maternal that Binx has milk on his mind as they take the ferry out to Ship Island. He is surrounded by "milk white" (*M* 219) country children, while the boat is "chuffing through the thin milky waters of Mississippi Sound" (*M* 129).[5]

Binx perfectly captures the excitement when one returns to the beach: "Over the hillock lies the open sea. The difference is very great: first, this sleazy backwater, then the great blue ocean. The beach is clean and a big surf is rolling in; the water in the middle distance is green and lathered. You come over the hillock and your heart lifts up; your old sad music comes into the major" (*M* 130). But Binx's especial excitement is suggested by a comment made by D. W. Winnicott about a line by Tagore, "On the seashore of endless worlds, children play":

40

In my adolescence I had no idea what it could mean, but it found a place in me, and its imprint has not yet faded.

When I first became a Freudian I *knew* what it meant. The sea and the shore represented endless intercourse between man and woman, and the child emerged from this union to have a brief moment before becoming in turn adult or parent. Then, as a student of unconscious symbolism, I *knew* (one always *knows*) that the sea is the mother, and onto the seashore the child is born. Babies come up out of the sea and are spewed out upon the land, like Jonah from the whale. So now the seashore was the mother's body, after a child is born and the mother and the now viable baby are getting to know each other. (Muensterberger 5–6)

With such an emotional investment, Binx easily fantasizes Sharon as Aphrodite, born of the white foam: "She wades out ahead of me, turning to and fro, hands outstretched to the water and sweeping it before her. Now and then she raises her hands to her head as if she were placing a crown and combs back her hair with the last two fingers. The green water foams . . ." (*M* 130). As Aphrodite—"originally a mother goddess," according to Michael Balint (93)—Sharon plays her role to perfection: "Come on, son. I'm going to give you some beer" (*M* 131). With his gustatory need met, no wonder that Binx can hardly wait for the next movement: "Once when she gets up, I come up on my knees and embrace her golden thighs, such a fine strapping armful they are" (*M* 132). Then he pays her full homage: "'Sweetheart, I'll never turn you loose.' Mother of all living, what an armful" (*M* 132). According to some etymologies, "mother of the living" is the meaning of the name *Eve*, so that Binx must be convinced that he is pretty close to Paradise. By the time the moon rises, Sharon has agreed to visit Binx's mother's fishing camp (*M* 136). While he has already admitted that Sharon, as a rotation object, is not so magnetic as she was, even so the pull of his mother's fishing camp as a locus of aesthetic repetition is so great that he still means to seduce her there, to fulfill Ferenczi's "situation of the penis in the vagina, the foetus in the uterus, and the fish in the water." He will return to the womb *on* his mother's place, if not *in* her place.

But his mother is at the camp, surrounded by the six surviving children of her second marriage. With justification, Binx thinks of the *Titanic*, another doomed maiden voyage. For the moviegoer, this

41

will not be *A Night to Remember*. Just moments before, Sharon had given him the penultimate promise: "She has become tender toward me and now and then presses my cheek with her hand" (*M* 136). Such caresses activate the infant's reflex to suck (Brazelton and Cramer 51–52). The welcome that Binx receives from his mother is of a different order:

> "Well, well, look who's here," she says but does not look.
>
> Her hands dry, she rubs her nose vigorously with her three middle fingers held straight up. She has hay fever and crabs make it worse. It is a sound too well known to me to be remembered, this quick jiggle up and down and the little wet wringing noises under her fingers.
>
> We give each other a kiss or rather we press our cheeks together, Mother embracing my head with her wrist as if her hands were still wet. (*M* 137)

In effect receiving a brush-off from his mother, Binx ponders their relationship: "Sometimes I feel a son's love for her, or something like this, and try to give her a special greeting, but at this time she avoids my eye and gives me her cheek . . ." (*M* 137–38). When, after a while, he tries again to talk to her, he gets the impression that she is "as old and sly as Eve herself" (*M* 142), but this is not the bountiful Eve he had earlier imagined Sharon to be, but the Great Mother, whose preeminence was destroyed by the Yahwist author of Genesis. That goddess was often accompanied by a son-lover who was sacrificed to die, in order to perpetuate her power.

Understandably, Binx jumps at the opportunity to take his half-siblings and Sharon to the Moonlite Drive-In (*M* 143–44). There he can patter about rotations and aesthetic repetitions, as if his life were nothing but moviegoing. But later the real moviegoing begins: "Three o'clock and suddenly awake amid the smell of dreams and of the years come back and peopled and blown away again like smoke. A young man am I, twenty-nine, but I am as full of dreams as an ancient. At night the years come back and perch around my bed like ghosts" (*M* 144).

Here dreams have the attribute of smell—appropriately, since the sense of smell, like the sense of taste, is first directed to the mother's breast (Brazelton and Cramer, 60–61), which is the place on which dreams originate. Binx had broached the subject of his dreaming with a similar image: "I dreamed of the war, no, not quite dreamed but woke with the taste of it in my mouth, the queasy-quince taste of 1951 and the Orient" (*M* 10). Since the wartime experience is a screen memory for his infantile trauma, it should be accompanied by a taste.

As would be expected, Binx's previous extended discussion of his disturbed sleep occurs when he speaks of *chez Naydre:*

> . . . sometimes before dawn I awake with a violent start and for the rest of the night lie dozing yet wakeful and watchful. I have not slept soundly for many years. Not since the war when I was knocked out for two days have I really lost consciousness as a child loses consciousness in sleep and wakes to a new world not even remembering when he went to bed. I always know where I am and what time it is. Whenever I feel myself sinking toward a deep sleep, something always recalls me: 'Not so fast now. Suppose you should go to sleep and it should happen. What then?' Clearly nothing. Yet there I lie, wakeful and watchful as a sentinel, ears tuned to the slightest noise. I can even hear old Rosebud turning round and round in the azalea bushes before settling down. (*M* 83–84)

The simple explanation will not, however, suffice. The basement apartment, "as impersonal as a motel room" (*M* 78), is a placeless place. Binx lives as an exile from Central Park, hounded by Rosebud, the witch's watchdog. Anyone caught in that situation would be tempted to regress, but fear that such regression might lead to extinction.

On the occasion in question, Binx had gotten up to walk to the lake. On his way he thought of another poor sleeper: "My father used to suffer from insomnia" (*M* 85). Binx's Aunt Emily has a memory of Binx's father as a "student prince" (*M* 50), taking "off helter-skelter up the Rhine . . . with a bottle of *Liebfraumilch* under one arm and *Wilhelm Meister* under the other." But apparently he never learned to wander from *Wilhelm,* nor did he find a sufficient supply of *Leibfraumilch,* even though he married a nurse. As Binx walks, he thinks of his mother's inability to respond to her husband's insomnia:

> Just at this hour of dawn I would be awakened by a terrible sound: my father crashing through the screen door, sleeping bag under his arm, his

eyes crisscrossed by fatigue and by the sadness of these glimmering dawns. My mother, without meaning to, put a quietus on his hopes of sleep even more effectively than this forlorn hour. She had a way of summing up his doings in a phrase that took the heart out of him. He dreamed, I know, of a place of quiet breathing and a deep sleep under the stars and next to the sweet earth. She agreed. "Honey, I'm all for it. I think we all ought to get back to nature and I'd be right with you, Honey, if it wasn't for the chiggers. I'm chigger bait." (*M* 85)

Binx's father continued his decline until he had no appetite at all. Then Binx's mother did mother her husband: "I got his book. I remember it—it was a book called *The Greene Murder Case.* Everybody in the family read it. I began to read and he began to listen, and while I read, I fed him" (*M* 152–53). But any reader of "The Man on the Train" knows that the effect of such a treatment is only temporary: "An Erle Stanley Gardner novel is a true exercise in alienation. A man who finishes his twentieth Perry Mason is that much nearer total despair than when he started" (83). Only the onset of World War II could rouse Binx's father from his torpor. Then—and this completes Binx's train of thought about his father—as a volunteer, Binx's father had died "in the wine dark sea" (*M* 25) off Crete. That his father had regressed to extinction is implied in Binx's bitter comment: "He found a way to do both: to please [the family] and please himself. To leave. To do what he wanted to do and save old England doing it. And perhaps even carry off the grandest coup of all: to die. To win the big prize for them and for himself (but not even he dreamed he would succeed not only in dying but in dying in Crete in the wine dark sea)" (*M* 157). That he knows the source of his father's alienation Binx implies by his assertion that his father died with a copy of *A Shropshire Lad* in his pocket, mother-haunted A. E. Houseman's great celebration of nostalgia (Wolfenstein).

When, then, Binx suddenly wakes at the fishing camp, he seems to experience nausea: ". . . my old place is used up (places get used up by rotatory and repetitive use) and when I awake, I awake in the grip of everydayness. Everydayness is the enemy. No search is possible. Perhaps there was a time when everydayness was not too strong and one could break its grip by brute strength. Now nothing breaks it—but disaster. Only once in my life was the grip of every-

44

dayness broken: when I lay bleeding in a ditch" (*M* 145). It was at that time that he had experienced two days of dreamless sleep (*M* 3–4)—probably a screen memory for his post-birth stupor—and he must be, as his father was, tempted to seek extinction, now that his moviegoing evasions no longer seem to work.

But then he acts like a stubborn infant: "In a sudden rage and, as if I had been seized by a fit, I roll over and fall in a heap on the floor and lie shivering on the boards, worse off than the miserablest muskrat in the swamp. Nevertheless I vow: I'm a son of a bitch if I'll be defeated by the everydayness" (*M* 145). And indeed he would be a son of a bitch (goddess) if he succumbed to an alienation which she had caused. He resolves to resume the search that he has occasionally mentioned, the existential repetition (or quest or return), which ends, according to "The Man on the Train," "before the house of one's childhood" (96).

Such resolution allows Binx to go back to sleep, a deep sleep, it may be inferred from his description of awakening: "It starts as an evil turn of events. There is a sense of urgency. Something has to be done. Let us please do something about it. Then it is a color, a very bad color that needs tending to. Then a pain. But there is no use: it is a sound that it is out there in the world and nothing can be done about it. Awake" (*M* 146–47). The description sounds more like an fetus trying not to be born or like a moviegoer at a movie with a bad projectionist. Then Binx is before the house of his childhood: "The world is like milk: sky, water, savannah. The thin etherlike water vaporizes; tendrils of fog gather like smoke; a white shaft lies straight as a ruler over the marsh" (*M* 147). As Binx listens to his stepfather going off to fish—Roy gets "the penis in the vagina, the foetus in the uterus, and the fish in the water"—he becomes aware of his isolation:

> The hull disappears into a white middle distance and the sound goes suddenly small as if the boat had run into cotton.
> A deformed live oak emerges from the whiteness, stands up in the air, like a tree in a Chinese print. Minutes pass. (*M* 147–48)

Binx can only wait: "Behind a screen door opens softly and my mother comes out on the dock with a casting rod. . . . 'Hinh-honh,' she says in a yawn-sigh as wan and white as the morning. Her blouse is one of Roy's army shirts and not much too big for her large breasts" (*M* 148). In fantasy Binx has pursued the mother-near-the-water during his entire narration, and now she stands before him, "her large breasts" lactating his world, like the Great Mother of old (Neumann 32) or like Juno, whose lactation created the Milky Way (Warner 196).

Binx pulls on his pants, to walk barefoot into "a cool milky world" (*M* 48):

> "Isn't it mighty early for you!" Her voice is a tinkle over the water.
> My mother is easy and affectionate with me. Now we may speak together. It is the early morning and our isolation in the great white marsh.
> "Can I fix you some breakfast?"
> "No'm. I'm not hungry." Our voices go ringing around the empty room of the morning.

Surely it comes as a surprise that Binx would refuse her gesture, for Binx has been speaking, ever since his memory of the movie out by Lake Pontchartrain (*M* 5), of the empty room that represents the womb and of the whiteness of the water locale and of the empty movie screen (soon to be discussed) that represents the breast. But Binx's next statement explains his reason for declining: "Still she puts me off" (*M* 149). Binx seems to realize that she will be his nurse no better than she was his father's. Binx notes that his mother "veers away from intimacy" (*M* 149), would prefer to talk about fishing. When he says that he does not like to fish, she replies, "You're just like your father." Binx stretches "out at full length," nestling his "head on a two-by-four," as if it were a mother's arm: "It is possible to squint into the rising sun and at the same time see my mother spangled in rainbows" (*M* 149–50), like a promise. The description of nursing by Kristeva offered earlier should be recalled.

Binx needs both nourishment and news. As if to tease him in both his desires, his mother tells of his father's one successful fishing trip, when he caught a *sac au lait,* so named by the Louisiana French in an attempt to pronounce the Choctaw *sakli,* their name for the fish known in English as *trout* (Mathews 1438). That *sakli* became *sac au lait* may speak volumes about Gallic psychosexual development. For

Binx's father the fish was no more a mamma than his wife would be. In time, Binx's mother turns the conversation to her father, who also was not a fisherman, though "[h]e owned a fleet of trawlers at Golden Meadow. But did he love pretty girls. Till his dying day" (*M* 155) Still squinting "up at her through the rainbows," Binx asks, "Does it last that long?" Her reply is sharp and conclusive: "Don't you get risque with me! This is your mother you're talking to and not one of your little hotsy-totsies." Apparently admitting defeat, Binx concludes, "Fishing is poor" (*M* 159), and there will be no "penis in the vagina" or "foetus in the uterus" at all.

What has been going on here? It should be remembered that Binx is constructing his narrative at least a year after the fact (for a violation of the "virtual present" of the narrative proper, see the anticipation of the "catastrophe Monday night" just as Binx and Kate arrive in Chicago on Monday morning [201]). It should be kept in mind, too, that Binx uses in his narrative either the same terms— rotation, (aesthetic) repetition—or closely equivalent terms—"malaise" for alienation, "search" for existential repetition—of the psychological system discussed in "The Man on the Train"; thus he implies that he is basing his interpretation and description of his earlier behavior on that system. Further, he makes in his narrative the same basic distinction that is made by "The Man on the Train"; for his narrative, the "vertical search" names the objective-empirical technique and the "horizontal search" (*M* 70) names the alienated response (and its putative deliverances). And, also, since he mentions Freud's *Interpretation of Dreams* in connection with his teenage curiosity and his mother's aloofness (*M* 138), he implies a long and close sensitivity to psychoanalytic literature, especially as it might benefit him. Finally, since he identifies himself as a "moviegoer" (*M* 109) and uses moviegoing and movie lore to illustrate his psychological theories and his impersonations, he implies a full knowledge of the psychoanalysis of moviegoing, as summarized in such recent studies as Robert Eberwein's *Film and the Dream Screen* and Judith Mayne's *Private Novels, Public Films*. With these considerations in mind, it is quite possible that Binx has relied upon a psychoanalytic theory formulated by Bertram Lewin to structure his narrative, especially the scene between his mother and himself on the dock. But even if Binx is not familiar with Lewin's research, it can, nevertheless, be used to gloss his mental and physical behavior.

Lewin introduced his theory in "Sleep, the Mouth, and the Dream Screen." His curiosity was aroused by Freud's comment in *The Interpretation of Dreams* that a wish to sleep is "the prime reason for all dreaming, the dream being the great guardian of sleep" (419). Lewin was also pondering M. J. Eisler's assertion "that sleep [is] a regressive phenomenon, a return to a hypothetical preoral or apnoeic stage, such as might be imagined for the unborn child" (419). Then a patient in session told him: "I had my dream all ready for you; but while I was lying here looking at it, it turned over away from me, rolled up, and rolled away from me—over and over like two tumblers" (420). Lewin was inspired to conceive of the "dream screen."

Lewin later reported, in "Inferences from the Dream Screen," that the analogy between the dream process and the moviegoing experience occurred to him immediately (226). (This is the same analogy that Mrs. Langer was to formulate later, except that she reversed the terms; it is also the same analogy that is undeveloped in Julia Kristeva's description of the nursing event.)[6] As refined and developed by Lewin and other analysts—Charles Rycroft, Joseph Kepecs, Gert Heilbrum, Mark Kanzer, Angel Garma, L. Bryce Boyer, and Carel van der Heide—the following model of the dreamer as moviegoer is widely used.

When a baby nurses, it wishes to nurse to gratification, then to drop into a dreamless, regressive sleep. The last visual impression that it receives before sleeping is the huge blank breast that is not far enough distant even to be perceived as an object separate from the ego. The baby therefore internalizes the breast as a blank dream, a blank screen with nothing on it. This internalization is not abandoned in time. As the ego develops, manifest content dreams—unconscious wishes that threaten to awaken the sleeper—are projected onto the dream screen, but that screen is ordinarily not recalled when the manifest dream is recalled. But as some people begin to awaken, the ego sometimes has the experience of seeing the dream screen—on which is projected a visual dream—receding, losing its flat appearance, assuming a smaller, curved shape. The experience of the dream screen seems more prevalent among those dreamers who have deep oral fixations. Such dreamers also have fantasies of intra-uterine regression, but there is also the possibility of a conflicting psychic energy, a death wish. Thus some such dreamers fight sleep, to the extent that "the tensions may be carried over into a dreamlike awakening in which the identifications and the instinctual goals remain confused" (Kanzer 519). In "Reconsideration of the Dream Screen" Lewin offers a composite of reports of the dream screen:

> The whitish, cloudy, endless wall is the breast or the ghost of a breast—thus sensed by the diplopic amblyopic baby, with its weak powers of accommodation and its confused depth and color perceptions. Notably the screen equivalent in such dreams is of badly defined thickness and consistency; it is thick or fluid, dark or whitish or milky, out of focus—indeed questionably visual at all . . . (183)

What does the model of the dream screen have to say about Binx's narrative? With his first description of moviegoing, Binx shows that a movie theater re-presents his fantasy of regression to the womb. When he comes out of his moviegoing, he generally heads for water, another image of intrauterine flight. Having denied the reality of his biological mother, he has split his fantasy figure: Mrs. Schexnaydre is the "bad mother," while each new secretary is the "good mother," as long as she represents pure possibility. Binx's oral fixation shows his need to nurse to satisfaction, so that he could sleep soundly (and thus see the dream screen) instead of the manifest content (such as the skaters in Central Park) which haunts his head. He suffers, instead, from dream disturbance, even as he fears relaxing his fragile grip on his ego so that he could sleep, for the regression might then be fatal.

In the scene at the fishing camp Binx suffers from dreaming, then makes a first effort to resist. Then he dreams the dream screen (*M* 146–47), even tries to prevent "color" and "sound" from occurring on the screen, thus waking him. The subsequent whiteness imagery indicates that the dream screen lingers, even as his mother appears through the "screen" (*M* 148)—it will be recalled that Binx described his "father crashing through the screen door, . . . his eyes crisscrossed by fatigue and by the sadness of these glimmering dawns" (*M* 85), such as Binx is now seeing. Then, by stretching out

49

on the dock, Binx positions himself as the child at the breast of the nurse. His rejection of her offer to make him breakfast reveals that he is coming to the realization that she simply cannot be a gratifying mother. He is progressing from a dependence upon ideal internal objects toward a more realistic response to things as they are, thus showing ego development.[7]

This is not to say that Binx's recovery will be quick and/or complete. On the way back to New Orleans on Sunday afternoon, he falls back into his rotational fantasy, seeking "the thickest and innerest part of Sharon's thigh" (*M* 166), which is just a *frisson* from fusion, fantasy's focus:

> She bats me away with a new vigor.
> "Son, don't you mess with me."
> "Very well, I won't," I say gloomily, as willing not to mess with her as mess with her, to tell the truth.
> "That's all right. You come here."
> "I'm here."
> She gives me a kiss. "I got your number, son. But that's all right. You're a good old boy. You really tickle me." She's been talking to my mother. "Now you tend to your business and get me on home."
> "Why?"
> "I have to meet someone."

Before they had started to the beach, Sharon had asked Binx, "Is Miss Cutrer any kin to you" (*M* 118), already suspecting that the romantic role of a Binx secretary is to be a tempo, not a permanent hire. Now, having talked with the real mother, who has been telling Binx for years that he should marry Kate (*M* 55), this hotsy-totsy realizes that she had better be getting out to "meet someone" of her own.

His fantasy of attainment having thus been rebuffed, Binx goes to the home of his Aunt Emily in the Garden District—certainly no garden district for him—there to suffer from his loss of sleep "during the past week" (*M* 82). Then, with Kate, he literally becomes "the man on the train," directed by his Uncle Jules to attend a convention in Chicago. His drowsiness had been but a prelude to his condition on the train: "The drowsiness returns. It is unwelcome. I recognize it as the sort of fitful twilight which has come over me of late, a twilight where waking dreams are dreamed and sleep never comes" (*M* 188). The sleep that never comes is also the penis that never comes. Back at Aunt Emily's, Sam Yerger had asked the departing Binx, "Brother Andy, is you getting much" (*M* 183). The fact is that, for all Binx's elaborate Don Juan behavior, he mentions not one orgasm, that experience whose existential drive is to achieve the same experience of fusion that he seeks through regression. Significantly, Binx alternates looking out the window and looking over the shoulder of his reading neighbor, both actions mirroring what is on his mind:

> We pause at an advertisement of a Bourbon Street nightclub which is a picture of a dancer with an oiled body. Her triceps arch forward like a mare's. For a second we gaze heavy-lidded and pass on. Now he finds what he wants. . . . Dreaming at his shoulder, I can make out no more than
> In order to deepen and enrich the marital—
> It is a counseling column which I too read faithfully. (*M* 188–89)

As the "train sways through the swamp" (*M* 189), Binx is miserable: "Staying awake is a kind of sickness and sleep is forever guarded against by a dizzy dutiful alertness. Waking wide-eyed dreams come as fitfully as swampfire." His condition like that earlier described by Mark Kanzer as "a dreamlike awakening," Binx has a waking dream of the sexologists Dean, whom he had seen at a Canal Street book-signing of their collaboration *Technique in Marriage,* one technique of which begins: "Now with a tender regard for your partner remove your hand from the nipple and gently manipulate. . ." (*M* 190). At this point in the life of the moviegoer/man-on-the train, a remark by Joseph Kepecs, in "A Waking Screen Analogous to the Dream Screen," is appropriate: "It is quite likely that many people are unable to perceive the real world clearly because between it and themselves they interpose a phantom of the maternal breast through which everything else is seen" (171). This scene once again confirms that the existential concerns of "The Man on the Train" are the psychosexual concerns of *The Moviegoer.*

Kate is herself in a serious crisis, part of a long-term condition that may have originated in deprivation of the object (*M* 110–11), for her mother, it is to be inferred, died before Kate was three years old. Binx

51

implies that they share the same condition, even as they share her roomette on the train. He observes the dream screen: "Outside a square of yellow light flees along an embankment, falls away to the woods and fields, comes roaring back good as new. Suddenly a perky head pops up. Kate is leaning forward hugging herself." He observes her observing the dream screen: "She is back at her window, moving her hand to see it move in the flying yellow square." He concludes: "We hunch up knee to knee and nose to nose like the two devils on the Rorschach card" (*M* 192).[8]

With such mutuality of misery, they begin to discuss marriage, a subject which has come up between them before (*M* 116). Since Kate is as alienated as Binx, it follows that she too has been dreaming of orgasm as fusion (*M* 199). They try, therefore, to consummate their relationship, hoping for deep, dreamless sleep: Binx imagines himself dispatching Kate into "as sweet a sleep as ever Scarlett enjoyed the morning of Rhett's return" (*M* 200). But "flesh poor flesh" failed them. Then Kate imagines herself as Ophelia (*M* 201), undone by another mother's boy, according to Freud.

Despite their sexual failure, Binx is developing the strength to express his love for Kate, who looks after him (*M* 201) much as a mother hen, "with many a cluck and much fuss" (*M* 202). He suffers not even "two seconds of malaise" (*M* 204). Then, in a bar on the Loop, Binx looks at Kate: ". . . I see her plain, see plain for the first time since I lay wounded in a ditch and watched on Oriental finch scratching around in the leaves—a quiet little body she is, a tough little city Celt; no, more of a Rachel really, a dark little Rachel bound home to Brooklyn on the IRT. I give her a pat on the leg" (*M* 206). Kepecs' comment about the "phantom of the maternal breast through which everything else is seen" is appropriate here. By calling Kate a Rachel, Binx may only mean that she is like a Jew, whom he has earlier epitomized as the alienated person (*M* 88–89), but there is the possibility that he is thinking of the Rachel who wept for her children. He knows that he needs that kind of wife who can feed his maternal deprivation. For once, he is free of the desire that is symptomatic of his nostalgia (*M* 207).

Even a visit to the home of some Wilmette suburbanites fails to dismay the couple: "Back to the Loop where we dive into the mother and Urwomb of all moviehouses—an Aztec mortuary of funeral urns and glyphs thronged with the spirit-presences of another day, William Powell and George Brent and Patsy Kelly and Charley Chase, the best friends of my childhood—and see a movie called *The Young Philadelphians*. Kate holds my hand tightly in the dark" (*M* 211). Looking back from his post-recovery vantage point, Binx now knows what the movie theater had meant to him before, the locus of all his repetitional fantasies, and can name it for what it had been. Ernest Becker says: "The dream mode, like the cinema, brings fantasied fulfillment in a shallowly lived present. The shortcomings of our world are remedied in fancy allowing one to transpose the body of his wife into that of his favorite movie star" (39). In his childhood loneliness, Binx had sought fantasy friends in the movie theater, the very locus of loss. But now he has found a fellow inhabitant in the city of love (as the movie title indicates); he even offers a synopsis of the movie, for he now realizes that it had foreshadowed his destiny: "Paul Newman is an idealistic young fellow who is disillusioned and becomes cynical and calculating. But in the end he recovers his ideals" (*M* 211). Then Paul is worthy of his Christian name—and so is Binx.

The forces of the past do not, however, give up their hold so easily. In his drowsy and dazed condition, Binx had neglected to tell his Aunt Emily of Kate's decision to go to Chicago with him. Outraged, she summons her nephew back to New Orleans for judgment. Her wrath is terrible, for, with one question, she reveals that she has absolutely no comprehension of her nephew's desperate condition ("What do you think is the purpose of life—to go to the movies and dally with every girl that comes along" [226]), for both behaviors originate in his mother-loss.[9]

Dismissed, Binx sees no future but Mrs. Schexnaydre's basement—but Kate tells him to wait there for her. While he waits, he is convinced that he will despair like his father; the future looks so bleak that he can only "fall prey to desire" (*M* 228), become once again a captive of nostalgia. He even tries to contact Sharon, to revive his fantasy quest for the "oceanic feeling"; standing in an "evil-smelling" telephone booth, he is mocked by a piece of playground equipment: "*Iii-oorr* goes the ocean wave, its struts twinkling in the golden light, its skirt swaying to and fro like a young dancing girl"

(*M* 231), like the vision of Aphrodite presented by the Sharon in the golden light on the beach. But, having found a "someone," Sharon is not at home; rather Binx talks to her roommate, Joyce, for whom he has harbored rotatory yearnings: "I've been wanting to meet you for some time" (*M* 229). But even she could be mocking Binx, for she replies, "The Lord of Misrule reigned yesterday [on Shrove Tuesday] . . ." (*M* 230). As Ian Suttie explains, the Lord of Misrule is a late survivor of the young male lover-victim who was sacrificed each spring in the Great Mother rites (130).

But then Kate proves loyal, does not abandon him as his fantasy-mother Sharon had. Kate's savior role had been foreshadowed earlier, when Sam Yerger tells Binx that when he saw Kate he said to himself: "My God, . . . there goes Natasha Rostov" (*M* 171). As Paul Friedrich notes: ". . . the striking thing about Natasha in *War and Peace* is her drastic shift from being an erotic adolescent to being a Slavic *Urmutter* . . ." (182–3). Since Binx has read "the novel of novels" (*M* 69), he should have had a little more confidence in Kate. At the playground they reaffirm their decision to marry. Such is the restoration of his spirit that he sees a sign of God's grace—a black man emerging from a Catholic church with his forehead marked with ashes—and converts, achieves an existential repetition.

In the "Epilogue" Binx reviews the events which have occurred since he and Kate decided to marry. The June marriage and his September entry into medical school indicate that he has escaped the hold of mother-loss and accepted the role at which his father had foundered, thus transcended both the preoedipal and oedipal conditions that had caused his psychic dysfunction. And since both actions were *doing the right thing*, in Aunt Emily's eyes, even if she does not understand them, he is reconciled to her. The next Mardi Gras, Uncle Jules, at the Boston Club, suffered a second heart attack, which proved fatal. Then in May Binx' stepbrother Lonnie died of a "massive virus infection" (*M* 237). Kate still suffers from severe anxiety. Binx refuses to say anything about himself—directly—for existential repetitions cannot be transmitted in literature. But he has endured the ordeal and received the four boons of reward described by Joseph Campbell—sacred marriage, father atonement, apotheosis, and elixir theft (246). He does not mention the movies (or screens, either dream or door). Nor does he mention his old hankering for Central Park; instead, he reveals that on the day of Lonnie's death, he took his brothers and sisters to ride the train in Audubon Park (*M* 240). Binx is still the man on the train, but his destination now is the City of God.

Figure 1. *Aphrodite*. Marble copy of fourth century B.C. Hellenistic original. The Metropolitan Museum of Art. New York City, Fletcher Fund, 1952. [52.11.5]

FOUR

The Moviegoer Dates the Love Goddess

In one of his last interviews, Walker Percy spoke of the two or three times when he felt that he had done a thing just right in a novel.[1] The one example he gave was the characterization of Sharon Kincaid, in *The Moviegoer:*

> Maybe Binx Bolling gets tired of going to the movies and he hires a secretary. His romantic life consists of hiring a series of secretaries. He's looking for the right girl. Finally, he hires one who looks and acts like a certain movie star and things happen just right. He takes her out to meet his family, his nephews, whom he likes very much. And the first secretary, Tiffany somebody, she was no good, she just stood around lumpy-looking and didn't know how to do anything, how to talk to the nephews. The second secretary squatted down—she was too gracious. She was like Joan Fontane [*sic*] visiting an orphanage. Finally, the third secretary does it just right. (Presson 220)

On this occasion Percy's memory for details was not too good. Binx's first secretary is named Marcia, not Tiffany. Further, in the interview Percy reversed the responses made to Binx's family by the first and the second secretary: "Linda [second secretary] . . . was nervous and shifted from one foot to the other and looked over their heads, her face gone heavy as a pudding. Marcia [first secretary] made too much over them, squatting down and hugging her knees like Joan Fontaine visiting an orphanage" (*M* 138). But, after all, it had been thirty years since he wrote *The Moviegoer*. And, besides, any reader of the novel will agree with Percy's larger judgment that in creating Sharon Kincaid he had given her as much animation as an "elfin creature, this sumptuous elf from Eufala" (*M* 122) could be expected to possess.

Binx's likening of Sharon to an "elfin creature" cannot be in response to her diminutive size. When he first describes her, he thus sizes her up: "She is a good-sized girl, at least five feet six and a hundred and thirty-five pounds—as big as a majorette—and her face is a little too short and pert, like one of those Renoir girls, and her eyes a little too yellow. Yet she has the most fearful soap-clean good looks. Her bottom is so beautiful that once as she crossed the room to the cooler I felt my eyes smart with tears of gratitude" (*M* 65). The next day, down in St. Bernard Parish, he again emphasizes her solidity: "Sharon stands astraddle, as heavy of leg as a Wac" (*M* 91). In a few minutes he adds: "She stands four-square, eyes rolled back a little, showing white. She is sleepy-eyed and frumpy; she looks like snapshots of Ava Gardner when she was a high school girl in North Carolina" (*M* 93).

Binx's description must, therefore, be occasioned by some other quality that Sharon projects, a quality to which her amplitude alludes. That she is physically *more* than the ordinary hints that, in some strange way, she is *spiritually* more than the ordinary. Both the definition and the etymology of *elf* provide a clue to Sharon's superabundant spiritual quality. An elf is a "small sprite or fairy, supposedly exercising magic powers and haunting woods and hills"; the word probably derives from Indo-European *albho*, "white," "prob. basic sense 'whitish figure' (in the mist)" (*Webster's* 470). In *The White Goddess* Robert Graves has a field day in discussing the many derivations of *albho* in his "historical grammar of poetic myth, "for their widespread occurrence supports his thesis that the white or moon goddess was worshipped throughout the prehistoric, matrilinear world of Eurasia and was therefore the inspiration of a poetry of

58

"magical language" (3–4, 97). That Sharon projects a spiritual quality will be taken up next; that she projects a whitish quality will be
taken up in the fullness of time.

In his interview Percy remembered that the third secretary,
Sharon, "looks and acts like a certain movie star." Since Binx likens
her to "Ava Gardner when she was a high school girl in North Carolina" (*M* 93), it is tempting to think that Percy had Ms Gardner in his
mind's eye when he created Sharon. But there is a greater likelihood
that Marilyn Monroe was his "certain movie star." Granted, Binx does
not mention Marilyn Monroe anywhere in his story, even though he
cites Eva Marie Saint (*M* 116) and Veronica Lake (*M* 209)—as well
as Joan Fontaine and Ava Gardner—as models for women he describes. Is it not surprising that a man who has been in a "life-long
trance of moviegoing," according to Percy in the same interview,
with a habit of using movie actors, actresses, and stories as visual
symbols for what he sees, does not mention the movie personality
who dominated American, indeed world, popular culture at the
time, 1961? *Time Magazine* had made her status official just a few
years before: "In Hollywood's pagan pantheon, Marilyn Monroe is
the Goddess of Love. . . . She bears, in fact, a sharp resemblance to
the airbrush Aphrodite known in the 30's as the Petty Girl" ("To Aristophanes" 74).[2]

Apparently the resemblance between Marilyn Monroe and Aphrodite did not depend merely on Ms Monroe's physical dimensions
as they appeared on the movie screen or in publicity photographs.
Her off-camera abandon, especially in sexual matters, was well
known. It was not a pose and was already characteristic of her when
she was a teenager, according to one of her first lovers, Ted Jordan
(17–26). Indeed, she seemed to incarnate those qualities of sexual
exuberance usually attributed to a goddess of love. The Jungian analyst Edward C. Whitmont goes so far as to say that Marilyn Monroe,
as a person, was overwhelmed by the archetype of divine eroticism:

> Even the most superficial of inquiries will reveal a correspondence be-
> tween Marilyn Monroe's life and the archetype represented by Aphrodite.
>
> Of course, this is not to claim that Marilyn derived this image from an
> esoteric study of mythology or from any other extraneous source. The
> objective psyche confronted her not only with the image but with the af-

fectivity of Aphrodite. Granted, she probably believed that her dream and her way of life belonged to her personally. Yet this only confirms the contention that she was grasped unconsciously and compulsively by the transpersonal element.

How completely she was under the sway of the archetype we cannot say, although society's response would indicate that she carried the image without rival and therefore must have been closely identified with it. Also the world related to Marilyn in an archetypal way. Without awareness of the mythological tag of Aphrodite, our nation simply regarded her as its sex symbol and as a "Love Goddess." Her own breezy response to this designation indicates its nonpersonal character. She said, "I never quite understood it—this sex symbol. I always thought symbols were those things you clash together." (100–1)

When it was first revealed that Ms Monroe preferred to be nude when she was at home, alone or with company, Whitmont's contention that she was under the spell of Aphrodite became hard to refute (Pepitone and Stadiem 16).

Since Marilyn Monroe had such a widely known symbolic value, it would have been impossible for Walker Percy not to think of her as he set about creating a character who was to symbolize the same kind of luxuriant eroticism to Binx Bolling. That Binx is not just a young bachelor with an ordinary liking for attractive women must be stressed. The need that Binx has for such a goddess figure had its origin in his youth. When he was eight, his older brother, Scott, died of pneumonia (*M* 3); then when Binx was ten, his father was killed in World War II (*M* 157). After his father's death, Binx's mother returned to work as a nurse, while he lived with his Aunt Emily (*M* 48), actually his great-aunt. In time his mother married again, providing Roy Smith with seven children, the first-born of whom, Duval, is already dead. Thus the deaths of Binx's father, older brother, and nearest stepbrother expose Binx as one who is vulnerable to death, even as his mother, as he might see it, has abandoned him. The effect of all these deaths on Binx's mother seems to have confirmed her in her undemonstrative handling of her children (*M* 142), as Binx realizes (*M* 158). But knowing why she thus behaves does not prevent Binx's feelings of maternal deprivation (*M* 137).

Confronted by the reality of a distinctly cool, distant mother, Binx has unconsciously split the mother image into a Bad Mother and a Good Mother. His landlady, Mrs. Schexnaydre, is the Bad Mother; her name announces her location, "she's nadir" (Cheney 693). Binx lives in Hell, in a basement apartment on a street called Elysian Fields. Each new secretary is apotheosized as the Good Mother whom Binx as a Don Juan then seduces and abandons, perhaps in revenge for his own abandonment. Most of his free time is spent going to the movies in an elaborate ritual of regression to a fantasy of original union between Binx as baby and movie screen as mother's breast. But he is, after all, a physically healthy young man, who occasionally is driven by his libido to need a secretary.

Binx now has Sharon, whom he has clothed from their introduction with the imagery of Aphrodite. Although he never refers to Sharon as Aphrodite, there is ample evidence that the goddess is active in his unconscious. Since he occasionally goes to the public library (*M* 100), perhaps he had been influenced by a recent article which discussed the better known statues of Aphrodite (or Venus as the Romans called her), on the occasion of the introduction of a statute of her at the Metropolitan Museum of Art, in New York (Barrett). The armless and legless statue had been acquired from a European estate in 1952, but it took until 1958 to construct plaster arms and legs (Fig. 1). The author also discusses the amplitude of the Aphrodite figure, saying that Marilyn Monroe, more than the average American woman, has goddess dimensions. And the author also refers to the "goldenness" of Aphrodite, a quality which gives her her most common epithet. This "diagnostic color . . . golden (i.e., yellow, tawny, and so forth)," explains Paul Friedrich, is appropriate because Aphrodite "more than any other goddess is unambiguously solar . . ." (93, 79). It was Sharon's solarity that first enticed Binx, as he tells her later, when they are at the beach: "Sweetheart, I can't get you out of my mind. Not since you walked into my office in that yellow dress. I'm crazy about you and you know it, don't you?" (*M* 133). Since the season is very early spring, Sharon would not be tanned, even in New Orleans. Hence her "goldenness" is more an emanation than an appearance; it promises "summer" to Binx, as he soon admits.

Sharon has been Binx's secretary for two weeks (*M* 65). Although

61

he was immediately infatuated with her, he has been as "aloof and correct as a Nazi officer in occupied Paris" (*M* 67). Now, though, on Thursday, he begins the seduction that he intends to consummate on Saturday. He decides on a method by which to fascinate her; he will "keep a Gregory-Peckish sort of distance" (*M* 68, 70, 71). Perhaps he remembers the Tom Ewell line in *The Seven Year Itch* (which is about a girl who looks like Marilyn Monroe played by Marilyn Monroe): "No girl in her right mind wants me; she wants Gregory Peck."[3]

Binx's appraisal of Sharon's appearance as he begins his campaign has already been given, but it includes another detail that must be noted. When Binx likens Sharon's face to that of a Renoir girl, it would be extremely appropriate if he was thinking of "Nude in the Sunlight," at the Louvre, for that painting represents Renoir's conception of Aphrodite (Fig. 2). As Renoir said, "The nude woman, whether she emerges from the waves of the sea, or from her own bed, is Venus, or Nini, and one's imagination cannot conceive anything better" (quoted in Pach 70). Renoir's phrase "whether she emerges from the sea" indicates that he is consciously placing his painting in succession to Botticelli's masterpiece "Birth of Venus," known to the vulgar as "Venus on the Half Shell," a peep show of which was exhibited at the Chicago World's Fair[4] that Binx attended (*M* 202); but since he was only five, he probably missed this introduction to Aphrodite. Now, though, he is ready to capture the "love goddess" as she emerges from the sea—this is precisely what he intends to do on Saturday afternoon, as he had done with Marcia and Linda (*M* 8) in their time. Walter Pach says of Renoir's "Nude in the Sunlight":

> The pearl-like shape and luster of the forms is the major theme, given in the round mass of the haunches and belly, the breasts, shoulders, head, and echoed in the roundness of arms and neck; and a dappled sunlight which plays across the arms and body sustains this motif. Nothing is allowed to distract from the fullness; notice how Renoir has virtually eliminated surface markings like the nipples and navel.
>
> The girl is completely a thing of nature; only Renoir's recurrent bracelet and ring betray a note of feminine vanity. (70)

While Pach may be correct about the bracelet as a reflection of vanity, the fact is that the bracelet is made of gold, thus emphasizing the

Figure 2. Pierre Auguste Renoir. *Nude in the Sunlight*. Musée d'Orsay, Paris.

diagnostic identification of the solar girl. It is that goldenness of Sharon—even to her eyes, "which are a little too yellow" (*M* 65)—that probably prompted Binx to think of Renoir in the first place.

Once Binx commits himself to the seduction, his increasingly feverished imagination attributes "goldenness" to every aspect of Sharon's presence. Thursday morning, in the office, Sharon has worn another yellow dress (*M* 67) or, perhaps, her interview frock. Binx immediately gets anatomical:

> . . . her arms come out of the armholes as tenderly as a little girl's. But when she puts her hand to her hair, you see that it is quite an arm. The soft round muscle goes slack of its own weight. Once she slapped a fly with her bare hand and set my Artmetal desk rinking like a gong. Her back is turned to me, but obliquely, so that I can see the line of her cheek with its whorl of down and the Slavic prominence under the notch of her eye and the quick tender incurve, shortening her face like a little mignon. (*M* 67)

The fullness of the upper arm looks back at an aspect of the Aphrodite figure that Pach emphasized about Renoir's version; the fussing with the hair looks forward to an aspect prominent in her classic statuary. That she is "like a little mignon" stresses Binx's visualization of her as a Renoir girl. Within minutes Binx is thinking of "the yellow-cotton smell of her and of the summer to come," as the music of *Der Rosenkavalier* accompanies his fantasy (*M* 68).[5] Thus inspired, he plans a "business trip" for Sharon and himself the following day.

The purpose of the trip on Friday is to visit "ten acres of a defunct duck club down in St Bernard Parish" (*M* 6) that Binx owns; the trip is actually unnecessary, but Binx really wants to return to the past, to the only inheritance that he has from his father. Binx would define such a trip as an aesthetic repetition (*M* 79–80), a trip to a time that is distorted by nostalgia (*M* 169–70); his memory of it has to be corrected by one who was there at the time, Mr. Sartalamaccia (*M* 91–92), the potential buyer. What Binx may not realize is that the trip is also another kind of regression, for he takes his Good Mother Aphrodite figure with him, perhaps to find that Edenic grove he knew before he knew alienation.

On the way back to New Orleans, Binx is overcome by desire for

Sharon, an emotion which is inspired by a nostalgia for paradise, according to Robert Romanyshyn (48–52). At a Shell gasoline station, probably managed by a Mr. Botticelli, Aphrodite appears to Binx as she did to the Cytherans, in a cockle-shell (Kerenyi 70). Standing in a bower of bliss formed by "a drift of honeysuckle sprouting through the oil cans" (*M* 95)—a variation of Percy's recurrent erotic setting of "love in the ruins"—Binx watches "Sharon with a coke balanced on her golden knee." He is mesmerized by "her knees doubled up in the sunshine, dress tucked under. An amber droplet of Coca-Cola meanders along her thigh, touches a blond hair, distributes itself around the tiny fossa." She seems to be, as Marilyn Monroe claimed to be, "blond all over." Binx is so enraptured by the tensions and torsions of her body that he describes it as if it were a statue: "By flexing her leg at a certain angle, she can stand the coke on a facet of her knee. What a structure it is, tendon and bone, facet and swell, and gold all over" (*M* 96). By then Binx has switched his persona: "I go home as the old [Clark] Gable, asweat and with no thought for her and sick to death with desire."

Late Friday afternoon Binx advances his scheme to the next degree by asking Sharon to work late. She agrees, but it is a wonder that Binx can even pretend to concentrate, for all he seems to notice is the "yellowness" of Sharon's eyes (*M* 103, twice). After a couple of hours their work-relationship has become intimate: "She watches closely now, her yellow agate-eyes snapping with interest. We are, all at once, on our way. We are like two children lost in a summer afternoon who, hardly aware of each other, find a door in a wall and enter an enchanted garden. Now we might join hands. She is watchful to see whether I see this too" (*M* 106). Like his creator, Binx appears to have read Kierkegaard's "Diary of a Seducer,"[6] which appropriately abounds in references to Aphrodite, particularly Aphrodite Anadyomene and Aphrodite Kallipygos,[7] of whom more later.

The "enchanted garden" is the paradisal locale of romantic regression to original symbiosis—so often represented in Percy's fiction as a gold course or a park, such as New York's Central Park, twin prints of which hang over Binx's bed (*M* 78) at Mrs. Schexnaydre's. But there is another, more pertinent allusion in this instance, to Aphrodite's garden. One tradition, through Ovid, is that Aphrodite had a garden in which she grew apples that were "plucked golden from a golden bough," which were really, according to Rendel Harris, apples of the mandrake plant capable of intense love-magic (122). Another tradition is that female devotees to Aphrodite, in mourning the death of Adonis, brought to his temple their little "gardens," thus quaintly defined by Karoly Kerenyi: "a symbol and picturesque expression, which was common in our tongue, as in others, for their own femininity. In eastern shrines they gave themselves to strangers. Whoever did not do this must at least sacrifice her hair to Adonis" (76). Binx does not seem particularly interested in Sharon's hair—it is the garden he seeks.

It should come as no surprise that Binx hears *Der Rosenkavalier* at this moment, namely "Baron Ochs' waltz" (*M* 106), at the end of Act II, when the Baron is so drunkenly certain of his seduction of "Mariandl" (who is really the young man Octavian) that he starts waltzing. But Binx refrains from waltzing; instead he virtuously delivers Sharon intact to her apartment. Still, there is a moment of regret: "At twilight it is good to come away from the open sky and into a yellow-lit place and sit next to a warm thigh. I almost violate my resolution and ask Sharon if she will have a drink. But I don't. Instead I watch her up into her house. She ascends a new flight of concrete steps which soars like a gangplank into a dim upper region" (*M* 107). Let the goddess spend her last night in the "dim upper region," for tomorrow she will come down the gangplank from her cockleshell, not at Cythera, but at Ship Island, Mississippi.

Saturday morning should be especially propitious to Binx's strategy, since it is the day of the week dedicated to Saturn, the god of "the golden age" and orgiastic revelry. But to Binx the actual morning is "dreary" (*M* 117), so filled with anticipation is he. As he looks out the window of his office, even "the gold lettering" of the company name reminds him of Sharon, who types behind him, turning his thoughts from the outer world to his inner fantasy. At eleven o'clock he asks Sharon if she wishes to go to the beach with him. Although she is a goddess, she is also a very sensible girl, so she asks about a frequent caller: "Sharon looks at me with a yellow eye. 'Is Miss Cutrer any kin to you?' she cries in her new scolding voice."

When Binx replies that Miss Cutrer is his cousin, Sharon replies: "Some old girl told me you were married to her. I said nayo indeed" (*M* 118). Binx says that he is not married to anyone and asks why she asked the question. She replies: "I'll tell you one thing, son. I'm not going out with any married man." Sharon may possess Aphrodite's beauty, but not her morals.

Satisfied that the conditions of the date are appropriate, Sharon is soon in Binx's little red MG, with "her big golden knees doubled up against the dashboard" (*M* 123). Apparently Sharon understands her psychological function as Good Mother, for she has already begun to address Binx as "son" and will continue to call him "son" or "boy" (*M* 132). She may even intuit her mythological function: if she is Aphrodite, then Binx could be Adonis, so she says, "Lordy lord" (*M* 124), the literal meaning of *Adonis* (Rose 124). She offers this salutation as the coltish car speeds along Elysian Fields, away from the house of Mrs. Schexnaydre, who assumes the mythological role of Persephone, who contended with Aphrodite for her son Adonis (James 147).

The last phase of the trip to the beach is by ferry boat from the mainland to Ship Island. Binx must be very conscious that he has nearly attained his objective, for he imagines a group of children who are fellow passengers as "milky white," indeed sees the very water through which the ferry travels as milk (*M* 129). Here Sharon projects her whitish quality, becomes the white goddess: as the Good Mother she represents the breast from which Binx was separated and to which, in fantasy, he as moviegoer has been trying to return.

Each physical movement forward is matched by a higher degree of excitement: ". . . first, this sleazy backwater, then the great blue ocean. The beach is clean and a big surf is rolling in; the water in the middle distance is green and lathered. You come over the hillock and your heart lifts up; your old sad music comes into the major" (*M* 130). It is to be suspected that more than Binx's heart lifted up, if there is any truth in this statement by Richard Sterba: "The major key . . . represents virility, the minor key is connected with the idea of castration. Our mood responses to the two decisive modes of major and minor key are then those of phallic strength and weakness" (107).

Then Binx awaits his epiphany:

> Sharon is already in, leaving her shirt and pants on the beach like a rag. She wades out ahead of me, turning to and fro, hands outstretched to the water and sweeping it before her. Now and then she raises her hands to her head as if she were placing a crown and combs back her hair with the last two fingers. The green water foams at her knees and sucks out ankle deep and swirling with sand. Out she goes, thighs asuck, turning slowly and sweeping the water before her. (*M* 130)

It is the foam of the water, already described as lather, which gives Aphrodite her name, "the foam born." Actually this version is a euphemism for the original version. In it Gaia, mother earth, became so abused by bearing the children of Uranos, the sky god, that she begged her son Kronos to protect her; so the next time Uranos tried to copulate with Gaia, Kronos rushed up, cut off his father's penis, and threw it into the sea. Hans Licht paraphrases Hesiod as to the consequences: "The member was borne a long time over the sea and round it was white foam, which came from the immortal member, and in it the maiden was nourished. The member, which was cut off immediately before the act, was already full of sperm; this now gushes out, and in and with the sea produces Aphrodite" (182 fn.). The strange origin of Aphrodite accounts for a certain masculinity that is associated with her tradition. It also may explain why Binx would become sexually excited by the sight of the lather of the water and why Sharon wants to play beach blanket bellicosity (*M* 132–33).

Many epithets were applied to Aphrodite, several of which inspired the poses that became traditional when she became the very popular subject of the sculptors. In his rapture at the beach Binx is so overwhelmed by Aphrodite's presence in Sharon that he imagines that the girl he sees—a Marilyn Monroe look-alike—is performing a series of *tableaux vivants* of the goddess. Actually, he had begun to see her in the pose of the goddess back in his office when he said, ". . . she has the most fearful soap-clean good looks. Her bottom is so beautiful that once as she crossed the room to the cooler I felt my eyes smart with tears of gratitude" (*M* 65). Here Sharon personifies Aphrodite Kallipygos, "the goddess with the beautiful buttocks"[8] (Fig. 3), a pose of Aphrodite which was worshipped in the temples of

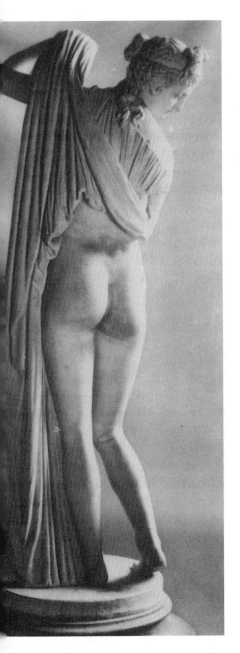

Figure 3. *Aphrodite Kallipygos*. Museo Nazionale, Naples, Italy.

Figure 4. *Marilyn Monroe*. Photograph by Eve Arnold. Courtesy of Magnum Photos.

Greece from one end to the other (Licht 201). Incidentally, Sharon is also personifying that other sex goddess, Marilyn Monroe, with this pose (Fig. 4 reveals Ms Monroe with body by Botticelli). Photographs of her, especially before she dyed her hair and underwent cosmetic surgery on her face, presented "the combination of fresh-faced young girl and voluptuous womanhood that so entranced men," according to the caption of one photograph (Jordan 120–21).[9] The statement that she was known throughout the world for her *derriere* cannot be rebutted; surely many men have experienced the response of Ted Jordan to seventeen year old Norma Jean Baker: "It was the kind of shape I used to stare at as a boy in the museums, which always had at least a few of those old Grecian statues showing the perfect female form. Alas, I discovered when I later began to look at girls more seriously, it seemed that no woman had that kind of shape. I began to be convinced that women simply did not meet that Grecian ideal—until I saw Norma Jean [Baker, later Marilyn Monroe]" (23).

At the beach—Aphrodite's sacred place, after all—Sharon's every gesture hints at her divinity. "She wades out ahead of me, turning to and fro, hands outstretched to the water and sweeping it before her" first of all recalls her callipygian feature, then suggests a familiar pose (Fig. 5) in which the arms are outstretched. There are various speculations as to the reasons that her arms are outstretched: that she is putting on a necklace or that she has a golden apple or mandrake root in her hand or that she is preparing to bind her sandal or that she is weaving. But these are only tentative explanations, for most of the arms have the hands broken off. "Now and then she raises her hands to her head as if she were placing a crown . . ." refers to the pose of Aphrodite Urania (Fig. 6), the heavenly goddess, as opposed to Aphrodite Pandemos, the goddess of all the people. The segment ". . . and combs her hair with the last two fingers. The green water foams at her knees . . ." refers to Aphrodite Anadyomene (Fig. 7), the goddess emerging from the sea—understandably the main cult statue, at least in some of the areas in which she was worshipped (Brinkerhoff 60).

Binx is so transfixed by Sharon's beauty that tears come to his eyes (*M* 130). She is quick to notice: "Why do you look at me like that?" (*M* 131). When he replies that he does not know, she good-naturedly accepts her role: "Come on, son. I'm going to give you some beer." Psychologically, she as the Good Mother offers him the milk that he seeks. Mythologically, she is offering an aphrodisiac, the word for a stimulant for desire coined by the Greeks in tribute to Aphrodite.

71

Figure 5. *Aphrodite*. Bronze, Greek, second century B.C. Courtesy of Museum of Art, Rhode Island School of Design, Museum Appropriation and Special Gift.

Indeed, the etymology of the original German *bier* is "foaming" (*Webster's* 133). In effect, the Aphrodite in Sharon offers herself to Binx.

With such enticement Binx can only resume his staring:

> Her suit is of a black sheeny stuff like a swim-meet suit and skirtless. She comes out of the water like a spaniel, giving her head a flirt which slaps

Figure 6. *Aphrodite Urania.* Terracotta, Greek, second century B.C. Courtesy Staatliche Museen, Berlin.

her hair around in a wet curl and stooping, brushes the water from her legs. Now she stands musing on the beach, leg locked, pelvis aslant, thumb and forefinger propped along the iliac crest and lightly, propped lightly as an athlete. As the salt water dries and stings, she minds herself, plying around the flesh of her arm and sending fingers along her back. (*M* 131)

Here Sharon appears to be giving a reprise of her entire Aphrodite role. ". . . giving her head a flirt which slaps her hair around in a wet curl . . ." recalls her attention to her hair as Aphrodite Anadyomene,

73

Figure 7. *Aphrodite Anadyomene*. "Venus of Courtrai." Bronze, Roman. Musee Royal de Mariemont, Belgium.

Figure 8. *Crouching Aphrodite*. Courtesy Archaeological Institute of Dodeca-nese, Rhodes, Greece.

who is so often represented as attending to her hair (Fig. 7). ". . . and stooping, brushes the water from her legs" suggests the Crouching Aphrodite (Fig. 8), who also characteristically attends to her hair. There may be an Aphrodite "with thumb and forefinger propped along the iliac crest," but it is unknown to this voyeur. The medita-

75

tive expression, locked leg, slanted pelvis, and minding of body are reminiscent of the Aphrodite in the Vatican Museum (Fig. 9). All those elements are present, too, in Botticelli's "Birth of Venus."

Binx has looked long enough. Soon they lie kissing, making the yin-yang figure that Percy's protagonists dream about. Then Binx makes his move: "Once when she gets up, I come up on my knees and embrace her golden thighs, such a fine strapping armful they are" (M 132). Apparently Sharon has taken off her crown as Aphrodite Urania, for Binx now addresses her as Aphrodite Pandemos, "Mother of all living, what an armful." As they leave the beach, Sharon agrees to go to the summer cottage owned by Binx's mother. As they walk as one through the marsh toward their tryst, a "lopsided yellow moon" (M 136), the white goddess, lights the path before them.

But Mrs. Smith is at the cottage, surrounded by her six children. In an instant, Aphrodite vanishes from the body of Sharon Kincaid, who, it will be remembered from the beginning of this essay, was praised by her creator for her domesticity. Binx notes: "Sharon is in the best of humors, rounding her eyes and laughing so infectiously that I wonder if she is not laughing at me. From the beginning she is natural with the children" (M 138). But in the presence of the real mother, who, her son feels, withheld her large breasts (M 148), Sharon becomes just another of Binx's dates, dismissed by his mother as a "hotsy-totsy" (M 155). When Binx's mother softly forces Binx and Sharon to attend Mass with the Smiths on Sunday morning, the would-be lovers must realize that their date is over (M 160). In the MG, on the trip back to New Orleans, Binx is easily dissuaded from resuming his seduction, even as Sharon says that she must get back to town to meet "someone" (M 166).

Thus Sharon as a person disappears from Binx's story—but the presence she had incarnated, Aphrodite, remains a while longer. Binx returns to his workaday life to become involved with Kate Cutrer, his great-aunt's stepdaughter. Kate is so desperately unhappy—perhaps from the same condition as Binx, since her mother died when Kate was a toddler—that she wishes to accompany Binx on the train to Chicago, whence he must go on business. That he is not over his infatuation with Aphrodite is apparent from the way that he

Figure 9. *Aphrodite*. Courtesy Monumenti Musei e Gallerie Pontificie, Vatican City.

stares at a newspaper picture of a Bourbon Street "dancer with an oiled body" (*M* 188) and dreams of a sex manual that he had read: "Now with a tender regard for your partner remove your hand from the nipple and gently manipulate . . ." (*M* 190). That he is more dominated by his late encounter with his mother, though, is apparent by the fact that he is impotent that very night with Kate. She seems to understand his real problem, for she drunkenly likens him to Hamlet, as very well known mother's boy, and likens herself to Ophelia: "Good night, sweet Whipple. Now you tuck Kate in. Poor Kate. . . . Good night, sweet Whipple, good night, good night, good night." (*Hamlet* V ii 369–70; IV iv 73–73).

If ever a man needed a mother, it is Binx when he and Kate step off the train in Chicago. And, despite his failure the night before—or perhaps because of it—Kate takes charge. Binx simply says, "Kate looks after me" (*M* 201). He is terrified by the "genie-soul," "the wind and the space" (*M* 203) of Chicago, and seems to be haunted by a trip taken to that city twenty-five years before with his father. But Freudian theory usually accepts landscape as symbolic of the mother, especially a landscape to which one is returning. In this case the locale is a Cartesian desolation to Binx because of his continued failure to make a connection, either with mother or with her romantic replacement. In the next few hours he falls in love with Kate. Before they left New Orleans, a mutual acquaintance had likened Kate to Natasha Rostov, in *War and Peace* (*M* 171), to Binx's skepticism, but now Kate undergoes Natasha's transformation from an immature self-centered girl to a confident mother figure. Her change accounts for Binx's happy discovery that he is free of the lure of Aphrodite, particularly Ms Kallipygos; he says he can "pass within a few feet of noble Midwestern girls with their clear eyes and splendid butts and never [have] a thought for them." Then he continues:

> What an experience, . . . to be free of it for once. Rassled out. What a sickness it is, . . . this latter-day post-Christian sex. To be pagan it would be one thing, an easement taken easily in a rosy old pagan world; to be Christian it would be another thing, fornication forbidden and not even to be thought of in the new life, and I can see that it need not be thought of if there were such a life. But to be neither pagan nor Christian but this: oh this is a sickness, . . . (*M* 207)

78

Drawn by his regressive needs, Binx has sought out pagan—Aphro-diticic—sexual connections with his secretaries as a substitute for his loss of the original object. But at the same time he has felt guilty for violating the Christian condemnation of sex outside marriage. Now he is to marry, to have the only sexual outlet that is countenanced by the church. But will he be free of desire, the temptation to taste the forbidden fruit? Not unless he accepts Christianity as the truth, the truth that there will be a new Eden to compensate for the loss of the old Eden, the mother's breast. That is why, when he looked out the window on the train, past Kate's face, he had a vision of "the holy city of Zion" (*M* 192). This twin conversion to marriage and to Christ anticipates Binx's resolution of his dilemma of loss and love.

That night in Chicago, Binx and Kate celebrate by going to the movies, in "the mother and Urwomb of all moviehouses" (*M* 211); in effect Binx is announcing that he has found the romantic-mother object to replace his lost maternal-mother object.[10] The movie title, *The Young Philadelphians*, the young citizens of the city of love, and Binx's plot summary—"Paul Newman [or Binx Bolling] is an ideal-istic young fellow who is disillusioned and becomes cynical and cal-culating. But in the end he recovers his ideals"—comment upon their exultation at that moment. But the other horn of the dilemma still poses a threat: he is summoned by his aunt, to account for his irresponsible behavior with Kate, in taking her off when she was so sick. Then Aunt Emily expressly asks, "Were you intimate with Kate?" (*M* 222). When he replies that, technically, he was, he is con-demned for his fornication. Aunt Emily's question, "What do you think is the purpose of life—to go to the movies and dally with every girl that comes along" (*M* 226), diagnoses his problem more percep-tively than she could ever know. Then she literally closes the book on him (*M* 226).

There is no place for him to go but to Mrs. Schexnaydre's, the lo-cale of Persephone. Although Kate had told him to wait there for her (*M* 227), he soon thinks that she has seen the wisdom of her step-mother's judgment and abandoned him. Hence he falls back into de-sire and tries to reach Sharon (*M* 228). The very landscape reveals that he is once again dreaming of the goddess on the beach; as he talks on the telephone he watches some children on a piece of playground equipment: "*Iii-oorrr* goes the ocean wave, its struts twinkling in the golden light, its skirt swaying to and fro like a young dancing girl" (*M* 231). Although it has only been three days since Binx had seen Sharon, she has gotten engaged (*M* 229)—Sharon seems to know that mortals, unlike goddesses, do not have all the time in the world. After Joyce, Sharon's roommate, tells Binx of this development, she mentions something about the Lord of Misrule reigning yesterday, Shrove Tuesday. Maybe Binx realizes that he is a modern day descendant of the Lord of Misrule, who derives from Adonis and the other son-gods who were sacrificed to Great Mothers like Aphrodite (Suttie 130–31). If so, this is the day of his sacrifice, Ash Wednesday. In desperation, Binx is trying to seduce Joyce when Kate drives up.

As Binx sits with Kate in her car, they decide to marry. She will support him, while he attends medical school, to pursue a career in medicine that his father had not been able to continue, because his father had been overwhelmed by a condition much like his son's, and had chosen to die "in Crete in the wine dark sea" (*M* 157).[11] Binx will support Kate by caring for her, in all senses of the word. Even so, he seems to realize that he cannot love Kate fully unless he also loves God. Watching a man come from a Catholic church after having received ashes, Binx converts.

At least a year later, when Binx is completing the story of that crucial week of his life, he summarizes what has happened in the interval. He and Kate are married, and he attends medical school: these responsible actions reconcile his aunt to him. Sharon is married. Lonnie, his oldest stepbrother, has died, an event which evokes a telling response from Binx. Lonnie was a cripple, and when the other stepsiblings ask Binx if Lonnie will rise whole on Resurrection Day, he assures them that he will. Thus Binx professes his belief in the new Eden and his new capacity to endure the loss of the old Eden. It should go without saying that he says not a word about a movie or a love goddess. What Binx's story says about its creator may be inferred by the fact that he told Martin Luschei that "writing it was better than three years of psychoanalysis" (16).

Regression in the Service of Transcendence in *The Moviegoer*

Occasionally there occurs a nearly perfect fit between an idea developed discursively and its counterpart represented in a work of fiction. When such a comparison happens, both ideas gain increased validation. The explicit theory is grounded and tested in the specific human context provided by the fiction; the implicit theme embodied in the fiction becomes significant as a representation of a general experience. In this mutually beneficial way, Michael Washburn's exposition of transpersonal theory, *The Ego and the Dynamic Ground* (1988), and Walker Percy's novel *The Moviegoer* (1961) constitute a dialogue, with each voice pursuing its distinctive theme until the two merge.[1]

The title of Washburn's study indicates its subject, the relation between the ego and the Dynamic Ground. The *dynamic* that results from the relationship between the ego and its ground is one perspective of the study (Washburn 4). Another perspective, the *triphasic,* is provided by the description of human development as a three-stage process, the pre-egoic, egoic, and transegoic, the latter of which an individual may or may not attain (Washburn 4). The movement through the stages is not an uninterrupted progress; thus the third perspective of the study is *dialectical* (Washburn 5–6).

Since there are three strands of thought which are occurring simultaneously but must be presented sequentially, the text is necessarily rich and complex. The following illustration, *which reads from bottom up,* effectively combines the three movements:

THE DYNAMIC-DIALECTICAL PARADIGM
OF TRIPHASIC DEVELOPMENT

INTEGRATION	The two poles of the psyche, having been reunited and their resources fused into higher forms, are integrated as a true bipolar system, a true two-in-one or *coincidentia oppositorum.* The power of the Ground, as spirit, is sovereign; the ego is subject.
REGENERATION IN SPIRIT	The ego, having ceased its resistance to nonegoic potentials, is now enhanced rather than assailed by these potentials; it begins to be regenerated by the power of the Ground: spirit.
REGRESSION IN THE SERVICE OF TRANSCENDENCE	Original repression gives way and the ego is resubmitted to the nonegoic pole, to which it regresses. The ego is assailed by resurging nonegoic potentials in their arrested, "pre-" form.

EGOIC OR MENTAL-EGOIC STAGE	The ego develops its operational functions in relative independence from the nonegoic pole, which, repressed and submerged, underlies the ego as the dynamic unconscious. The nonegoic pole is the not-self or id; the egoic pole is the mental or Cartesian ego.
ORIGINAL REPRESSION	At this turning point, the ego wins its individuated selfhood but only by repressively dissociating itself from the nonegoic pole, the potentials of which are arrested at the pre-egoic level and submerged into unconsciousness.
PRE-EGOIC OR BODY-EGOIC STAGE	Pre-Oedipal childhood is a period during which the ego begins to be differentiated from the Great Mother but is still under the sway of nonegoic forces. The nonegoic pole is a primordial Self; the egoic pole is a body-ego.
ORIGINAL EMBEDMENT	The neonatal condition is a state prior to any differentiation of the egoic from the nonegoic pole, of the ego from the Dynamic Ground. The Dynamic Ground is here the aboriginal source prior to all selfhood.

(Washburn 24)

Since an actual life is not known beforehand, but must be lived and then recovered, the plot of *The Moviegoer* does not follow the "Original Embedment" to "Integration" movement of Washburn's paradigm. Rather the reader discovers only after he has read the entire novel that only in the Epilogue (*M* 236–42) is the present described and that all the previous narrative describes a time at least a year in the past. Several revelations—to be discussed later in this essay—argue that in the present of the Epilogue the narrator, John Bickerson "Binx" Bolling, has achieved the phase of "Regeneration in Spirit" and is anticipating the phase of "Integration." Now, though, it is essential to mention only one phenomenon of "Regeneration" that Washburn cites, "The harnessing of the creative process" (Washburn 202–5), especially its conclusion:

> In sum, regeneration in spirit is a time during which factors that were seriously disruptive of mental functioning become factors that make a positive contribution to mental functioning. It is a time during which potentials that had precipitated a mental breakdown become elements of a higher organization. Specifically, it is a period during which dynamic, intuitive, autosymbolic, and infusive/absorptive phenomena, which had broken through into consciousness in ways resembling serious psychopathology, are reassembled on a higher level, bringing into being the highest of all cognitive capacities: contemplation. (Washburn 204–5)

Only because Binx Bolling has reached the stage of contemplation could he compose the account of his "Regression in the Service of Transcendence."

Binx's story describes a period of eight days that culminates on his thirtieth birthday, which occurs on Ash Wednesday. During that period the bachelor New Orleans stockbroker goes to four movies, refers to twelve specific and several unidentified movies, and mentions thirty-seven actors and eight actresses. As a self-identified "moviegoer" (*M* 109) he might appear to others to be happy and carefree, but as a self-identified "bin x," he confesses that he is profoundly alienated. His symbolizing of himself as "the moviegoer" means that he is not engrossed by, but distanced from the world spectacle. Washburn offers a thorough explication of Binx's implication:

> The world of the alienated mental ego is flat throughout, since, in withdrawing from the world, the mental ego has ceased intersecting in depth with the world.
>
> A perfect example of what it is like for the world to go flat is available from the domain of the cinema. Everyone is familiar with what happens when one is suddenly drawn out of the action of a film. Let us consider a possible case. Let us suppose that a man and a woman are viewing a mys-

tery-suspense film. The man is totally absorbed. The world of the film is, for the present, his own world. He is identified with the hero, caught up in the action, and so forth. The woman in contrast, having already seen the film on a previous occasion, is not absorbed, and let us suppose that, out of boredom and impatience, she reveals the film's conclusion to the man—which conclusion, let us also suppose, the man finds disappointing. It is reasonable to assume that under these conditions the man would suffer disillusionment and would lose interest in the film. That is to say, he would become alienated from the *world* of the film. Simultaneously, the film itself, as everyone has experienced, would go flat. Without the depth factor provided by outreaching thought and feeling, the film would cease being a self-contained world, a reality unto itself, and would become instead only a film, a fiction. The hero would be reduced to a mere actor saying lines, and what was a compelling drama would be reduced to a mere plot or story line. The world of the film would no longer be engaged, and so it would cease being an engaging reality. It would become only a setting, a sequence of scenes.

The experience of the mental ego as it suffers disillusionment and then alienation is virtually identical with that of our moviegoer. (Washburn 162–63)

Washburn identifies two constituents of alienation, *"derealization"* (Washburn 160) and *"deanimation of the self-concept"* (Washburn 163); the former term has the same title and properties as in traditional psychoanalysis, while the latter is very similar to the traditional "depersonalization." Washburn then explains *"derealization"*: "Generally stated, the world during the process of alienation undergoes *derealization:* it loses its substance and meaning, its credibility and compellingness. It loses its familiarity, aliveness, and sense and becomes, by gradual deterioration, distant, dead, and 'absurd.' It is reduced to an arid and meaningless landscape—a wasteland" (Washburn 160). In so doing, Washburn provides an explanation for Binx's response to the suburb in which he lives. Washburn's explanation also gives significance to Binx's single-book library, *Arabia Deserta* (*M* 78): what Binx continually reads reflects what he continuously sees.

Washburn thus explains the second property of alienation:

The deanimation of the self-concept brings the mental ego to perceive itself (i.e., its worldly self) in the same way that it perceives others. Like

85

everyone and everything else in its derealized world, the mental ego sees itself as flat and dead. The mental ego senses that it is no longer a real person in a real world, but only an assemblage of traits, habits, routines, and roles that are played out on a lifeless stage. Just as the mental ego now sees other people only as facades without foundations, so, too, it sees itself as but a set of poses. It therefore ceases to believe in itself, to take itself seriously, for it has become only a disguise, a mask. (Washburn 163–64).

This description greatly enhances Binx's response to the Lovells, his cousin Nell and her husband Eddie. Binx introduces an encounter with Nell with this generalization: "For some time now the impression has been growing upon me that everyone is dead" (*M* 99). After Nell has nattered on about her delight with the world as it is, an infatuation inspired by *The Prophet* (*M* 101), Binx wonders, ". . . why does she talk as if she were dead? Another forty years to go and dead, dead, dead" (*M* 102). Thus the encounter ends: "We part laughing and dead" (*M* 102). The same description also accounts for Binx's disassembly of Eddie, when they meet:

Look at him. As he talks, he slaps a folded newspaper against his pants leg and his eye watches me and at the same times sweeps the terrain behind me, taking note of the slightest movement. A green truck turns down Bourbon Street; the eye sizes it up, flags it down, demands credentials, waves it on. A businessman turns in at the Maison Blanche building; the eye knows him, even knows what he is up to. All the while he talks very well. His lips move muscularly, molding words into pleasing shapes, marshalling arguments, and during the slight pauses are held poised, attractively everted in a Charles-Boyer pout—while a little web of saliva gathers in a corner like the clear oil of a good machine. Now he jingles the coins deep in his pocket. No mystery here!—he is as cogent as a bird dog quartering a field. He understands everything out there and everything out there is something to be understood. (*M* 18–19)

The same description by Washburn also accounts for Binx's persistent interest in actors and actresses, as typified by his comments upon observing William Holden on the street: Holden possesses a "resplendent reality" (*M* 16), has a "plenary . . . existence" (*M* 16), emanates an "aura of heightened reality" (*M* 16). Also explained by the same description is Binx's habitual close observation of anyone with whom he happens to be engaged (*M* 31, 49, 57). And, finally, it clarifies Binx's cataloguing of "an assemblage of traits, habits, routines, and roles that are played out on a lifeless stage" (Washburn 164) to introduce himself:

> Life in Gentilly is very peaceful. I manage a small branch office of my uncle's brokerage firm. My home is the basement apartment of a raised bungalow belonging to Mrs Schexnaydre, the widow of a fireman. I am a model tenant and a model citizen and take pleasure in doing all that is expected of me. My wallet is full of identity cards, library cards, credit cards. Last year I purchased a flat olive-drab strongbox, very smooth and heavily built with double walls for fire protection, in which I placed my birth certificate, college diploma, honorable discharge, G.I. insurance, a few stock certificates, and my inheritance: a deed to ten acres of a defunct duck club down in St Bernard Parish, the only relic of my father's many enthusiasms. It is a pleasure to carry out the duties of a citizen and to receive in return a receipt or a neat styrene card with one's name of it certifying, so to speak, one's right to exist. (*M* 6–7)

An outsider could see all these habits, as well as Binx's recreational behavior, "go[ing] to the movies and dally[ing] with every girl that comes along" (*M* 226), as his aunt puts it, and could conclude that Binx has an attractive life.

Privately, though, Binx is in despair, the kind that Kierkegaard describes: ". . . the specific character of despair is precisely this: it is unaware of being despair." (Binx had not realized his condition *then*, but he does by the time he writes his story, for he uses Kierkegaard's definition as the motto of *The Moviegoer*.) What Binx had not realized at the time is well described by Washburn:

> The mental ego's inability to stem the tide of alienation deprives it of hope and brings it finally to despair. Despair signals that all recourses within the mental-egoic system have been exhausted. It signals that the world is irrevocably lost and that the self-concept (and the shadow, too) is completely defunct, beyond all possibility of reanimation. It signals that the mental ego has been totally dispossessed. Despair, that is, indicates that alienation has run full course and that the mental ego has arrived at its nadir. This nadir point—at which there is no world and no self—I will call *zero point*. Despair, then, is the state of mind of the mental ego at zero point. (Washburn 169)

87

Mrs. Schexnaydre lives on "Elysian Fields, the main thoroughfare of Faubourg Marigny" (*M* 9); perhaps *then*, in alienation, Binx saw no irony in either the landlady's name—she's nadir (Chaney 693)—or the street's name, but he must, *now*, in the stage of "Regeneration in Spirit," for thus he describes his response when his uncle had sent him to Chicago on business: "Oh sons of all bitches and great beast of Chicago lying in wait. There goes my life in Gentilly, my Little Way, my secret existence among the happy shades in Elysian Fields" (*M* 99).

At the beginning of the story of his past crisis, Binx is at the end-point of Washburn's "mental-egoic stage." Later he tells us when his alienation had reached that acute phase:

> There was a time when [*Arabia Deserta*, disguised in a Standard and Poor binder (*M* 69)] was the last book on earth I'd have chosen to read. Until recent years, I read only 'fundamental' books, that is, key books on key subjects, such as *War and Peace*, the novel of novels; *A Study of History*, the solution of the problem of time; Schroedinger's *What is Life?*, Einstein's *The Universe as I See It*, and such. During those years I stood outside the universe and sought to understand it. I lived in my room as an Anyone living Anywhere and read fundamental books and only for diversion took walks around the neighborhood and saw an occasional movie. Certainly it did not matter to me where I was when I read such a book as *The Expanding Universe*. The greatest success of this enterprise, which I call my vertical search, came one night when I sat in a hotel room in Birmingham and read a book called *The Chemistry of Life*. When I finished it, it seemed to me that the main goals of my search were reached or were in principle reachable, whereupon I went out and saw a movie called *It Happened One Night* which was itself very good. A memorable night. The only difficulty was that though the universe had been disposed of, I myself was left over. There I lay in my hotel room with my search over yet still obliged to draw one breath and then another. (*M* 69–70)

Washburn's description of the mental ego closely captures Binx's ego when it is under the influence of the "vertical search":

> The mental ego, no longer buffered from the world by the Great Mother [i.e., in the stage of body-ego], needs a reliable conceptual map with which to test and explore reality. It therefore works hard to rid the rudimentary meanings inherited from the body-egoic period of their limita-

tions and aberrations. And in time the mental ego succeeds in putting together a framework of fully abstracted concepts that define things consistently and along essential lines—whether essential intrinsically or relative to human needs and purposes. These concepts are hierarchically interwoven, with higher levels possessing greater generality and lower levels greater specificity. Room, logical space, is available for the inclusion of new concepts, and concept already a part of the system are, in principle, open to revision or amendment. Hence, the system has both sufficient scope to assimilate the new and sufficient flexibility, usually, to accommodate anomalies and counterinstances. (Washburn 104)

When Binx gives his "cousin" Kate a Cartesian catechism, he has the spirit of Washburn's words, indeed almost the letter:

"If you walk in the front door of the laboratory, you undertake the vertical search. You have a specimen, a cubic centimeter of water or a frog or a pinch of salt or a star."
"One learns general things?"
"And there is excitement to the search."
"Why?" she asks.
"Because as you get deeper into the search, you unify. You understand more and more specimens by fewer and fewer formulae. There is the excitement. Of course you are always after the big one, the new key, the secret leverage point, and that is the best of it."
"And it doesn't matter where you are or who you are."
"No."
"And the danger is of becoming no one nowhere."
"Never mind." (*M* 82–83)

When he despairs of the "vertical search," at that moment becoming "the moviegoer," Binx is the personification of the victim of "Cartesian Dualism" (Washburn 89): "The mental ego, associated with the head, stands above the body and commands it from on high, and in doing so the mental ego takes on airs of incorporeality and independence ['Anyone living Anywhere']. It adopts the Cartesian stance and assumes the role of *res cogitans*" (Washburn 89–90).

From the narrative it is impossible to say precisely when Binx entered the "mental-egoic stage." But entering it "is an almost inescapable eventuality of early childhood development" (Washburn 68), an eventuality activated by the onset of "[o]riginal repression . . . , the last act of the body-ego" (Washburn 61). "It is hard to say exactly when this corner is turned, although, generally speaking, the event can be said to occur sometime in the second or third year of life" (Washburn 54). The need for "original repression," which is not to be seen only in a negative light (Washburn 66), results from two sources:

> The struggle is at once an interpersonal conflict by which the child seeks to extricate himself from the dominance of the mothering parent and an intrapsychic conflict by which the ego resists, and finally contains, the power of the Dynamic Ground. The first or interpersonal side of the struggle has as its chief consequences a withdrawal by the child from the mother's affections and, as a means to this, a burying by the child of his needs ("vulnerabilities") for openly flowing and intermingling love. And the second or intrapsychic side of the struggle has as its chief consequences a repressive alienation of the Dynamic Ground and, as a means to this, a repression of the body and of physico-dynamic life. (Washburn 55)

These two sources are, it must be understood, as one for the young child:

> . . . the mothering parent and the power of the Ground are, for the body-ego, inseparable dimensions of a single phenomenon. From the very beginning, it is one and the same experience for the body-ego to yield to the love of the mother and for it to give way to the power of the Ground. The body-ego knows nothing of the independence of these two dimensions of the maternal reality [the Good Mother and the Terrible Mother], and even if it did, given the causal interactivity of these dimensions and their etiological equivalence as magnetic-solvent forces, the body-ego would not be able to undertake an action with respect to one dimension without simultaneously undertaking the same action with respect to the other. Moreover, . . . the body-ego's action against the mother is of necessity also an action against the Ground because the very same bodily posture that distances the body-ego from the mother also has the consequence of severing the body-ego from the Ground. For these reasons, then, the body-ego's alienation of the mother's affections is perforce also an alienation of the power of the Ground. (Washburn 57)

That the child Binx repressed his dependence upon both his parents and the Dynamic Ground is clear from the story that he tells.

What is significant about his memory of his mother is his silence: he never talks about their having shared a moment of affection. On the contrary, when Binx unintentionally visits his mother, he comments on her cool greeting: "Sometimes I feel a son's love for her, or something like this, and try to give her a special greeting, but at these times she avoids my eye and gives me her cheek and calls on me to notice this about Mathilde or that about Thérèse" (*M* 137–38).

Binx tells Aunt Emily that he cannot remember his father (*M* 56), who died when Binx was twelve, yet he does volunteer several memories, particularly one in which he all but admits being motivated by original repression:

> Some years later, after Scott's death, we came my father and I to the Field Museum, a long dismal peristyle dwindling away into the howling distance, and inside stood before a tableau of Stone Age Man, father mother and child crouched around an artificial ember in postures of minatory quiet—until, feeling my father's eye on me, I turned and saw what he required of me—very special father and son we were that summer, he staking his everything this time on a perfect comradeship—and I, seeing in his eyes the terrible request, requiring from me his very life; I, through *a child's perversity or some atavistic recoil from an intimacy too intimate*, turned him down, turned away, refused him what I knew I could not give. [my emphasis] (*M* 204)

The tableau itself is doubly the picture of what original repression represses, the primacy of the family triangle—not separated even by a comma—and the Dynamic Ground, as symbolized by the "fire of the hearth" (Washburn 53). Not that Binx is oblique in his rejection of the Dynamic Ground: "My unbelief was invincible from the beginning. I could never make head or tail of God. The proofs of God's existence may have been true for all I know, but it didn't make the slightest difference. If God himself had appeared to me, it would have changed nothing. In fact, I have only to hear the word God and a curtain comes down in my head" (*M* 145).

Since the original repression which initiated the "mental-egoic stage" is precisely "the sealing of the Ground and the submerging of it (together with the nonegoic pole of the psyche!) into unconsciousness" (Washburn 57), Binx has no direct memory of his "body-egoic stage": "The act of original repression disconnects the ego from the

91

network of archetypes that belong to the Great Mother system. These archetypes, then, which are active in the conscious life of the body-ego, are alienated from the conscious life of the mental ego. For the mental ego, these archetypes belong to the prepersonal unconscious; they are part of a separate psychic system, a system that is invisible and unknown—except, usually, in sleep and dreams" (Washburn 83). Thus Binx's consciousness of the period of his crisis, as he reconstructs it later, consists of the "internal dialogue" (Washburn 97–99) of Cartesian dualism and of the haunting appeal from archetypes, which determines much of his emotional state and his subsequent unconscious behavior.

It is the latter aspect of Binx's consciousness which constitutes the "pre-history" of the plot of his story, a "pre-history" which closely parallels the "pre-history" of the "mental-egoic stage" offered by Washburn:

> The body-ego goes through several phases of development. These phases are governed by many different factors. In this chapter, I will concentrate on the psychodynamic and interpersonal factors, giving specific consideration to the following: (1) the pre-egoic fusion state, i.e., original embedment, immersion in the Dynamic Ground; (2) the body-ego's ambivalence toward the Ground and the maternal parent, and the differentiation of the Ground/mother complex (the Great Mother) into positive and negative poles (viz., the Good Mother and the Terrible Mother); (3) the dynamically charged character of the body-ego's experience, which is manifested diversely as polymorphous sensuousness, overall intensity, and numinosity; (4) the phases of psychosexual development, culminating in the Oedipal conflict; and (5) the conflict with the material and paternal powers (as Terrible Mother and Oedipal Father), leading to original repression. (Washburn 41)

There seems to be nothing at all special about the day that Binx chooses as the opening for his story. Living with Mrs. Schexnaydre, he would have awakened to the same sight: "My apartment is as impersonal as a motel room. I have been careful not to accumulate possessions. My library is a single book, *Arabia Deserta*. The television set looks as if it took coins. On the wall over the bed hang two Currier and Ives prints of ice-skaters in Central Park. How sad the little figures seem, skimming along in step! How sad the city seems!" (*M* 78).

Those prints of Central Park announce "an early experience of the Good Mother as a complex archetypal network expressed in such images as . . . the luxuriant environment of the garden of paradise . . ." (Washburn 82). But the archetype gives little solace, if any, to Binx, when it descends upon his dreams, for in his wakeful mental-egoic state, he has this to say:

> Our neighborhood theater in Gentilly has permanent lettering on the front of the marquee reading: Where Happiness Costs So Little. The fact is I am quite happy in a movie, even a bad movie. Other people, so I have read, treasure memorable moments in their lives: the time one climbed the Parthenon at sunrise, the summer night one met a lonely girl in Central Park and achieved with her a sweet and natural relationship, as they say in books. I too once met a girl in Central Park, but it is not much to remember.(*M* 7)

The rare, dimly remembered experience of original embedment may be cinematic: "Sights are unrelated to sounds, sounds to kinesthetic sensations, music movements to visual cues, and so on. The perceived world is something like a living movie being shown without synchronization of events in space and time" (Cowan, quoted in Washburn 44–45). But the mental-egoic Binx, to whom archetypes are "invisible" (Washburn 83), prefers movies of the Hollywood variety, even if they ultimately turn out to be "flat."

On the second page of his text Binx is ready to speak of going to the movies:

> It reminds me of a movie I saw last month out by Lake Pontchartrain. Linda and I went out to a theater in a new suburb. It was evident somebody had miscalculated, for the suburb had quit growing and here was the theater, a pink stucco cube, sitting out in a field all by itself. A strong wind whipped the waves against the seawall; even inside you could hear the racket. The movie was about a man who lose his memory in an accident and as a result lost everything: his family, his friends, his money. He found himself a stranger in a strange city. Here he had to make a fresh start, find a new place to live, a new job, a new girl. It was supposed to be a tragedy, his losing all this, and he seemed to suffer a great deal. On the other hand, things were not so bad after all. In no time he found a very picturesque place to live, a houseboat on the river, and a very handsome girl, the local librarian. (*M* 4–5)

93

The plot would be compelling to Binx, for it could be construed as an allusion to the original repression of which Binx must have some faint knowledge:

> After the movie Linda and I stood under the marquee and talked to the manager, or rather listened to him tell his troubles: the theater was almost empty, which was pleasant for me but not for him. It was a fine night and I felt very good. Overhead was the blackest sky I ever saw, a black wind pushed the lake toward us. The waves jumped over the seawall and spattered the street. The manager had to yell to be heard while from the sidewalk speaker directly over his head came the twittering conversation of the amnesiac and the librarian. It was the part where they are going through the newspaper files in search of some clues to his identity (he has a vague recollection of an accident). (*M* 5)

But while the movie character wishes to recover from his amnesia, Binx thinks that amnesia would be the most desirable state of consciousness, for it would guarantee a constant rotation: "A rotation I define as the experiencing of the new beyond the expectation of the experiencing of the new" (*M* 144). Washburn offers a helpful analysis of Binx's need of rotation: "A fugitive from 'nothingness,' the mental ego is forever after something new. The novelty of the new attracts the mental ego's attention and, in doing so, facilitates its distraction from self. And the novelty of the new also generates excitement, which is the mental ego's pale, but manageable, substitute for the native dynamism of life" (Washburn 94).

It is not, however, the virtual reality of the movie—which appeals to Binx's mental ego—which is the more significant aspect of Binx's account at this point. Rather it is the physical presence of the theater itself which draws Binx to the movies nearly every day, which presents an archetype that appeals to Binx's now unconscious body-ego. Washburn's text is here very pertinent:

> The circulation of the power of the Ground affects the infant in two main ways. First, since the power of the Ground is an energy that amplifies psychic processes, its unimpeded flow quickens and enhances the infant's experience across all dimensions. And second, since the power of the Ground is a force of a magnetic and fluidic nature, its free ascent buoys, lulls and entrances the infant, keeping him in a state of unmindful absorption. Viewed in this light, original embedment is a state analogous to the

intrauterine condition. It is a womb outside the womb, a condition sustained and suspended in "maternal fluid." It is a condition of immersion and dissolution, which, as such, is aptly called an oceanic state. Original embedment, then, to put it succinctly, is a liquidlike plenum or, as Neumann calls it, a pleroma, a condition of dynamic fullness and fulfillment. (Washburn 43)

Washburn accounts not only for Binx's delight in the nearly empty theater but also for his "oceanic experience" outside the theater: "It was a fine night and I felt very good. Overhead was the blackest sky I ever saw; a black wind pushed the lake toward us. The waves jumped over the seawall and spattered the street." These images, among others, constitute the "archetype of the collective unconscious" (in original embedment): "an enveloping darkness prior to the dawning of light (ego) and, therefore, prior to the alternation of day (consciousness) and night (unconsciousness, sleep)" and "an oceanic depth out of which are born the myriad forms of life" (Washburn 44). There is yet another motive to Binx's moviegoing; within the womb-theater he regards the movie screen as a dream screen, a symbol for the maternal breast (whose sufficiency provides undisturbed sleep), first analyzed by Bertram Lewin. For the infant, the breast in the mouth is another instance of the outside inside.

It is vitally important to note here a clarification about the original embedment of the ego in the Dynamic Ground-Great Mother, the significance of which will appear in the fullness of time:

> The well-being experienced during original embedment is never entirely forgotten, and the ever-so-faint memory of it lives on to haunt us in later life. Our nostalgia for paradise reflects a longing for this original state, the undividedness and ebullience of which constitute for us an implicit paradigm of wholeness and happiness. However, this nostalgia can be misleading if it is taken to imply that original embedment is the proper standard of fulfilled existence. For original embedment is only a foreglimpse of the truly fulfilled state; it is the pre-egoic correlate of the transegoic state that is the proper goal of life. It is true that original embedment is a condition of unqualified unity and bliss, but it is equally true that it is a condition that is wholly undeveloped and therefore primitive. Specifically, original embedment is a state the unity of which is completely undifferentiated: it is a state of at-one-ment without an ego that is at one.

And original embedment is a state the bliss of which, although real and of lasting importance, is completely blind, i.e., unpossessed and unappreciated.

Original embedment is, then, only a primitive precursor of (transegoic) paradise, not paradise itself. This means that the real point of the nostalgia for paradise is not that the ego should return to its original prediffterentiated unity with the Dynamic Ground, but rather that the ego should reroot and thereby regenerate itself in this Ground. Hence, if regression in the service of transcendence would draw the ego back toward the first source of its being, it does so not to dissolve and re-embed the ego in the Ground, but rather to open a permanent channel to the Ground so that the ego can be replenished by the power-spirit that issues from the Ground. (Washburn 45–46)

Like any other ego, Binx's ego emerged from the Dynamic Ground into a body-ego dependent on the Great Mother, "instantiated in the person of the mothering parent, with her physical embrace and lactic fluids" (Washburn 47). At first the Great Mother is the Good Mother, willingly responsive to every need of the infant, but in time that Great Mother must, for a variety of reasons, unavoidably disappoint the growing child. Gradually the Great Mother becomes bivalent, both the Good Mother and the Terrible Mother. When this split occurs the Great Mother is transformed: "To be sure, the body-ego continues to need the mother and to interact with her in an affectionate manner. But it never again surrenders itself to her totally; the period of unconditional openness and completely intimate mutuality is over" (Washburn 56).

As a defense against the continuing internal need for the Good Mother and against the rigors imposed by the Terrible Mother, the child learns to repress the "power of the Ground" (Washburn 58). But at the same time the mother representative is split, so is the child's representation of self, into the "good child" and the "terrible child," with the "terrible child" being identified with the body-ego which is being frustrated. Thus the developing mental-ego must repress its own body-ego, so as to develop a defense against the Terrible Mother. Since in either condition, "good" or "bad," the child is still dependent upon the mother, the child is jealous of the father, who is "an independent intimate" of the mother (Washburn 62)—Washburn's version of the Oedipus complex. So the child identifies with the father, assigning to him opposite values from those of the mother, who is still associated with the body-ego. Hence the father is associated with the mental ego. Once again original repression leads to Cartesian dualism (Washburn 64).

When Binx's father was killed in World War II, Binx's mother, a nurse (her occupation another irony, as Binx may now see), returned to her former job in a Biloxi hospital, thus in effect vacating the maternal position, which, theoretically, had already been split into the Good Mother and Terrible Mother representations. As if to emphasize her withdrawal, she quickly remarried and started having a large second set of children. Binx has spent "much of the past fifteen years" (*M* 26) in the house of his Aunt Emily, who can be seen as something of a Terrible Mother, although she has relinquished part of that role to Mrs. Schexnaydre. There is no mention of an early representation of the Terrible Mother, nor is there a mention of early Good Mother representatives. But recent Good Mother representatives have been Binx's succession of secretaries, Marcia, Linda, and now Sharon.

Very early in his narrative Binx discusses his romantic project:

> Naturally I would like to say that I had made conquests of these splendid girls, my secretaries, casting them off one after the other like old gloves, but it would not be strictly true. They could be called love affairs, I suppose. They started off as love affairs anyway, fine careless raptures in which Marcia or Linda (but not yet Sharon) and I would go spinning along the Gulf Coast, lie embracing in a deserted cove of Ship Island, and hardly believe our good fortune, hardly believe that the world could contain such happiness. (*M* 8)

This succession of avatars of the Great Mother represents the archetype "of sirens and nymphs (who would lure the ego back into oceanic immersion)" (Washburn 82). The trouble begins when each victim of seduction, ignorant of her archetypal role, languishes in frustration at Binx's disinclination to say the right words. Binx's mental-egoic way of looking at his secretaries would be cynical, if it were not so sad: "It is not a bad thing to settle for the Little Way, not the big search for the big happiness but the sad little happiness of drinks and kisses, a good little car and a warm deep thigh" (*M* 136).

When Binx had exhausted the mental-egoic stage, the "vertical search" he calls it (*M* 70), he becomes "the moviegoer," undertakes "a different kind of search, a horizontal search. As a consequence, what takes place in my room is less important. What is important is what I shall find when I leave my room and wander in the neighborhood" (*M* 70). The "horizontal search" he also calls "[his] life in Gentilly, [his] Little Way, [his] secret existence among the happy shades in Elysian Fields" (*M* 99). The aimless "horizontal search" suggests that he stoically accepts his alienation. But his reference to the "Little Way" argues that he has at least a very faint awareness of the archetype of the Way, as it is described by Washburn:

> There are many other archetypes that bear upon the unfolding of the ego/Ground interaction, including, for example, archetypes of descent into the underworld, the beast of the abyss, demonic evil and angelic good, death and resurrection, purgation and transfiguration, damnation and salvation, and liberation and apotheosis. However, these archetypes, in being invisible to the mental ego, do not belong to the unconscious by way of inheritance from the body-ego. They are not buried remnants of the pre-egoic past, but rather still-latent potentialities of the transegoic future. Jung, who undertook an in-depth study of archetypes such as these, understood them to be spontaneous prefigurations of spiritual development, signposts of the Way. In the terms being used here, they are heralds of events that await the mental ego if and when it quits its repression of the Dynamic Ground and begins the journey that would lead it ultimately to a higher reunion with the Ground. These archetypes of the Way, then, are unconscious in a different sense than are the archetypes that make up the Great Mother system. Indeed, both groups of archetypes pertain to the ego's ontogenesis in relation to the Dynamic Ground, and both belong to the collective unconscious in the broadest sense of the term. But whereas the archetypes constituting the Great Mother system are vestiges of a prepersonal past, the archetypes of the Way are harbingers of a transpersonal future. (Washburn 83)

The only time Binx directly mentions "the Way," he is specifically referring to *Tao* (Chinese for "the Way") and he is so embittered by impotence (induced by his mental-egoic condition) that he mocks the libidinal superabundance supposedly possessed by successful seekers of the spirit:

> . . . he . . . is a seeker and a pilgrim of sorts and he is just in from Guanajuato or Sambuco where he has found the Real Right Thing or from the

East where he apprenticed himself to a wise man and became proficient in the seventh path to the seventh happiness. Yet he does not disdain this world either and when it happens that a maid comes to his bed with a heart full of longing for him, he puts down his book in a good and cheerful spirit and gives her as merry a time as she could possibly wish for. Whereupon, with her dispatched into as sweet a sleep as ever Scarlett enjoyed the morning of Rhett's return, he takes up his book again and is in an instant ten miles high and on the Way. (*M* 199–200)

Binx is particularly bitter at his impotence because it seems to be the culmination of a series of setbacks that has frustrated his efforts to mount a new kind of search. His impotence occurs with Kate (whom he, mental-egoically, has not been able to admit he loves), not with a secretary; Kate, he seems to understand, is not just a diversion, but a woman whom he could trust, who could, in other words, be an authentic replacement for the Great Mother (and thus be an accessory to the opening of the Dynamic Ground).

On Wednesday, the first day of his narration, Binx reports that "the possibility of a search" (M 10) had occurred to him. Since he makes this announcement soon after saying that he had received a request from his Aunt Emily to come to lunch, there is a likelihood that it is the anticipation of confronting the Terrible Mother that propels the idea of a search into his mind. Such a thought has not occurred to him in ten years; that time was in 1951 when he awakened "bleeding in a ditch" (*M* 145) in Korea, so near death that he vowed to search for a new life if he lived. The declivous locale of his original awakening suggests that it represented the archetype of expulsion from the womb. Binx himself is very vague about the nature of the search, but the inference is that it was the possibility of physical death that awakened him to the actuality of spiritual death (*M* 11). When he returned to the States, he promptly forgot about the search. Now, though, seeing himself merely as the possessor of the things that he puts into his pockets, he says: "[a] man can look at this little pile on his bureau for thirty years and never once see it. It is as invisible as his own hand. Once I saw it, however, the search became possible" (*M* 11). The "thirty years" duration reinforces the inference that he is responding to the loss of the Dynamic Ground, for his thirtieth birthday is a week away. He then likens himself to a corpse, further hinting that he vaguely realizes that he is spiritually dead: "I bathed,

99

shaved, dressed carefully, and sat at my desk and poked through the little pile in search of a clue just as the detective on television pokes through the dead man's possessions, using his pencil as a poker" (*M* 11).

But no sooner does Binx get on the bus than he is distracted from the search by the sight of "a very fine looking girl" (*M* 12), whom he immediately incorporates into his standard fantasy: "What good times we could have! This very afternoon we could go spinning along the Gulf Coast" (*M* 12–13). Apparently the fantasy is so visual that Binx pictures himself on the beach, which prompts him to think of himself as "a castaway," an analogue of the existential image of the shipwrecked man. By this chain of images he returns to the subject of the search; in his "internal dialogue" he asks himself: "What do you seek—God? you ask with a smile" (*M* 13). But again he refuses to answer: ". . . it is the fear of exposing my own ignorance which constrains me from mentioning the object of my search" (*M* 14).

When Binx arrives at his aunt's house, he immediately makes his way to the mantelpiece of the living room, where there are photographs of the family:

> One picture I never tire of looking at. For ten years I have looked at it on this mantelpiece and tried to understand it. Now I take it down and hold it against the light from the darkening sky. Here are two brothers, Dr. Wills and Judge Anse [the former his grandfather, the latter his grand-uncle] with their arms about each other's shoulders, and my father in front, the three standing on a mountain trail against a dark forest. It is the Schwarzwald. A few years after the first war they had gotten together for once and made the grand tour. Only Alex Bolling is missing—he is in the third frame: an astonishingly handsome young man with the Rupert Brooke-Galahad sort of face you see so often in pictures of World War I soldiers. His death in the Argonne (five years before) was held to be fitting since the original Alex Bolling was killed with Roberdaux Wheat in the Hood breakthrough at Gaines Mill in 1862. My father is wearing some kind of fraternity blazer and a hard katy straw. He looks different from the brothers. Alex too is much younger, yet he is still one of them. But not my father. It is hard to say why. The elder Bollings—and Alex—are serene in their identities. Each coincides with himself, just as the larch trees in the photograph coincide with themselves. . . . But my father is not one of them. (*M* 24–25)

The picture frame is shadowed because of the approaching storm; the pictured human subjects are shadowed because of their background. But Binx's father is the real shadow, as Washburn describes that aspect of the "personal submerged unconscious" of the mental ego:

> . . . The shadow is the alter ego of the mental ego's self-concept. The mental ego has a vested interest in seeing itself in a certain way, namely, as possessing those facticities that enter into its self-concept, which is surrogate body and being. These facticities are introjected and identified with as self, and everything incompatible with them is alienated and denied to awareness. The result of this alienation is the shadow, the psychic subsystem containing the dark and disowned dimensions of the personality. (Washburn 130)

Binx later acknowledges (*M* 157) that his father so severely suffered from the despair of the mental-egoic stage that he contrived to get himself killed. Thus, in the photograph, he looks at his son from beyond the grave, knowing more about the torment that Binx is going through than Binx does himself.

When Aunt Emily enters the room, Binx unconsciously feels the impact of her Terrible Mother representation: "In a split second I have forgotten everything, the years in Gentilly, even my search. As always we take up again where we left off. This is where I belong after all" (*M* 26). Later in his visit, he does, however, try to tell her of his new search: " 'As a matter of fact I was planning to leave Gentilly soon, but for a different reason. There is something—' I stop. My idea of a search seems absurd" (*M* 54). So formidable is Aunt Emily's Terrible Mother personality that Binx thinks no more about the search until Friday morning, but even then, in a kind of mental-egoic behavior, he offers a backdoor discussion of the subject:

> Jews are my first real clue.
>
> When a man is in despair and does not in his heart of hearts allow that a search is possible and when such a man passes a Jew in the street, he notices nothing.
>
> When a man becomes a scientist or an artist, he is open to a different kind of despair. When such a man passes a Jew in the street, he may notice something but it is not a remarkable encounter. To him the Jew can only appear as a scientist or artist like himself or as a specimen to be studied.
>
> But when a man awakes to the possibility of a search and when such a

man passes a Jew in the street for the first time, he is like Robinson Crusoe seeing the footprint on the beach. (*M* 89)

Such a mental-egoic abstractness is appropriate on Friday, though, for Binx has been preoccupied with his seduction of Sharon since Thursday morning (*M* 67), anticipating the beach that is his archetypal seduction site. By Friday afternoon at 4:00, he decides "to set in motion my newest scheme conceived in the interests of money and love, my love for Sharon" (*M* 102), by asking her to work late. With the intimacy that results, Binx has no difficulty in persuading Sharon to go to Ship Island with him, when they finish work before noon on Saturday (*M* 118). The pre-consummation phase of the seduction rivals any described in Kierkegaard's *Diary of the Seducer:* Binx has obviously had a two-book library sometime in the past. All the while, as if knowledgeable of her archetypal role, Sharon is calling Binx "son" or "boy." Given the fantasy that activates Binx's romantic project, it is appropriate that the consummation is to take place at his mother's fishing cottage. But reality intrudes: Binx's mother, with her six Smith children, is actually there.

Binx masterfully hides his frustrated ardor, but alone on the cot that his mother makes up for him on the porch, he has, as expected, troubled sleep. His thoughts are not on Sharon, as expected; rather he thinks of the search: ". . . when I awake, I awake in the grip of everydayness. Everydayness is the enemy. No search is possible" (*M* 145). Figuratively, this is the bed that his mother has forced him to occupy all his conscious life. His pain is increased by his loneliness: "Neither my mother's family nor my father's family understand my search" (*M* 145). The former think that he has lost his faith (whereas he claims never to have had any), while the latter "think that the world makes sense without God and that anyone but an idiot knows what the good life is and anyone but a scoundrel can lead it" (*M* 146). Completely baffled, he makes a note for himself to follow:

Starting point for search:
It no longer avails to start with creatures and prove God.
Yet it is impossible to rule God out.
The only possible starting point: the strange fact of one's own invincible apathy—that if the proofs were proved and God presented himself, noth-

ing would be changed. Here is the strangest fact of all.

Abraham saw signs of God and believed. Now the only sign is that all the signs in the world make no difference. Is this God's ironic revenge? But I am onto him. (*M* 146)

Although his seduction of Sharon is a failure, Binx profits from an unexpected benefit by going to the beach. He had thought to engage in a rotation, an admittedly temporary respite from his alienation, with a mother-surrogate, but instead he must confront the original woman on the beach. He is forced to regress to infancy in his effort to understand his relationship with his mother.

The confrontation is foreshadowed when Binx refers to Abraham, not specifically to the Biblical Abraham, but to the Abraham created by Kierkegaard in *Fear and Trembling* (Kierkegaard 1941). There Kierkegaard presents his version of Genesis 22, the story of Abraham's willingness to follow God's command that he sacrifice his son Isaac, the willingness to transcend the ethical that characterizes "the knight of faith." In the edition that Binx would have read, in the Introduction, the Translator, Walter Lowrie, quotes a passage in Kierkegaard's *Journal* which offers the germ of the entire book. One paragraph of the passage is particularly relevant to Binx's search:

> When the child has to be weaned the mother blackens her breast, but her eyes rest just as lovingly upon the child. The child believes it is the breast that has changed, but that the mother is unchanged. And why does she blacken her breast? Because, she says, it would be a shame that it should seem delicious when the child must not get it.—This collision is easily resolved, for the breast is only a part of the mother herself. Happy is he who has not experienced more dreadful collisions, who did not need to blacken *himself,* who did not need to go to hell in order to see what the devil looks like, so that he might paint himself accordingly and in that way if possible save another person in that person's God-relationship at least. This would be Abraham's collision. (Kierkegaard 1941 12)

In the "Prelude" of *Fear and Trembling* (Kierkegaard 1941 26–29), in order to project a psychology for Abraham, Kierkegaard recurs several times to the figure of the mother who blackens her breast. Kierkegaard imagines Abraham, at the moment he is to sacrifice Isaac, assuming the look of a monster, blackening *himself,* so as to achieve this result:

103

He seized Isaac by the throat, threw him to the ground, and said, "Stupid boy, dost thou then suppose that I am thy father? I am an idolator. Dost thou suppose that this is God's bidding? No, it is my desire." Then Isaac trembled and cried out in his terror, "O God in heaven, have compassion on me. God of Abraham, have compassion on me. If I have no father upon earth, be Thou my father!" But Abraham in a low voice said to himself, "O Lord in heaven, I thank Thee. After all it is better for him to believe that I am a monster, rather than that he should lose faith in Thee." (Kierkegaard 1941 27)

Abraham is thus like Kierkegaard's last figure of the mother who blackens her breast: "When the child must be weaned, the mother has stronger food in readiness, lest the child should perish. Happy the person who has stronger food in readiness!" (Kierkegaard 1941 29).

Also alluding to *Fear and Trembling*, by speaking of "the knight of faith," Washburn, in his discussion of regression, makes a point which explains Binx's crisis on the porch:

. . . the ego eventually realizes that, in combating the Terrible Mother, it is really only hurting itself. And, in time, the ego also realizes why this is so, namely, because it is somehow related to the Terrible Mother as to a larger part of itself. The ego, that is, arrives at the insight that its adversary is not something inherently alien and evil, but rather something that only appears such because it has been alienated and condemned. For these reasons the ego at last concludes that it cannot—indeed, should not—continue to struggle against the power that has set upon it.

This is a momentous decision, which saves the ego from disaster. Putting this decision into practice, the ego reverses its stand. It ceases being the hero who would slay the dragon—that, after all, was the role of the body-ego—and becomes the knight of faith, the hero who submits himself to the awesome power of the dragon so that, through an atoning death, spiritual rebirth can be earned. The ego, therefore, quits its fight and flight and begins instead to surrender and return to the underlying sources of its being. (Washburn 183)

But there is a warning: "Before this turn [to regeneration] can be made, the ego must suffer many encounters with the terrible maternal power" (Washburn 184).

Binx must come to the realization that the Good Mother *must be* blackened into the Terrible Mother, for otherwise the ego would never evolve. And if the ego never evolves, it would never have the opportunity to regenerate in spirit so as to achieve integration in the Dynamic Ground. At the same time, though, Binx will try to remember that his mother is, after all, not only his "internal object" but as well a sovereign person who has lost a husband, two sons, and is close to losing another.

In the morning after his "dark night of the soul" (Washburn 155), Binx awakens to confront his mother. "The world is milk: sky, water, savannah" (*M* 147), as Binx anticipates his mother's arrival, "as old and sly as Eve herself" (*M* 142). She comes through the screen door, as she has so often come through his dream screen: "'Hinh-honh,' she says in a yawn-sigh as wan and white as the morning. Her blouse is one of [her husband's] army shirts and not much too big for her large breasts" (*M* 148). Binx lies down on the dock: "I stretch out at full length, prop my head on a two-by-four. It is possible to squint into the rising sun and at the same time see my mother spangled in rainbows" (*M* 149–150). Binx is ready to nurse the nurse.

But instead his mother tells about how, for one morning, she had helped Binx's father to escape his alienation by taking him fishing. But the next day Binx's father relapsed into his despair. She says that on another occasion she spoon-fed him for six months (*M* 153); but there was again a relapse. Then she says that Binx is very much like his father (*M* 154): if Binx accepts this identification, he must think that he will eventually follow his father's path to self-destruction. So he rejects her implication at once by hinting that he is too suffused with libido (which can be transformed into spirit) to die. Sharply she replies: "Don't you get risque with me! This is your mother you're talking to and not one of your little hotsy-totsies" (*M* 155). Then, more softly, she says that Kate Cutrer, not a hotsy-totsy, is his destiny: even a Terrible Mother sometimes knows what is best for her son. So the weekend concludes. Binx has achieved at least a partial regression. Even so, on the trip back to New Orleans, he falls victim to the malaise, "the pain of loss" (*M* 120), and tries to cope by making a pass at Sharon:

"Son, don't you mess with me."
"Very well, I won't," I say gloomily, as willing not to mess with her as mess with her, to tell the truth. (*M* 166)

As Washburn writes, before "the turn from regression in the service of transcendence to regeneration in spirit" can be made, "the ego must suffer many encounters with the terrible maternal power" (Washburn 184).

On Sunday afternoon, then, Binx, having been defeated in his "Little Way," returns to his aunt's house, still under the spell of the Terrible Mother. There he finds Kate in such a state of anxiety that she proposes to accompany him that very night on his Chicago business trip. Having had very little sleep (and having been subjected to "the fury of the return of the repressed" [Washburn 170]), Binx is pretty much in an "exceptional state": must of what he experiences on the trip is dreamlike. He becomes "the man on the train" that Percy had written about in his study of alienation, "The Man on the Train." As Binx fights his miserable condition, he thinks: ". . . in the past few days my own life has gone to seed. I no longer eat and sleep regularly or write philosophical notes in my notebook and my fingernails are dirty. The search has spoiled the pleasure of my tidy and ingenious life in Gentilly" (*M* 190). And Binx is aware that Kate is no better off: "We hunch up knee to knee and nose to nose like the two devils on the Rorschach card (*M* 192). Later they try to make love, but Binx is impotent (*M* 200–1). Since Kate alludes to herself as Ophelia, then Binx must be Hamlet, and thus she might be implying that she suspects the reason for Binx's impotence.

But Kate does not scorn him; rather, Binx says, "Kate takes charge with many a cluck and much fuss, as if she had caught sight in me of a howling void and meant to conceal it from the world" (*M* 202). Binx's trite image of Kate as a mother hen does not alleviate his experience of the "dead void of the mental-egoic system" (Washburn 171–72)—instead it emphasizes just how close to infantile defenselessness he really is. When they take shelter in a tiny bar, Binx has a moment of clarity: "There I see her plain, see plain for the first time since I lay wounded in a ditch and watched an Oriental finch scratching around in the leaves—a quiet little body she is, a tough little city Celt; no, more of a Rachel really, a dark little Rachel bound home to Brooklyn on the IRT" (*M* 206). According to his use of the Jew as a litmus test, previously cited, Binx is announcing that he recognizes Kate as one like himself, who can join him in the search. He prefigures their marriage by alluding now to *The Taming of the Shrew:* "'Sweet Kate,' say I patting her" (*M* 206). So triumphant are they that they celebrate: "Back to the Loop where we dive into the mother and Urwomb of all moviehouses . . . and see a movie called *The Young Philadelphians*" (*M* 211). The title, "the young inhabitants of the city of love," says it all—but Binx's summary of the movie underlines it: "Paul Newman is an idealistic young fellow who is disillusioned and becomes cynical and calculating. But in the end he recovers his ideals" (*M* 211). Yet there is another layer of meaning: his entry into the Urwomb with a woman who can truly be an alternative to the Terrible Mother suggests that Binx is close to complete regression-and-turn.

There is a hint at the ever-increasing "fury of the return of the repressed" when Binx and Kate emerge from the Urwomb: "Outside, a new note has crept into the wind, a black williwaw sound straight from the terrible wastes to the north. 'Oh oh oh,'" wails Kate as we creep home to the hotel, sunk into ourselves and with no stomach even for hand-holding. 'Something is going to happen'" (*M* 211). Their presentiment is borne out when they get to the hotel: Binx is commanded to call his aunt, who upbraids him for his behavior with Kate (*M* 212). When Binx stands before his aunt in New Orleans, the Terrible Mother's fury reaches hurricane strength. Then he is spiritually disowned, with no place to go but to the house of Mrs. Schexnaydre. Kate tells him to wait for her there.

Binx is quickly overcome by despair:

> Today is my thirtieth birthday and I sit on the ocean wave in the schoolyard and wait for Kate and think of nothing. Now in the thirty-first year of my dark pilgrimage on this earth and knowing less than I ever knew before, having learned only to recognize merde when I see it, having inherited no more from my father than a good nose for merde, for every species of shit that flies—my only talent—smelling merde from every quarter, living in fact in the very century of merde, the great shithouse of scientific humanism where needs are satisfied, everyone becomes an anyone, a warm and creative person, and prospers like a dung beetle, and one hundred percent of people are humanists and ninety-eight percent believe in God, and men are dead, dead, dead; and the malaise has settled like a fall-out and what people really fear is not that the bomb will fall but

that the bomb will not fall—on this my thirtieth birthday, I know nothing and there is nothing to do but fall prey to desire.

Nothing remains but desire, and desire comes howling down Elysian Fields like a mistral. My search has been abandoned; it is no match for my aunt, her rightness and her despair, her despairing of me and her despairing of herself. Whenever I take leave of my aunt after one of her serious talks, I have to find a girl. (*M* 228)

Binx has clearly reached "the second stage of regression," the "encounter with the prepersonal unconscious" (Washburn 170–85). He thinks of nothing, for his "internal dialogue" has ceased because his mental-ego can no longer repress the Dynamic Ground (Washburn 170). He thinks of nothing because he *is* nothing. All he is is "the self that [he] has not wanted to be (the shadow)" (Washburn 171), so he identifies with his father. Nothing is the world, a "dead void" (Washburn 171). Likening the malaise to a fall-out, he responds to the apocalypse archetype (Washburn 172–73), particularly its image of *merde,* "which mean[s] that the rawest and rudest aspects of life are about to break loose" (Washburn 173). As always, after being assailed by the Terrible Mother, Binx "fall[s] prey to desire." Washburn explains Binx's need for a girl:

> In re-encountering the power of the Ground, then, the ego has the experience of renewing its relation with the maternal principle. Moreover, given its long-standing negative stance toward nonegoic life, the ego has the experience more specifically of renewing its relation with the *negative* side of the maternal principle: the Terrible Mother. The ego finds itself once again in face of an abysmal, dark-dreadful-doomful-devouring reality. This awful female presence is in many respects similar to the Terrible Mother experienced years ago by the body-ego. But there are the two major differences just mentioned: this new Terrible Mother is not confused with a specific human person and she is intimately associated with the sexual and aggressive instincts. Unlike the old Terrible Mother, this new Terrible Mother is not an outer or material presence but is rather exclusively an inner, psychic or spiritual reality. (Washburn 182–83)

When, after nearly an hour, Kate has not come, Binx concludes that she has sided with the Terrible Mother aunt. Desperately he tries to telephone Sharon, for erotic dialogue might replace the missing "internal dialogue": ". . . the wire thrills and stops and thrills and in the interval there comes into my ear my own breath as if my very self stood beside me and would not speak" (*M* 229). Sharon is not at her apartment, so Binx even tries to infatuate Joyce, who shares the apartment, so urgent is his need. As he talks, he has the impression that the apocalypse has occurred: "A watery sunlight breaks through the smoke of the Chef and turns the sky yellow. Elysian Fields glistens like a vat of sulfur; the playground looks as if it alone had survived the end of the world" (*M* 231). Then Kate comes: "There she sits like a bomber pilot, resting on her wheel and looking sideways at the children and not seeing, and she could be I myself, sooty eyed and nowhere" (*M* 231). Binx says that for a long time he has "hoped for the end of the world," but Kate's faithfulness gives him another kind of hope: "Is it possible that—it is not too late?" (*M* 231)

Binx's recognition of Kate as a reflection of himself is a major achievement of his regression in service of transcendence. Such is the bivalence of the Great Mother for him that he has assigned an archetypal value, either "graceful maiden" or "ugly witch" (Washburn 121), to every woman significant to his life. But with the proof of Kate's faith in him and his consequent faith in a future, Binx discovers a thrilling possibility. As Washburn describes the process of reconciliation: ". . . as the ego does this, it finds that the beast eventually becomes tame (the instincts are pacified) and that, more generally, the instinctualized Terrible Mother is slowly transformed into a goddess of love and light (libido is transformed into spirit)" (Washburn 183–84). Binx concludes his conversation with Joyce by saying that he will bring his fiancée, Kate Cutrer, to a party she and Sharon plan.

Then Binx and Kate discuss their marriage, which will be even more complicated than marriage necessarily is. As Binx listens to Kate confess her feelings of insecurity and dependence on him, he watches people entering a church for the imposition of ashes. At this moment Binx must realize the inseparable connection between the Great Mother and the Dynamic Ground (out of which he was taken and to which he desperately hopes to return).

When Binx constructs his narrative over a year later, he says:

> As for my search, I have not the inclination to say much on the subject. For one thing, I have not the authority, as the great Danish philosopher declared, to speak of such matters in any way other than the edifying. For

another thing, it is not open to me even to be edifying, since the time is later than his, much too late to edify or do much of anything except plant a foot in the right place as the opportunity presents itself—if indeed ass-kicking is properly distinguished from edification.

Further: I am a member of my mother's family after all and so naturally shy away from the subject of religion (a peculiar word this in the first place, *religion;* it is something to be suspicious of). (*M* 237)

Despite his refusal to admit his "conversion" (Washburn 196), it is certain that he has experienced one and probably that it occurred there before the church on Ash Wednesday. For Binx describes a Black man who enters the church and emerges while Binx and Kate are discussing their plans. Binx watches "him closely through the rear view mirror" (*M* 35), which is the same as saying that he is talking about himself. Then he says of the Black man: "It is impossible to say why he is here. It is part and parcel of the complex business of coming up in the world? Or is it because he believes that God himself is present here at the corner of Elysian Fields and Bons Enfants? Or is he here for both reasons: through some dim dazzling trick of grace, coming for the one and receiving the other as God's own importunate bonus?" (*M* 235). Much of that meditation is sufficiently vague to apply to anyone, but only someone who has experienced grace and knows the richness of its workings would be capable of such a brilliant description of it.

There is a final proof of the success of Binx's regression in the service of transcendence. In the Epilogue Binx says that in the May of the year after his crucial Ash Wednesday his stepbrother Lonnie Smith fell fatally ill. The day before Lonnie died, Binx was taking care of his other stepsiblings. When one of them asks if Lonnie is going to die, Binx tells the truth. Then another asks: "When Our Lord raises us up on the last day, will Lonnie still be in a wheelchair or will he be like us?" Binx replies: "He'll be like you" (*M* 240). It is as if Binx has been waiting since that Ash Wednesday to proclaim that it will be followed by Easter, the Resurrection. In asserting that Lonnie will rise unblemished, Binx is acknowledging the grace that supports his total commitment to the Dynamic Ground. He is also testifying to his escape from Cartesian dualism into "mind-body integration":

The body is "resurrected" during regression in the service of transcendence, and then the ego is "reincarnated" during regeneration in spirit. By these means the mind/body alienation characteristic of the mental-egoic period is overcome and a higher mind/body whole is brought into being. This is a whole that, objectively, is immediately present in outer physical space and that, subjectively, is intimately familiar with inner psychic space. It is a whole that has its anchor in the body and yet is capable of ascending to abstract intellectual heights. And it is a whole that has firm command of mind and will and yet is capable of enjoying the polymorphous pleasures of bodily life. But this much was already said in the last chapter.

What was not said in the last chapter is that, as the transition to integration is made, the ego begins to become aware of itself as having *two* bodies, namely, not only the physical body (which is now awakened) but also an energetic or spiritual body, namely the circulating power of the Dynamic Ground. That is, the ego begins to realize that it is not just a solid substance but also a moving, dynamic one. It becomes evident to the ego that, as an extended being, it is not only the body proper but also the spiritual force that enlivens the body. This second, ethereal body is recognized by most of the world's religions. For example, it is, I suggest, what is meant by the resurrection body (*soma pneumatikon*) in Christianity . . . (Washburn 216)

In this final assistance, Washburn explains how in his final accounting Binx can flirt with his wife ("You are very good-looking today" [*M* 239]), speak spiritual truth to the children, and say not one word about the movies.

Will Barrett under the Telescope

It is, of course, possible to be both a physician and a scholar of consciousness, yet not write like either one. In his fiction Walker Percy has brilliantly illustrated that possibility. So when he creates a narrator who calls attention to his medical and psychoanalytic knowledge, as he does in *The Last Gentleman* (1966), we had better pay attention to such an aberration.

Percy's narrator immediately introduces his main character, Williston Bibb Barrett, aged twenty-five, just at the moment ready to look through a telescope. The place is the Great Meadow in New York's Central Park; the time is early summer, 1964. Although the narrator occasionally reveals the thinking of other characters, he discloses nothing of significance by such omniscience. It is clear that his only real concern is to render both the subjective experience and the objective behavior of Will Barrett, to which he adds, in a kind of "voice-over" technique, his own commentary. Such interpretation can of course be made only after reflection—say a generation later. It is possible that the narrator is viewing his twenty-five-year-old self through forty-seven-year-old eyes.

There is another reason that Walker Percy does not merely use the technique of first-person point of view. As the narrator describes Will Barrett's business with the telescope, he also provides a medical history. As a child, Will

had had "spells," occurrences which were nameless and not to be thought of, let alone mentioned, and which he therefore thought of as lying at the secret and somehow shameful heart of childhood itself. There was a name for it, he discovered later, which gave it form and habitation. It was *déjà vu*, at least he reckoned it was. What happened anyhow was that even when he was a child and was sitting in the kitchen watching D'lo snap beans or make beaten biscuits, there came over him as it might come over a sorrowful old man the strongest sense that it had all happened before and that something else was going to happen and when it did he would know the secret of his own life. Things seemed to turn white and dense and time itself became freighted with an unspeakable emotion. Sometimes he "fell out," and would wake up hours later, in his bed, refreshed but still haunted. (*LG* 11)

Will's adult condition cannot be said to have improved: "To be specific, he had now a nervous condition and suffered spells of amnesia and even between times did not quite know what was what" (*LG* 11). There will be more, but at this point the narrator is content with this summary: "A German physician once remarked that in the lives of people who suffer emotional illness he had noticed the presence of *Lücken* or gaps. As he studied the history of a particular patient he found whole sections missing, like a book with blank pages" (*LG* 12). The "German" physician was Sigmund Freud, who used not once but often the image of *Lücken* to characterize mental life. More uses of the image, more than a dozen occur in *The Interpretation of Dreams* than in any of his other works.

Soon the narrator prefaces an assertion with the inclusive structure "as every psychologist knows" (*LG* 29). Now "psychologist" is rather a modest title in the current hierarchy of mental health practitioners; it seems hardly a title to suggest that the narrator himself is a specialist in such matters or, at the very least, that he is a very knowledgeable layman. But he knows that when Freud wrote his classic work on dreams, which is the foundation of psychoanalysis, he was still referring to himself as a psychologist. And the narrator

113

does want to tie himself to *The Interpretation of Dreams,* for he intends to use the famous telescope of Chapter 7, Freud's scientific model for the "psychic apparatus."[1]

At the conclusion of that long book, after all his analyses of dreams, desperate to be accepted as a scientist, Freud, in "The Psychology of the Dream-Process," offers an explanatory model, although well aware of the danger that it would be taken too literally. Perceptions enter the psychic apparatus through the clear glass of primary awareness, passing through unhindered, to leave impressions or "memory traces" on the various lenses that convey images to the unconscious system. Here images associate, to form memories, which if energized become dreams or other innervations.

My description of the model has the virtues of vagueness and crudity; rather than invite a point by point comparison, it merely suggests that Will Barrett's mental life is "layered" like the mental life illustrated by Freud's telescope. Will *is*, in a sense, the telescope that he uses on the very first page of the narrative, an instrument whose German origin is repeatedly emphasized. Now it is clear why the narrator could not use the first-person point of view: after Freud, the concept of mental activity was no longer just consciousness, but had annexed the vast countryside of which consciousness was not conscious. If the narrator intends to describe the fullness of his mental life at twenty-five—or at least as much of it as he is now aware or willing to acknowledge—he must describe unretentive immediate perception *and* the hallucinations, dreams, screen memories, *déjà vus*, and fugues which were then blocked from consciousness by repression. Much later he directly refers to the distinction between "layers" of mentality: "For a long time [Will] gazed at the temple. What was it? It alone was not refracted and transformed by the prism of dreams and memory" (*LG* 238).

Quickly the narrator traces Will's path to the purchase of the telescope. He begins with the revelation, already cited, of Will's childhood "spells"—for which he offers no explanation, even though he implies by placement that the "spells" marked the origin of Will's "nervous condition." His silence frees us to go our own way; his subsequent reference to Freud suggests a way for us to choose to go, to Freud's essay "Dostoevsky and Parricide." There Freud speculates that Dostoevsky's childhood "spells" were caused not by disease of the brain, but hysteria of the mind. He theorizes that such "spells" resulted from melancholy induced by fear of death. He then dogmatizes that such "spells" signify an identification with a dead person, "either with someone who is really dead or with someone who is still alive and whom the subject wishes dead" (*SE* 21 182–83). That "someone," according to psychoanalysis, is usually the father. Such a wish, says Freud, accounts for the extreme epilepsy that began to attack Dostoevsky after the murder of his father, when Dostoevsky was eighteen. The guilt that resulted from the fulfillment of his secret wish, Freud asserts, undoubtedly influenced Dostoevsky to treat the theme of the murdered father in *The Brothers Karamazov,* a favorite novel of Walker Percy since high school (M. Smith 136)[2] and without a rival as Freud's favorite (Roazen 147).

Childhood amnesia is so strong that Will apparently remembers very, very little. He is provoked only once to think of his mother, when he observes Rita Vaught run her hand through Jamie Vaught's hair (*LG* 232). He relates to his analyst that, while still a boy, he had run away from the camp to which his father and stepmother had sent him while they went to Europe (*LG* 13), though he never thinks of the disappearance of his mother, which is an anomaly considering the frequency of his unconscious thoughts about his father. His rather more frequent memories of D'lo, the cook, may result from two related causes: he spent the preponderance of his time with her and that time was not invested with the kind of emotional significance that would require repression. One memory that he does not share with Binx Bolling, in Percy's earlier novel *The Moviegoer,* is that of reading *The Interpretation of Dreams* and reading about Jackson's Valley Campaign (*M* 138). But his flirtation with psychoanalysis, his recurrent reading of Freeman's *R. E. Lee,* and his fugue to the Shenandoah suggest that Will had shared Binx's reading. Although he thinks that he can remember every detail of "a conversation with his father fifteen years ago" (*LG* 138), he actually is provoked to remember very little until the summer of his father's death.

Will must have been, like Dostoevsky, about eighteen when his father died. At sixteen he had been sent to Princeton, to follow his father and his father before him. In the fall of his junior year, on the Saturday of the Harvard-Princeton game, he had, in his (before him, his grandfather's) room, been "assaulted by stupefying *déjà vus*" (*LG* 14), which produced an intense melancholy. The contents of the *déjà vus*—in *The Psychopathology of Everyday Life* Freud thought them to be the intrusions of day or night dreams from the unconscious (*SE* 6 265–68)—conveyed the impression that he had seen every game in the series. Thus, in danger of losing his identity to the Platonic form of Barrett-at-Princeton, Will had experienced the suffocating weight of tradition, "and he moved like a sloth" (*LG* 15). Immediately he had left school, to live in the Manhattan Y.M.C.A. as a young Christian man—that is, presumably, as a virgin.

Then there is, literally, a "gap" in the text (*LG* 16). It is probable that Will embarked on a fugue—an unconscious flight, believed to be caused by trauma, epilepsy, or hysteria, followed by amnesia. If Freud is correct, the latter two causes are probably related, and doubtless caused Will's decampment, though it should be acknowledged that one would not have to be neurotic to want to escape from the Y.M.C.A.

"The following summer, in deference to the wishes of his father, who hoped to arouse in him a desire to complete his education and particularly to awaken a fondness for the law, he worked as a clerk in the family law firm" (*LG* 16). The only other detail given about his employment is that Will suffered from hay fever the entire summer, whether in reaction to pollen or to some other cause is not stated. "At the end of the summer his father died" (*LG* 16). Will thereafter suffered not only from hay fever but also from "a long fit of melancholy and vacancy amounting almost to amnesia" (*LG* 17). Soon he was drafted, serving two years before he was "honorably and medically discharged when he was discovered totally amnesic and wandering about the Shenandoah Valley between Cross Keys and Port Republic, sites of notable victories of General Stonewall Jackson" (*LG* 18).

The preceding summary was presented in all its numbing lack of effect because it is probably the way that Will offered his history to the psychiatrist to whom he immediately submitted himself. Upon discharge, he resumed residence at the Y, deciding that he needed therapy and a job to pay for it. Thus he engaged Dr. Gamow for treatment, which was to last "for forty-five minutes a day, five days a week, for the following five years, at an approximate cost of $18,000" (*LG* 18), and, after six months training at L.I.U., he became a humidification engineer, his most recent employment, for two years, being at Macy's, where he monitored instruments three floors underground on the graveyard shift. Such aspects of deadness about his job did not bother him, though; he liked his work and felt that he was making real headway with his analysis, though he had continued over the years to fall into a fugue state from time to time, just at a moment when he had thought he was identifying very successfully with some larger group, such as southern expatriates, Greenwich Village interracial liberals, or Ohioans.

Dr. Gamow thinks otherwise. Although his treatment of choice seems to be the pursuit of imagined slips of the tongue, he does have sense enough to realize that Will has mounted a monstrously successful campaign of resistance (*LG* 32). According to Freudian theory, consciousness wishes to protect itself from invasion by terrifying ideas from the unconscious (by way of the preconscious, which is to the psyche what Atlanta is to Delta Airlines). Will has used a most simple tactic to keep Dr. Gamow from breaking down his repression of threatening memories: anticipating each attack that his analyst will mount—he is like Lee in the Wilderness Campaign—Will then cheerfully "becomes" the patient he would be if that attack had been successful. Without "working through" emotionally, he acquiesces vocally. He is, indeed, as Dr. Gamow thinks, "a Southern belle . . . light on his feet and giving away nothing" (*LG* 32). Rather than betray himself by a sullen resistance, he is so terrified by emotion that he projects such a good humor that the analyst, quite unprofessionally, is the partner who gets hostile.

Will, meanwhile, gets his telescope. He had been window-shopping it for some weeks, but apparently decided to buy it only after an incident at the Metropolitan Museum of Art (*LG* 26–28). Unable to attach meaning to what he sees (because, remember, he "forgets" what he sees, immediately), Will has gone to the museum, there to look over another viewer's shoulder, perchance to achieve, secondarily, a response to the seen. While he is there, a skylight falls, and creates such a departure from everydayness that even he can experience a painting directly. It is a sign—but Will gets the wrong meaning from it. When the glass breaks, the real may be recovered. But Will decides to buy the telescope, for glass (instrumentation) will confirm that what sight sees is the really real: "It was as if the telescope created its own world in the brilliant theater of its lenses" (*LG* 5).

Once he has the telescope, Will feels that each of his "five senses was honed to a razor's edge and attuned like the great Jodrell Bank antenna to the slightest signal of something gone amiss" (*LG* 41). Not just any telescope, he is the largest radio telescope in the world, ready to explore farthest space. Soon he begins to imagine himself a "radar" (*LG* 93), without understanding the transmission. That failure apparently results from his deafness in one ear, a deficit with a hysteric origin.

Now that Will has a telescope, he too can be a specialist, a visualizer who deals in range and in depth. Having set up his new purchase, he takes his first look:

> He focused on a building clear across the park and beyond Fifth Avenue. There sprang into view a disc of brickwork perhaps eight feet in diameter. Now stripping to his shorts, he drew up a chair, made himself comfortable, and gazed another five minutes at the bricks. He slapped his leg. It was as he had hoped. Not only were the bricks seen as if they were ten feet away; they were better than that. It was better than having the bricks there before him. They gained in value. Every grain and crack and excrescence became available. (*LG* 31)

Although imprisoned in the Y, he is convinced that science will cure his alienation by drawing him near the world (whereas it has really extended space, hence pushed him farther away, and, on top of that, made the world visible merely as discrete particles). He has become a scientist like Dr. Gamow, so he does not need him any more. All the "talking cure" does is traffic in the subjective—no wonder that when Will looks through his telescope he soon sees a headline, "parley fails" (*LG* 5)

Thus the narrator presents Will's twenty-five year-old consciousness as he descends from Gamow's rarefied suite: "I am indeed an engineer, he thought, if only a humidification engineer, which is no great shakes of a profession. But I am also an engineer in a deeper sense: I shall engineer the future of my life according to the scientific principles and the self-knowledge I have so arduously gained from five years of analysis" (*LG* 41). Of course the narrator, knowing that Will has learned nothing of the past from his five years and that he will therefore act out unconscious behavior rather than conscious plans, has already offered this commentary: "So it was that Williston Bibb Barrett once again set forth into the wide world at the age of twenty-five, . . . in possession of $8.35, a Tetzlar telescope, an old frame house, and a defunct plantation. Once again he found himself alone in the world, cut adrift from Dr. Gamow, a father of sorts, and from his alma mater, sweet mother psychoanalysis" (*LG* 41).

Will immediately begins to reveal that his motives come not from purpose but from past. The day after abandoning analysis, he begins to haunt the southwest quadrant of Central Park, which the narrator says "he knew as his own backyard" (*LG* 107). The very centralness of the place argues that it is the navel of the world, the image of Paradise, while its backyardness asserts that Will's unconscious yearning is for the peacefulness of earliest childhood. His fugues have taken him to, among other places, Memphis and Cincinnati. Even the narrator is confused about what Will did where: at one point (*LG* 12) he says that Will worked in a bakery in Cincinnati and in a greenhouse in Memphis, but later (*LG* 269) Will is said to have worked for a florist in Cincinnati. In *The Second Coming* Will remembers that he worked for six months in a Cincinnati greenhouse (*SC* 107–8), probably in Krohn Conservatory, one of the world's largest public greenhouses, which is in Eden Park, appropriately. Small wonder, too, that Will falls in love at first sight in Central Park (through the telescope, yet): "It was not so much her good looks, her smooth brushed brow and firm round neck bowed so that two or three vertebrae surfaced in the soft flesh, as a certain bemused and dry-eyed expression in which he seemed to recognize—himself! She was a beautiful girl but she also slouched and was watchful and dry-eyed and musing like a thirteen-year-old boy. She was his better half" (*LG* 7–8). At least since Plato, the hemisoul has dreamt of being one once again. With such communion, "It would be possible to sit on a bench and eat a peanut-butter sandwich with her and say not a word."

When Dr. Gamow spies Will's new telescope, he suspects that in buying it Will has performed a symbolic action, an action that is primarily meaningful considered as an unconscious wish fulfillment. The narrator then violates the confidential relationship between doctor and patient:

> "A telescope," mused the analyst, sighting into the farthest depths of the desk. "Do you intend to become a seer?"
> "A seer?"
> "A see-er. After all a seer is a see-er, one who can see. Could it be that you believe that there is some ultimate hidden truth and that you have the magical means for observing it?"
> "Ha-ha, there might be something in that. A see-er. Yes."
> "So now it seems you have spent your money on an instrument which will enable you to see the truth once and for all?"
> The patient shrugged affably. (*LG* 37)

The narrator calls Will "the patient," for Will, ever intent to act his role, would be thinking of himself as the patient: as patient he can only agree with the expert.

But there is another, even deeper reason for Will's impulsive purchase. Will is drawn to Central Park at night, also:

> Lamps made gold-green spaces in the rustling leaves.
> He strolled about the alp at the pond, hands in pockets and brow furrowed as if he were lost in thought. It was a dangerous place to visit by night, but he paid no attention. (*LG* 99)

Quite unconsciously he acts out his father's mannerisms. Presently he experiences a *déjà vu:* "Yonder was not the alp but the levee, and not the lamp in the trees but the street light at Houston Street and De Ridder. The man walked up and down in the darkness under the water oaks. The boy sat on the porch steps and minded the Philco, which clanked and whirred and plopped down the old 78's and set the needle hissing and voyaging. Old Brahms went abroad into the summer night" (*LG* 99).[3]

This scene is but the first of Will's returns, either in memory or in dream, to a night seven years before. In later scenes, Will remembers that his father frequently would speak "of the galaxies and of the expanding universe and take pleasure in the insignificance of man in the great lonely universe." Then he might quote "Dover Beach" as a coda (*LG* 309, 330). And in later scenes Will frequently registers awareness of a star: Canopus (*LG* 239), Andromeda (*LG* 358), Scorpio in Antares (*LG* 327), and Pegasus (*LG* 347). Most interestingly, he even dreams of seeing the Pleiades and hearing Brahms and watching his father walk under the water oaks (*LG* 238). It seems a fair inherence that Will, in identifying himself as a telescope, is also unconsciously identifying himself with his father, who, given his astronomical interests, must have had his own telescope. (Such an heirloom of his father Percy possessed [Tolson 38].) Those "green-gold spaces" could be a sufficient likeness to "the galaxies" to trigger a restless mind backward. Will's frequent awareness of a star must be evidence of a repressed memory of a time when his father instructed him about the heavens.

Here follows a conglomeration. The character Lawyer Barrett is based in part upon Walker Percy's adoptive father, William Alexander Percy, whose traits had also been passed on to Binx Bolling's Aunt Emily, in *The Moviegoer.* Aunt Emily loves Chopin, also philosophizes peripatetically, speaking of the "going under of the evening land" (*M* 54), sharing the Bolling belief in "the new messiah, the scientist-philosopher-mystic who would come striding through the ruins with the *Gita* in one hand and a Geiger counter in the other" (*M* 181–82). At the same time, Binx's father is like Percy's biological father: Binx recalls that his father "bought a telescope and one night he called us outside and showed us the horsehead nebula in Orion" (*M* 91). Lance Lamar also remembers that his father had showed him Arcturus: "Think of it, . . . The light you are seeing started thirty years ago!" (*L* 56–57).

From these data, several traits for a composite father figure in Percy's fiction may be detected, traits that, even if they are unspecified in *The Last Gentleman,* can fairly be ascribed to the character Lawyer Barrett. From an observation of Aunt Emily it is possible to discern much more fully the role that music plays in revealing the emotional cast of the father figure's mentality. The restrained Binx Bolling has this to say of Chopin: "Now Aunt Emily, fingernails click-

121

ing over the keys, comes back to the tune, the sweet sad piping of the nineteenth century, good as it can be but not good enough" (*M* 48). The narrator of *The Last Gentleman* reacts much more violently to Brahms. Thus he describes Will experiencing a *déjà vu* before his father's house: "The boy listening: what was the dread in his heart as he heard the colloquy and the beautiful terrible Brahms which went abroad into the humming summer night and the heavy ham-rich air?" (*LG* 329). Then he struggles to cope with a clearer image: ". . . there was a dread about this night, the night of victory. (Victory is the saddest thing of all, said the father.) The mellowness of Brahms had gone overripe, the victorious serenity of the Great Horn Theme was false, oh fake fake. Underneath, all was unwell" (*LG* 331).

It could be that the love of such music is merely a clue to the romantic idealism that dominates the father figure's outlook. But there is probably even more significance. When Aunt Emily refers to "the going under of the evening land," she is consciously making a literal translation of the title of Oswald Spengler's monumental universal history, entitled in English *The Decline of the West*.[4] His ideas, like those of Toynbee and Yeats, echo in the secularist counter-theme of *The Moviegoer*, and all of Percy's other novels. According to Spengler, a culture, no less than a human or a year, is bound to a cycle of growth and decline: Spring, Summer, Fall, Winter. He proclaims that Western, or "Faustian," culture is in its Winter phase and therefore its death spasm. Culture, the spiritual world, must face the same Second Law of Thermodynamics that binds the physical world—Aunt Emily implies as much: "I don't quite know what we're doing on this insignificant cinder spinning away in a dark corner of the universe" (*M* 54). Spengler's description of Stoicism as an "end-phenomenon" (*Decline* I 356–59) clarifies Aunt Emily's choice of Marcus Aurelius as a guide for Binx's conduct and William Alexander Percy's recommendation that his adoptive sons accept "the unassailable wintry kingdom of Marcus Aurelius, which some more gently call the Kingdom of Heaven" (*Lanterns* 313). The father figure is, of course, very aware of himself as a captive in a cycle: such self-consciousness gives birth to his *Schadenfreude*, which ultimately demands destruction of the seen—or the self. Faustian culture, Spengler asserts, is driven by the desire to expand into infinite space. Such a desire was inevitable, once man knew the infinitesimal calculus created by Newton and Leibnitz. The greatest artistic expression of the Faustian yearning for infinity is the fugue, in which Mozart and Beethoven use counterpoint to teach the soul to feel measureless distance. Thus, while the Percy father figure is associated with a degenerate, spurious musical expression of the spirit of Faustian man, he nevertheless still has enough authority to project his son into a world considered as space. *The Last Gentleman,* consisting of disjunct conscious-segments of time and place, *is* a fugue that counterpoints Will Barrett's nostalgia for the South and his exile into the Southwest, his yearning for basic unity and his sadness over his fall.

The fact that Central Park is haunted by his father's ghost also accounts for another mood that plays through Will Barrett's unconsciousness. While it may be the Eden of his deepest past, it is also the desert of his second coming. Heir to a belief in the expanding universe, Will is therefore imprisoned in possibility, for if all is expansion, then the self never reaches the limit by which actuality is established. As the narrator generalizes: "If a man lives in the sphere of the possible and waits for something to happen, what he is waiting for is war—or the end of the world" (*LG* 10). At one level, then, Will yearns for the contraction of space, the final term of the Second Law. Since like many another soul he is impatient of the end, he dreams of the man-made model, war, the Bomb. Reading in the Sunday *Times* (what better Bible for secular man?) that ground zero lies just inside the southeast corner of Central Park, he fantasizes that "It" has already occurred (*LG* 47–48). If so, he as a member of the surviving few can crawl out of his cave under Macy's, to find love in the ruins, in a new world that will be the Eden of the new cycle. He would be "the seer or saint" long anticipated by William Alexander Percy: ". . . he will come, even if he must walk through the ruins" (*Lanterns* 321). Dr. Gamow's speculation that Will wants to be a seer so that he can become a seer (*LG* 37) is not so farfetched, after all.

A seer must have a sign of the last days. So the narrator says of Will: "Often nowadays people do not know what to do and so live out their lives as if they were waiting for some sign or another. This young man was such a person" (*LG* 6). Despite its residence, Will's consciousness is not Christian; the Word being unheard, Will does

123

not perceive the peregrine that he first observes as a sign, a statement of man's wayfaring condition (*LG* 5). Thus he cannot leave the Park: "Being of both a scientific and a superstitious turn of mind and therefore always on the lookout for chance happenings which lead to great discoveries, he had to have a last look . . ." (*LG* 5). That look reveals a woman, who both reads "parley fails" and sends a secret message. Intercepting the message, Will is so intrigued that he must observe the recipient, who turns out to be the girl with whom he immediately falls in love (*LG* 7). Still, this extraordinary event is not a sign. It is only when he grounds the occurrence in his own belief system, scientific romanticism, that he perceives significance:

> The bench, where the Handsome Woman had sat, was exactly at ground zero.
> He smiled again. It was a sign. (*LG* 48)

The girl caught in Will's telescope, then, is not just another pretty face, not even just the goddess of the grove, but the Eve of the apocalypse. Since a scientist, in thinking absolutely, is no different from a romantic, Will begins at once to think of the two women by using language either appropriately categorical, "Handsome Woman," or romantic, "a radiance from another quarter, a 'certain someone' as they used to say in old novels" (*LG* 541). The luminous one turns out to be Miss Katherine Gibbs Vaught, twenty-one, of Alabama, cute and therefore "Kitty" to one and all.

Ironically, it is at this point that vision—so clean, so distant, so scientific, so romantic—is replaced by olfaction—so primordial, so intense, so personal—as the sense that dominates Will Barrett's psyche.[5] Through the technique of the accidental encounter, Will is led to a hospital room, which is, beside his Kitty, littered with various Vaughts, including the focus—sick, sixteen-year-old Jamie. But, besides his Kitty, her father probably has the greatest impact on Will's unconscious. To be sure, her mother soon roars, "Lord, I knew your mother, Lucy Hunnicutt, the prettiest little thing I ever saw" (*LG* 53), but those are only words, and to a fairly deaf young man at that. Mr. Vaught also claims to have known Will's father and to know Will's Uncle Fannin.

With his unquenchable thirst for Coca Cola, Chandler Vaught is the very picture of mid-South paterfamilias. His appearance is underscored by his smell: "His suit, an old-fashioned seersucker with a broad stripe, gave off a fresh cotton-and-ironing board smell that pierced the engineer's memory. It reminded him of something but he could not think what" (*LG* 50–51).[6] Freud would understand Will's reaction, for he thought that smell, the primary sense in animals, had become subordinated to other senses, psychogenetically, in human beings. Since the sense of smell is so intimately associated with sexual arousal, the repression of the sense of smell must have been the price that the human being paid for abandoning his polymorphous sexuality. Freud believed that there was an increased sense of smell in hysteria, presumably since the condition has its origin in the throes of childhood sexuality.[7] Will the hysteric is to be led by his nose back to the repressed planes of home, family, father.

The self-styled "engineer" (*LG* 41), having abandoned father Gamow and "sweet mother psychoanalysis" (and, implicitly, an admission of the neurosis that they attended), wants to do what any other normal adult American male wants to do, make love to the girl he loves. It is true that he still thinks of her romantically: "What he wanted to tell her but could not think quite how was that he did not propose country matters. He did not propose to press against her in an elevator. What he wanted was both more and less. He loved her. His heart melted. She was his sweetheart, his certain someone. He wanted to hold her charms in his arms. He wanted to go into a proper house and shower her with kisses in the old style (*LG* 71). This fact does not, however, contradict my previous statement; it demonstrates, instead, that his behavior is alternately dominated by contradictory impulses, which he attempts to reconcile with disastrous results.

"Country matters" aside, he is more of a Hamlet than he can be aware. On a night when he has had a *déjà vu* in Central Park, a memory of his father's fulminations against fornication (*LG* 100), Will finds himself calling upon Kitty, first to declare his desire to marry her (*LG* 104). But at the same time he begins to suffer a stuffy nose, supposedly from dander, but perhaps an emotional reaction to his father's strictures, just as his hay fever of his summer in his father's law office probably was. The nose problem is surely an upward displacement, something that Freud would appreciate, even if Will does not: "Do I love her? I something her. He felt his nose" (*LG* 104). Damnable embarrassment: "He tried to blow his nose but the mucous membranes had swelled against each other like violet eiderdowns. 'I think I'll be going'" (*LG* 105). At that point Kitty becomes amorous: "Her lips were parted slightly and her eyes sparkled. His nose was turning to concrete" (*LG* 105). Will also frequently displaces downward, too; then he is handicapped by a leaping leg.

Kitty will go out with him into the night, and the only place that he can think to take her is into the southwest quadrant, a place with contradictory psychic overlays, being in his unconscious both the Eden of his infantile desire and the front porch of his father's injunction ("Don't treat a lady like a whore or a whore like a lady" [100]), not to mention the site where he fancies himself a scientist and a ground-zero romantic. There Kitty strips, then gives him a Mae West purr: "What about you, you big geezer" (*LG* 109). Upon such wantonnesse, big geezer detumefacts. A much older narrator considers the impact this turn of events must have had on Kitty: "The poor girl could not get the straight of it: the engineer's alternating fits of passion and depression" (*LG* 109). Now safely again a romantic, Will ponders the same dilemma: "But is love a sweetnesse or a wantonnesse" (*LG* 110)? The tryst ends with his nose intact and hers somewhat out of joint.

Failure to connect is, to be sure, the essential ingredient for successful romanticism. Will is avid to follow Kitty (and Mr. Vaught, though Will is not aware of his allure) when the family returns South. He accepts a job as a companion for the sick Jamie, like himself of a scientific bent, only more so, as Will discovers: ". . . like me he lives in the sphere of the possible, all antenna, ear cocked and lips parted. But I am conscious of it, know what is up, and he is not and does not. He is pure aching primary awareness and does not even know that he doesn't know it" (*LG* 162). There are, in effect, no lenses in Jamie's telescope.

Put on salary to become a part of the family, to go home, Will is to pilot "Ulysses," a camper that was bought, the Handsome Woman says, "to lead us beyond the borders of the Western world and bring us home" (*LG* 96). No doubt Spengler would be the talking book on

126

the tape deck. Will is already in the Western (Southwestern) world culturally, and he thinks he likes it. The television room at the Y, "a room done in Spanish colonial motif with exposed yellow beams and furniture of oxidized metal" (*LG* 18), implies where he is when he looks at the world. He is delighted to learn that Macy's occupies the most valuable space on earth—appraisal, "ninety dollars per cubic inch" (*LG* 44): "it gave him pleasure to stand in Nedick's and think about the cubic inch of space at the tip of his nose, a perfect little jewel of an investment" (*LG* 44). Most people would think that the location is so treasured because it is so peopled, but for Will-the-scientist space is empty, as when he uses Nedick's as his observatory: "The canyon of Seventh Avenue with the smoking rays of sunlight piercing the thundering blue shadow, the echoing twilight spaces as dim and resounding as the precipice air of a Western gorge . . ." (*LG* 45). Even Central Park, it should be remembered, had been originally his conscious choice as a place of observation.

But most of his trips to Central Park are really mini-fugues, flights from the Western (Southwestern) world just like his more extended stays in the hinterland. And his constant feeling of being bombarded by "noxious particles" (*LG* 39) comes from his underlying dissatisfaction with the world viewed as nothing but masses of discrete energy bits. Although he does not know it, then, it is the mention of "home" in the Handsome Woman's statement that really strikes a vibrant chord in his psyche.

Somehow it is fitting that it is the Handsome Woman who sees to it that Will gets left when the Southern exodus takes place. Thus he has to chase after the family, even as he has longed for one all his life. The trip itself becomes a fugue: there is many a psychic pothole in U.S. 1 between Gotham and Williamsburg, the first Southern oasis for the Vaughts. Thereafter, Will and Jamie make short forays to do science, while the main column, roughly reversing Sherman's march, invests one antique shoppe after another; Will and Jamie rendezvous occasionally with the other Vaughts at a motel, an aphrodisiac atmosphere for Will—until he is alone with Kitty.

Once the Vaught "castle" (*LG* 189) is reached, the narrator resumes his sketch of a young man haunted by his father. Will himself is reasonably responsive to the immediate demands of home and school (he, Jamie, and Kitty have enrolled in the university), but the narrator now knows that such normality was jarred by the tremors of the unconscious. Will must be thoroughly confused, for Mr. Vaught habitually calls him son (*LG* 154, 155); if that is the case, then Kitty is his sister, and intercourse would be all the more forbidden. Even such a domestic scene as a servant at work has its mysterious aura: "Damnation, David couldn't even polish silver. There was always silver cream left in the grooves. Still, the engineer liked to watch him at work. The morning sunlight fell among the silver like fish in the shallows. The metal was creamy and satiny. The open jar of silver cream, the clotted rag, the gritty astringent smell of it, put him in mind of something but he couldn't say what" (*LG* 197). Since it is through smell that Will's father seems most accessible to him, Will's nose (and sometimes, to paraphrase a remark allegedly made by Dr. Freud, a nose is just that) will no doubt become more prominent.

On one occasion, Will, ever drawn to Eden (which now appears as the country club golf course adjacent to the "castle"), has found a garden to nap in (*LG* 205). But his sleep is troubled by anxiety: "He was dreaming his old dream of being back in high school and running afoul of the curriculum, wandering up and down the corridors past busy classrooms. Where was his class? He couldn't find it and he had to have the credit to graduate." That dream is succeeded by another: "Someone kissed him on the mouth, maybe really kissed him as he lay asleep, for he dreamed a dream to account for the kiss, met Alice Bocock behind the library stacks and gave her a sweet ten-o'clock in the morning kiss." Easily aroused, he awakens to eavesdrop on Kitty and the Handsome Woman. But at that moment he discovers that he is being observed: "Some thirty feet away and ten feet above him a balcony of the garage overhung the garden, not a proper balcony, but just enough ledge to break the ugly wall and give a pleasant cloistered effect to the garden; not for standing on, but there stood a man anyhow, with his hands in his pockets, looking down into the garden" (*LG* 206). That man, Sutter Vaught, will, as a father-figure, shadow Will's garden from now on, if for no other reason but that he concocts twenty-minute assignations in the woods off number 7 fairway (*LG* 349).

Will knows quite a bit about Sutter, for the family has talked of little else. After learning of Jamie's illness the summer before, Sutter had taken him camping in the New Mexico desert. It was almost a miracle that they were found alive, after they were lost for several days, during which time their water mysteriously vanished. Then Sutter had shot away half his face in a suicide attempt. Now, stripped of his liability insurance and therefore forbidden to touch a live body—at least medically—he drinks constantly, works as a pathologist, and recreates as a roué.

Will's first close-up glimpse of Sutter is through what he assumes is a knothole. Having just dismounted his telescope with a vow not to be an eavesviewer anymore, he closes himself in his closet (*LG* 214); thus he can see into the next room, where Sutter, massaging his cheek with the muzzle of an automatic pistol, is talking with his sister, Val, whose response to Jamie's illness had been to become a nun. Quickly Will can stand to see or hear no more; since there is no available release for his agitation, he can only pace his room. When Val leaves abruptly, there is a shot. Will rushes to Sutter's room, though the narrator specifies that Will must not have known, that his "dismay" (*LG* 216) was more for himself than for Sutter.

Who had not shot himself, but rather The Old Arab Physician, a poster which has been shot a good many times before. One outlying hole was in fact Will's "knothole." For all intents Will is simply not there, so strong is a memory: "His eyes were fixed vacantly on the dismantled gun barrel. The fruity steel smell of Hoppe's gun oil put him in mind of something but he couldn't think what" (*LG* 217). Will's repression machine must be going full-throttle now. He cannot, therefore, allow himself to think of Sutter as father—but he can think of him as physician and fornicator. Very indirectly he begins to ask Sutter about the cause of amnesia (*LG* 219). All the while, Sutter is getting Hemingwayish with the automatic, pulling back the "breach" (*sic*) and ringing up a cartridge. At the same time, he asks Will about his sex life (*LG* 220). Silence is Will's answer.

Sutter knows that Will has been in analysis for five years and therefore knows that Will probably blames all of his problems on the inhibition of sexual activity. Sutter must conclude that amnesia occludes Will's consciousness of a powerful negative force from the past. One of his questions suggests that he has a pretty good idea of the identity of the force: "What sort of man was your father" (*LG* 221). (The conversation between Val and Sutter, previously, suggests that the Vaughts knew Will's father rather well, so that Sutter knows that he is dead and perhaps more.) Such is Will's repression that he has not been able to ask a direct question; he thus rises to leave. Even though he is the one leaving, he suddenly says, "Wait" (*LG* 224). That word, spoken just after he had thought of one of his father's injunctions, announces that he is unconsciously repeating the traumatic scene of his life. That he can then ask a direct question is quite a breakthrough: "I want to know whether a nervous condition could be caused by not having sexual intercourse" (*LG* 224). Sutter's answer can only frustrate. For Sutter, thinking that Will has asked him only because he thinks Sutter, as a fornicator, will tell him to fornicate, refuses to play psychiatric games.

The frustration boils up that night. Will dreams of his father and himself: "The man walked up and down in the darkness of the water oaks, emerging now and then under the street light, which shed a weak yellow drizzle. The boy sat on the steps between the azaleas and watched. He always imagined he could see the individual quanta of light pulsing from the filament" (*LG* 237). The astronomical intimations of the dream scene should be noted. In the dream, Will is afraid that some unidentified men will kill his father and pleads with him to go around to the garden, where the music can be heard just as well. Then he dreams of a gunshot (oblivious of the "gap" in the narrative of the dream), a dream so vivid that it awakens him (*LG* 238). Or does it? For he goes from his garage room into the "castle":

> . . . through the dark pantry and into the front hall, where he rounded the newel abruptly and went up the stairs. To the second and then third floor as if he knew exactly where he was, though he had only once visited the second floor and not once been above it. Around again and up a final closeted flight of narrow wooden steps and into the attic. It was a vast unfinished place with walks of lumber laid over the joists. He prowled through the waists and caverns of the attic ribbed in the old heart pine of the 1920's. The lumber was still warm and fragrant from the afternoon sun. He shone the flashlight into every nook and cranny. (*LG* 239)

That is also what he must do to his past.

130

Controlled by his repression, though, Will can only be wistful about the past. He may continue to wish that he were as uncomplicated as Rooney Lee (*LG* 265), according to Henry Adams' characterization of Lee, but to no avail (actually, in his mind, there could be a strong resemblance, but of a different sort: both were poor copies of their father). He may continue to read Freeman's *Lee* (*LG* 267), certainly the hagiography of the Southern father-figure, but he cannot change the way things turn out. It is only a matter of time before he once again seeks help from Sutter, so intent that he seems unmindful of the smell of "fruity Hoppe's gun oil" (*LG* 270), saying that he fears that he is going into a fugue. This time Sutter acts, placing Will under hypnosis and implanting a suggestion for Will to follow (*G* 271). Sutter's act may not be all that impersonal. He is to take Jamie away to New Mexico the next morning; out there Jamie may not survive and if Jamie does die, Sutter will want someone else present.

At this time there is a great deal of social disturbance in Will's world, but only the narrator could describe it, for Will literally does not know where he is (*LG* 292–93). He looks only for any sign that will lead him toward his destination, actually being pulled forward by Sutter's post-hypnotic suggestion (*LG* 294). His trip takes him farther south (which is deeper into the heart of darkness, his past) to Val's mission: "It was a frosty morn. The old corn shucks hung like frozen rags. A killdeer went crying down a freshly turned row, its chevroned wing elbowing along the greasy disced-up gobbets of earth. The smell of it, the rimy mucous cold in his nostrils, and the blast of the engine-warm truck air at his feet put him in mind of something—of hunting! of snot drying in your nose and the hot protein reek of fresh-killed quail" (*LR* 295).

This is all of Will's memory trace. The narrator will not be ready to say more for about fifteen years. There is only the most tenuous link to Will's father: "Either I have been here, he thought, perhaps with my father while he was trying a case, or else it was he with his father and he told me about it" (*LG* 295). In *The Second Coming* the memory-trace becomes an extended, recurrent memory.

Suffering from confusion, Will visits Val for a few hours. He learns nothing from her; Sutter and Jamie have been there, before departing for Santa Fe; but he knew their ultimate destination already.

Mostly Will is just ill at ease, especially embarrassed at the way that Val feeds a hawk (*LG* 296, 297, 303). The scene, then, is important for what it does not say. The narrator, not Will, knows that Val had taken a religious name, Johnette Mary Vianney, that indicated her decision to go to the country to work; probably she read William James' *Varieties of Religious Experience* while she was still at Columbia and thus found Father Vianney cited as an example of holiness. Will does not consider that Val had faced the onset of Jamie's illness by going south, rather than southwest, Sutter's destination. She chose the peregrine, to accept herself as a wayfarer; but Will does not see her hawk as a sign. Nor can Will accept the smell of an outhouse that Val offers as a sign (*LG* 302): but the death of the flesh must be acknowledged before the life of the spirit can be gained. Until Will sees signs—the narrator is saying—he will not be able to recover from the illness that originated in the relationship with his father in south Alabama.

For Will, the road to Santa Fe goes through Ithaca, his hometown. Once again he becomes deeply involved in the affairs of others, but since he cannot remember where he has been for the last month (*LG* 304), he can hardly be expected to be very alert to his present location. The townspeople are amused to see that he is still out of it (*LG* 311). If anything, he is more out of it, for he has an epileptic seizure (*LG* 310), as he walks into town on the levee. So powerful is the place as an evocation of past that Will alternates unconsciously among perhaps half a dozen levels of time. All the while he is being drawn toward the traumatic scene before the house of his childhood: a summer evening under the street light and water oaks, with Brahms accompanying his father's condemnation of the fornicators, as he paces off his line of defense, to the corner and back (*LG* 328–31).

This time Will remembers more. Although he had pleaded with his father not to leave him, Lawyer Barrett had gone up to the attic, there to fit the muzzle of a double-barrel twelve gauge Greener into the notch of his breastbone. Will is now drawn to reenact his own behavior (*LG* 331–32)—he hears this shot, thinks that he turns off the Philco, and goes up to the attic: "The old clear-glass 25-watt bulb shed a yellow mizzling light, a light of rays, actual striae. . . . He

132

picked up the Greener, broke the breech and sighted at the yellow bulb. The bore was still speckled wity powder grains." All the astronomical images from Central Park onward are now clarified: Lawyer Barrett's act had ripped his son loose from place and tossed him into space. The polishing and cleaning smells that have appealed to Will have pulled him toward that shotgun. He sits there for two hours, following "the yellow drizzle of light into every corner of the attic room" (LG 334). But he leaves without cleaning the gun, cleaning up his problem. Perhaps the gun must be used again before it can be cleaned?

Although there is no resolution of Will's condition, certain inferences about its nature may now be drawn. Its origin is to be found in early childhood, perhaps in the lack of memory of the vanished mother. Will's response to his father's suicide must be double-barrelled: he would mourn the death of his father, yet he would probably also feel guilt. For if his early "spells" resulted from his identification with one whom he wished dead, how much more might that wish have been intensified by the threatening father who railed against sexual activity to a teenager, especially since—Freud held—the earliest experience of desire was directed toward the mother. But as the narrator describes it, Will lacks any emotion at all at that time—which is curious. Will's psyche has every reason to hide in amnesia—and since Will has worked through nothing, he cannot stay in the South, but must continue on to the Southwest.

Will is now pulled across the Mississippi—where South begins its slow change into Southwest—to Shut Off, Louisiana, where his Uncle Fannin, attended by his faithful Merriam, still uses shotguns for their legitimate purpose, to shoot birds (and, occasionally, a goofy dog). Such a version of the Southern past is as fake as the TV westerns that the two old men love, as fake as the Captain Kangaroo version of childhood that they cackle over with their "breakfast of brains and eggs . . ." (LG 346). Will is but slightly bothered by such discrepancies, however; he had "slept ten hours dreamlessly and without spansules," apparently still under Sutter's suggestion.

Even so, Will fugues across Texas, at one point having a dream memory in which he and his father talk with Senator Oscar Underwood, who had just lost the 1924 Democratic nomination because of

133

the opposition of the Ku Klux Klan (*LG* 348). As time thus unravels, Will continues to read the casebook that Sutter had purposely left for him—actually it's a "dialogue" between Sutter and Val that the narrator was afraid to use because it would simply be incredible; no one as sick as Will could *listen* to such a debate, but Will can *read* it, even if the words make no sense to him. By the time he reaches the other river, the Rio Grande, he has completed the transition to the Southwest, having reached such absolute space that "[a] single leaf danced on its pedicle, mysteriously dispensed from energy laws" (*LG* 355). Arriving at Sutter's ranch, Will is bombarded by cosmic references: "The silence was disjunct. It ran concurrently with one and did not flow from the past. Each passing second was packaged in cottony silence. It had no antecedents. . . . Here one was not watched. There was no one. The silence hushed everything up, the small trees were separated by a geometry of silence. The sky was empty map space" (*LG* 357). The South is long gone, for "[t]here was no grits to be had, and he had to buy Cream of Wheat" (*LG* 358). In this kind of Cartesian/Newtonian environment, it is hardly surprising that Will suddenly unlimbers his telescope.

True to his alternating nature, Will makes a conscious effort to choose place over space, present over past: "He shivered. I'm through with telescopes, he thought, and the vast galaxies. What do I need with Andromeda? What I need is my Bama bride and my cosy camper, a match struck and the butane lit and a friendly square of light cast upon the neighbor earth, and a hot cup of Luzianne between us against the desert cold, and a warm bed and there lie dreaming in the one another's arms while old Andromeda leans through the night" (*LG* 358). He can even mark the Confederate high tide at Valverde, without, as previously, lapsing into body English that might forestall the defeat (*LG* 358).

But—even if he could act upon such a healthy decision—he chances upon Sutter. His salutation, "Wait, sir" (*LG* 359), shouts out that he is once again precipitated into his search for a father. It is understandable, though, that he must repress this reason, to be mystified by his presence in Santa Fe. When Sutter asks why he has come, the "engineer passed a hand across his eyes. 'I—think you asked me, didn't you? I also came to see Jamie'" (*LG* 360). The time has come to say that Will's interest in Jamie is no less personal than his pursuit of Sutter. Although for the best of reasons, Sutter *had* tried to kill Jamie; and now Jamie lies dying. Will must watch Jamie die, for he may think that he himself has been dying for years, after someone tried to kill him. If he had thought, away back in Central Park, that Kitty was his "better half," certainly Jamie is his "worse half." Indeed, each of the four Vaught siblings comes to symbolize some aspect of himself, either now or later, as the narrator, speaking from the vantage of the future, well knows.

Once again, as he sits with Jamie, Will is overwhelmed by space: "Outside in the still air, yellow as butter, the flat mathematical leaves of the aspens danced a Brownian dance in the sunlight, blown by a still, molecular wind" (*LG* 369). Jamie, though, is protected by the innocence of primary awareness. Even when he tells Will to call Val, his intention is not to ask a question, but to clinch an argument: "Give her a hard time about the book. She promised to send it to me. Tell her I think she lost heart in the argument. She claims there is a historical movement in the direction of negative entrophy. But so what? You know" (*LG* 370). Caught up in science, he thinks that the meaning implied by negative entropy is meaningless. Or, at least that is all the poor kid lets himself say. Maybe, like many another kid, he needs someone to say the words for him.

Back in the Trav-L-Aire, Will finishes Sutter's casebook without finding an answer. When Will had recently accosted him, Sutter had asked, "Are you Philip and is this the Gaza Desert?" (*LG* 359); as it turns out, he is the Philip who will not explain the text to Will the eunuch. As Will throws the pad into "the trashburner of Alamo-gordo Motor Park" (*LG* 373), he must think that he is as close to hell as he has been. But then a "retired fire inspector from Muncie," not a bad euphemism for a devil, takes him a little closer by forcing Will to inspect his customized rig. The man so illustrates the rootless Westering man, swinging like a star between Key West and Victoria, B.C., yearly, that Will is driven to utter despair, horny for any immanence to escape transcendence: "returning to his own modest camper, he became at once agitated and lustful. His heart beat powerfully at the root of his neck. The coarsest possible images formed themselves before his eyes" (*LG* 374). Alamogordo Motor Park, ground zero, will do that to you.

This time, "instead of throwing a fit or lapsing into a fugue as he had done so often in the past" (*LG* 374), presumably as evasive tacks to escape lust, Will has a perfect memory:

> He recalled everything, even a single perception years ago, one of a thousand billion, so trivial that it was not even remembered then, five minutes later: on a college field trip through the mangy Jersey woods looking for spirogyra, he had crossed a utility right-of-way. When he reached the farther woods, he had paused and looked over his shoulder. There was nothing to see: the terrain dipped, making a little swale which was overgrown by the special forlorn plants of rights-of-way, not small trees or bushes or even weeds exactly but just the unclassified plants which grow up in electric-light-and-power-places. That was all. He turned and went on. (*LG* 374–75)

It is quite remarkable that Will's memory on this occasion is "perfect," yet of a scene so "trivial." It might be that the eeriness of the scene depends upon the premonition that something is about to happen because he crossed a "right-of-way." For the New Jersey locale could be a "screen memory" for a south Alabama scene. Certainly it is noteworthy that the locale is an "electric-light-and-power-place," when both electric light (visual image) and power (kinetic image) recur in his dreams of his father. If he goes out to fornicate now, he risks what might hit him from behind, not a flaming sword, but the scatter from a Greener. It may be that the Central Park setting is so iconic because ultimately it stands for that place in which he had been so traumatically punished. There was paradise lost.

Before his repression could get working properly, he jumps into "Ulysses," not apparently to sail "beyond the borders of the Western world" (*LG* 96), but to chase girls, for he yells to the fire inspector, "I'm going over to Albuquerque" (*LG* 375). He leaves so abruptly that he snaps all "umbilical connections" for the truck—and apparently for himself, as well. Then, just as abruptly, he stops, to tell the "still astounded Hoosier," "Pardon, . . . I think I'll call Kitty—' and nodded by way of further explanation to a telephone hooked contingently to a telephone pole. Could he call Kitty from such a contingent telephone?" (*LG* 375). So he is after all still connected to the South. He talks to Kitty for two hours, we later learn (*LG* 380). Perhaps the love of a "Bama bride" (*LG* 358) will save him from a fornicator's fate.

But at the end of the conversation, which settles many things, Will says, he is nevertheless drawn to seek out Sutter once more. And he is back in the sphere of science: "Sutter gazed into the empty sky, which instead of turning rosy with sunset was simply going out like a light" (*LG* 386). Will lays out his reasons for the domestic life in Alabama, at Confederate Chevrolet, in Cap'n Andy's house on South Ridge, with Kitty. Then he offers his justification: "It is better to do something than do nothing—no reflection, sir" (*LG* 384). Sutter, appreciating Will's delicacy, but the irony more, repeats, "No reflection." For he knows that Will could only live such a life if he had no reflection. Then Will asks him about one of his former patients, "the Deke from Vanderbilt—with the lovely wife and children—you know" (*LG* 386), who had suffered a breakdown. Since Will will not recognize that the Deke's illness resulted from the condition of concreteness to which he aspires, Sutter knows that it is hopeless to respond. Instead, he tells Will to call the family, that Jamie's time has come.

One look at Jamie, and Will calls Val, to get someone who is competent to deal with such an outlandish situation. But she, disregarding *his* condition, orders him to get Jamie baptized. Such is his distress, the narrator now understands, that Will could act only by reverting unconsciously to the persona of the legendary Barrett male:

> All at once time fell in, bent, and he was transported over the Dutch sort of door—it didn't seem to open—flew over it like a poltergeist and found himself inside the station. He seemed to be listening. "You hear me, goddamn it," thundered a voice terrible and strange. It was for the two of them to listen as the voice went on. "—or else I'm going to kick yo' ass down there." An oddly Southern voice, then not his surely. Yet her glassy eyes were on *him*, round as a dollar watch, the lids nictitating from below like a lizard's. Her smile, stretching open the rugae, the troughs of which he noticed were bare of lipstick, proffered a new ghastly friendship for *him*. Now as he watched, dreaming, she was using the phone again. (*LG* 394–95)

137

This certainty soon deserts Will; he becomes the "engineer" once again, but an "engineer" who is happy that the priest has come, so that someone else can engineer the situation. Sutter has also arrived, but acts only as a doctor, engineering within his small compass, unwilling to act as an older brother. At that moment, Jamie throws all engineering into utter chaos: "After a moment there arose to the engineer's nostrils first an intimation, like a new presence in the room, a somebody, then a foulness beyond the compass of smell. This could only be the dread ultimate rot of the molecules themselves, an abject surrender. It was the body's disgorgement of its most secret shame. Doesn't this ruin everything, wondered the engineer . . . The stench scandalized him. Shouldn't they all leave?" (*LG* 401–2). Will must have known that he would face this scene, ever since he blundered into Jamie's hospital room in New York.

Will cannot, of course, see that this smell is a sign, any more than he understood that the smell of Val's outhouse was a sign. Only the visual—certainly not the heard or the smelled—is a legitimate, valid part of the scientific picture of the world. Molecules may be energy or they may be matter in a scientific model, but in the shared, existential world the really important molecules eventually rot.

The narrator then offers the climactic scene of his story, an elaborate allusion to Mark 8:18. At that point in Mark's narrative, the Pharisees have just demanded a sign from Jesus. Refusing them, Jesus enters the ship, to discover that his disciples have forgotten to provide bread for the voyage across the Sea of Galilee. When Jesus warns his followers to beware of the leaven of the Pharisees and of Herod, they think that he is angry about the lack of bread. Impatiently Jesus says, "Having eyes, see ye not? and having ears, hear ye not? and do ye not remember?" Then he reminds them of the two miracles by which he had provided bread for the multitudes. If they will but renounce secular considerations, He is implying, He will provide the Bread necessary for wayfarers.

As the baptism begins, Jamie, the pure scientist, cannot hear or speak; thus Will is forced to talk and listen for him. In this way, Jamie hears the good news, though the content does not register in Will's consciousness. Having been deaf, then, he is unprepared to accept the sign of Jamie's salvation that his eyes visually registered: "Outside in the night the engineer saw a Holsum bread truck pass under the street light" (*LG* 404). As far as Will is concerned, Jamie's "Don't let me go" (*LG* 406) is a "Wait" ignored. What he sees is the image of death, a sign repugnant to the secular mind: although the priest holds them, "four white vermiform fingers" capture Will's attention.

Once Will and Sutter reach the street, Will is in a panic to find some security. He has just seen someone like himself die, and he can see nothing but what he saw. He thus needs Sutter more than Jamie did, he says, for Jamie had Val too. Five times, he pleads with Sutter, "wait." Once he even grabs Sutter's sleeve, only to have Sutter shake himself free (*LG* 408). It is only after Sutter has started to drive off in his Edsel that Will's fifth "wait" causes him to stop and let Will get in. The only people who could be optimistic about this closure do not know Detroit.

So the narrator concludes. Surprisingly, the story is, in retrospect, not unpleasant; this is precisely because of the point of view taken. The mere fact that a person has survived to write about an earlier life is cause for joy—witness just about anybody's "ordeal" account. There is, as well, the experience of liberation when a person talks himself loose from his past. The "secret and somehow shameful heart of childhood" (*LG* 11) is the heart of the novel, the confession that Will Barrett had not been able to make to Dr. Gamow. And the story has to be whatever is the opposite of tragic, for, at the end, nothing has been inevitably decided.

But what of Walker Percy? Splitting himself in endowment—giving Will Barrett his experience and the narrator his knowledge—he must have hoped to talk himself loose from the past, by telling us the story that he had not been able to tell Dr. Rioch and Dr. Booth, his analysts in his early twenties. I would not be misunderstood here: the manifest story of Will Barrett is quite immaterial and its application to Walker Percy's personal history is none of our business; what has been confessed in the novel is the terror of childhood, the story that lurks in all of us which only a few ever tell. That shock of recognition—unique to literature—is essential to full consciousness.

Even though the cure is presented in *The Last Gentleman*—Walker Percy did not ignore the Holsum bread truck—the disease of childhood had not been extirpated. He was impelled to write *The Second*

Coming (1980), to reveal that Will Barrett, rich and retired, is, still because of the past, worse off than he had been at twenty-five. Such desperation demands even more desperate confession, but the reward is definite closure: the discovery of Allie Huger in the greenhouse that Will Barrett has dreamed of all his life.

SEVEN

"The parent in the percept" in *The Last Gentleman*

Walker Percy's *The Last Gentleman* opens with this scene:

> One fine day in early summer a young man lay thinking in Central Park. His head was propped on his jacket, which had been folded twice so that the lining was outermost, and wedged into a seam of rock. The rock jutted out of the ground in a section of the park known as the Great Meadow. Beside him and canted up at mortar angle squatted a telescope of an unusual design. (*LG* 3)

Such an introduction announces three aspects of the subject of the novel. First and foremost, as the first sentence brazenly announces, the narrative is to be about the young man's thinking, especially as his thinking is colored by fantasy. As Freud (whose theories provide a prominent subtext for the novel) said, fantasy (or primary process thinking) is for realistic response (or secondary process thinking) as a natural preserve, like Yellowstone Park, is for the mental health of urbanized society.[1] Second, the specific setting, Central Park, suggests that the mental setting is to be colored by a nostalgia for *the* Central Park, the Garden of Eden.[2] Third, the telescope reveals the intention of both the young man's conscious thinking and his unconscious thinking, as later analysis will reveal.

Then the narrator intrudes his presence with this description: "In the course of the next five minutes the young man was to witness by chance an insignificant, though rather curious happening. It was the telescope which became the instrument of a bit of accidental eavesdropping. As a consequence of a chance event the rest of his life was to be changed" (*LG* 3). What is established here is that the scene just described is not immediate, but is mediated. For all its circumstantiality, the scene is not in the present, but in the past. The scene is therefore being viewed through the consciousness of the narrator. Since the narrator then offers an unqualified prediction about the totality of the young man's future, it is likely that the narrator is a self describing his former self to his self which is just coming into existence. Such a narrative technique would be consistent with the model of consciousness that Walker Percy implies in his essays in *The Message in the Bottle*.[3]

The narrator then describes the "chance event" that was to change the rest of the life of the young man, soon to be identified as Williston Bibb Barrett, hereafter Will. Hoping to photograph a peregrine falcon in its mid-air attack on a pigeon, Will had focused his newly purchased telescope skyward. Since he thinks of the falcon coming down "at two hundred miles an hour, big feet stuck out in front like a Stuka" (*LG* 5), he must think that he holds a picture of reality that is dominated by the viciousness of both man and nature. Instead, Will had accidentally focused on this scene:

> His heart gave a leap. He fell in love, at first sight and at a distance of two thousand feet. It was not so much her good looks, her smooth brushed brow and firm round neck bowed so that two or three vertebrae surfaced in the soft flesh, as a certain bemused and dry-eyed expression in which he seemed to recognize—himself! She was a beautiful girl but she also slouched and was watchful and dry-eyed and musing like a thirteen-year-old boy. She was his better half. It would be possible to sit on a bench and eat a peanut-butter sandwich with her and say not a word. (*LG* 7–8)

142

The immediate evocation of this scene is that of the romantic discovery of the soul mate, that complement to one's self for whom one always longs.[4] There is yet another evocation, though, that of a longing that begins much earlier in life, one which may be the foundation of romantic longing. To see oneself in another is to reexperience the "mirror phase" of infancy, when one first experiences consciousness by focusing upon the mother's face while nursing the mother's breast. This phase, just preceding but inextricably connected with language acquisition, is the last time that communication can rely simply upon silence, on affect without cognition.[5] Such is the import, then, of the narrator's concluding statement above; "It would be possible to sit on a bench and eat a peanut-butter sandwich with her and say not a word."

Although the narrator is speaking of the past, he realizes that the past had had a past lurking in it. He therefore offers a short, very selective summary of Will Barrett's life before he had set up his telescope. Of Will's mother virtually nothing is said, at this time or in subsequent narration. Of Will's father a good deal is said, though what is said, both here and hereafter, is elliptic and oblique. Will's life in public is given in a somewhat more straightforward order, even if the dating of specific events can only be approximated. Probably at fifteen, Will had, like the Barrett men before him, entered Princeton University. In the fall of his junior year he had dropped out, going to New York City, "where he lived quite contentedly at the Y.M.C.A." (*LG* 16). His choice of residence probably publicizes his virginal state; such is his confused state of mind that he accepts identification from the institution in which he finds himself (here as young male Christian, but later as expatriate Southerner or Ohioan [*LG* 20–21]). The following summer he had come home to Mississippi to read law in his father's office. At the end of the summer his father had died, of a cause not given in this summary (*LG* 16–17). Then Will had been drafted into the army, to serve two years before being medically discharged because of amnesia. He had returned to the Y.M.C.A. presumably still virginal, to submit himself to five years of psychiatric treatment and to become a "humidification engineer" (*LG* 18) at Macy's.

But the "talking cure" fails for Will; no wonder that his telescope had quickly told him that "parley fails" (*LG* 5). The failure must have resulted, at least in part, from the fact that Dr. Gamow, his rather orthodox Freudian analyst, had never talked to Will as a subject, but had recorded his notes about Will for his private observation. Thus Will had had to sneak a reading of the notes (*LG* 39); in effect Dr. Gamow had increased Will's alienation by presenting Will to himself as an "object of technique" (*LG* 35). In his quest for Freudian slips (*LG* 34), Dr. Gamow only exacerbates Will's dysfunction with language, the basis of intersubjectivity. Thus he had driven Will deeper into a reliance upon the subject/object model of the world formulated by Descartes. Will signals this new state of mind by purchasing the telescope. A recent generalization explains Will's specific inappropriate act: "Cartesian dualism is . . . the separation of the mind and the body into a disembodied spirit and an object it can use as an instrument—whether as a lever or a pair of binoculars" (Dilman 7).

This reconstruction of Will's public behavior might be taken to imply that Will, like many of his peers, had, after a difficult adolescence, then settled down. But the narrator immediately offers evidence that all is not as it might appear:

> A German physician once remarked that in the lives of people who suffer emotional illness he had noticed the presence of *Lücken* or gaps. As he studied the history of a particular patient he found whole sections missing, like a book with blank pages.
> Most of this young man's life was a gap. (*LG* 12)

The "German" physician was really an Austrian, Sigmund Freud. According to his basic theory, a person who suffers traumatic childhood experiences will repress the memory of those experiences from the conscious to the unconscious mind. Thus such a person has many gaps in the life story that he can tell. At the same time, though, the repressed memories attempt to manifest themselves through neurotic symptom-formation, distorted conscious thinking, and apparently inappropriate physical behavior. Both of Will's activities on the day that he sets up his telescope can be scanned by the previous sentence. He has been in analysis for five years, five days a week, but so strong has been repression that he has been unable to tell his analyst any of the memories which traumatize him. He has chosen his occupation, which involves monitoring a larger computer system which reports such data as temperature and humidity, because it signifies to him the kind of unmediated relation which he would like to have with a mechanistic world. As a result, he suffers from delusions that "noxious particles" (*LG* 25) fill the air and from deafness (probably hysteric in origin) and, episodically, from *déjà vu*, fugue states, and spasms of the left leg.

The narrator offers no explanation for these symptoms, many of which are termed "Depersonalization Phenomena" by the *American Handbook of Psychiatry*. The narrator may or may not know what his past self is repressing. It is possible that he knows more than he is telling and that he does not know all that could be told. Since he does not tell, however, we are forced to interpret his narration for ourselves.

The earliest account of Will Barrett that the narrator gives us is undoubtedly the most revealing in the entire sequence: "As a child he had had 'spells,' occurrences which were nameless and not to be thought of, let alone mentioned, and which he therefore thought of as lying at the secret and somehow shameful heart of childhood itself. There was a name for it, he discovered later, which gave it form and habitation. It was *déjà vu*, at least he reckoned it was" (*LG* 11). This memory is most revealing, even though it is, for the narrator, a screen memory, that is, a memory that is not in and of itself significant, but significant insofar as it is a sign for an experience that the narrator cannot allow himself to remember or—if he can remember it—tell it.

A short elaboration of the event by the narrator may contain a vital clue:

What happened anyhow was that even when he was a child and was sitting in the kitchen watching D'lo snap beans or make beaten biscuits, there came over him as it might come over a sorrowful old man the strongest sense that it had all happened before and that something else was going to happen and when it did he would know the secret of his own life. Things seemed to turn white and dense and time itself became freighted with an unspeakable emotion. Sometimes he "fell out" and would wake up hours later, in his bed, refreshed but still haunted. (*LG* 11)

145

What is so haunting here is the manifest absence of the mother, either in the kitchen or, later, at the bedside. What is so haunting in the entire novel—a recollection, remember—is the absent mother, of whom Will thinks only once (*LG* 237). What is significant here is that the narrator thinks the experience was a *déjà vu*, if Freud's contention be accepted that a *déjà vu* of a specific locale always indicates the desire of consciousness to return to the mother's genitals (*Interpretation* 399). Such a latent meaning would account for the extreme emotion the narrator invests in the experience, "the secret and somehow shameful heart of childhood itself."

The mother is, to labor the obvious, the original object with whom the self has a relation. The nature of this relation, according to many thinkers, determines the nature of all subsequent relations that the self establishes.[6] Such a view is well known in the study of child psychology. It is, though, a novel idea in the study of phenomenology, being introduced by Mel D. Faber, in *Objectivity and Human Perception* (1985). Faber's thesis is that the original relationship determines the self's way of seeing the world. He is speaking literally, not merely figuratively. What the self sees is affected to some degree or another by "the parent in the percept,"[7] by the effect of the unconscious upon actual vision. Will's desire to see as through a telescope, then, is a telling clue to his sense of object loss; he believes that the telescope will provide a restitution: "It was as he had hoped. Not only were the bricks seen as if they were ten feet away; they were better than that. It was better than having the bricks there before him. They gained in value" (*LG* 31). Not only does the telescope reduce the vastness that the alienated person experiences, but it also, as an instrument of science and technology, confirms a hitherto subjective experience.

There is but one eventuality for the first relationship: the self is separated from its original object, to begin a life-long search for an object or complex of objects to replace the lost original.[8] The narrator may be describing some such condition for Will when he says that Will had "fallen . . . into a long fit of melancholy and vacancy amounting almost to amnesia" (*LG* 17), fallen in the way that the story of the Garden of Eden speaks of the Fallenness that led to expulsion. The loss of the original object also teaches the self about the immensity of space—the original object was a body as close as a gaze and a caress, experienced sensuously as well as cognitively, but when it recedes, the newly bodiless self is introduced to the immensity of space, to itself, as the "mental-ego," as Washburn calls it. Will Barrett's registering of stars and other cosmic phenomena in his flow of consciousness may result from the "scientific" view of the world forced upon him by his earliest trauma.[9]

So infatuated with his scientific outlook has he become that he decides to abandon "his alma mater, sweet mother psychoanalysis" (*LG* 41)—a therapy often described as a process attempting to replicate the mother-infant symbiosis—to become a scientist, spending his last $1,900 to buy a telescope, which will be his way of announcing that the world can be viewed directly through technology. It is ironic that while he must have bought the telescope as a symbol, that instrument has another well-known symbolic significance, one which undercuts the significance that Will had intended. In Chapter 7 of *The Interpretation of Dreams* Freud uses the telescope as his model for the "psychic apparatus." In his model, perceptions of phenomena pass through the clear glass of primary awareness, to lodge on one or another of the planes of the lenses, the unconscious. What is seen by the viewer, then, is perception as it is affected by past perceptions, none of which ever escapes from its lodgement on a lens.

When Will first sets up his telescope, it does what he had expected it to do: "These lenses did not transmit light merely. They penetrated to the heart of things" (*LG* 29). Will's happy thought may be true in more ways than one, for soon enough he is drawn to use the telescope in a place that appeals to his unconscious quest for paradise, Central Park. There, quite by chance, he glimpses first a woman older than himself and then a younger woman, who comes to retrieve a message left by the other woman. Both of these women are to be parents in Will's percept. The older woman, Rita Vaught, will act as the Bad Mother; motivated by her desire to control the younger woman, Kitty Vaught, Rita will try to frustrate Will's pursuit of Kitty, whom he unconsciously sees as the Good Mother. When Will discovers that the bench on which he had first seen the women is "ground zero" (*LG* 48), he delightedly takes it as a sign that he would see them again—he can of course have no way of knowing that they

147

represent "ground zero" of his consciousness, awakening his infantile need for mother and home, "the heart of things."

Together the women provide a trail that leads Will to more Vaughts, Poppy (*LG* 63), Mama (*LG* 53) or Dolly (*LG* 97), and Jamie, their fatally ill sixteen-year-old son, Kitty's younger brother. (Rita is divorced from Sutter, the Vaught's thirty-four-year-old miscreant doctor son.) It turns out that Poppy knew Will's father (*LG* 51–52) and that Mama knew Will's mother, Lucy Hunicutt (*LG* 53). The fact that the Vaughts come from Birmingham only intensifies Will's flirtation with the idea that he has finally found his true family.

Although Will is drawn to Kitty because of his psychic need for an idealized mother figure, that does not mean that he cannot associate her with "country matters." Despite his residence in the Y.M.C.A., Will has been driven by carnal desire, of a peculiar nature, as is revealed in his relationship with Midge Auchincloss. Will had simply not been able to advance his relationship with Midge to what Desmond Morris calls the twelfth and final stage of sexual intimacy, *"genitals to genitals"* (78)[10]: "Though they liked each other well enough, there was nothing to do, it seemed, but press against each other whenever they were alone. Coming home to Midge's apartment late at night, they would step over the sleeping Irishman, stand in the elevator and press against each other for a good half hour, each gazing abstractedly and dry-eyed over the other's shoulder" (*LG* 23–24). Even after an extraordinary "date," during which Will and Midge had rescued a lost child (!) and actually talked, they had returned to Park Avenue, to creep "into the selfsame lobby and over the sleeping Irishman and into the elevator where they strove against each other like wrestlers, each refusing to yield an inch" (*LG* 26). The censorious Irishman may be asleep, but Will's "censor" clearly is not. Will's arrest in the penultimate stage of sexual intimacy argues that his psychic need for merger—rather than a genital need for penetration—has its origin back in the symbiotic phase.[11]

Perhaps Will's immediate conviction that he has fallen in love through the telescope provokes a fire in the loins that he had never experienced for Midge. He soon begins to fantasize about Kitty: "Luck would be this: if he saw her snatch a purse, flee into the park pursued by the cops. Then he would know something and could do something. He could hide her in a rocky den he had discovered in a wild section of the park. He would bring her food and they would sit and talk until nightfall, when they could slip out of the city and go home to Alabama" (*LG* 64). It should be noted, though, that even in his standard "rescue scenario" there lurk the park and home, both places seemingly essential to any thinking that he does. The park as context for his imagined action and for his point of departure for home probably prompts him to specify a "den" for their refuge; in *Remembering*, Edward Casey points out that "[f]or St. Augustine, memory is precisely place-like in its capacity—as is attested by an entire metaphorics of 'cave,' 'den,' 'cavern,' 'treasure-house,' etc" (343). Will, who has earlier confessed to Kitty that he suffers from a faulty memory (*LG* 56), must share St. Augustine's "metaphorics" of place. We learn that his bouts of amnesia often culminate with a fugue to a park-like place (*LG* 12).

So strong is his attraction to Kitty that Will's thinking leaps farther into the future than it has ever gone before: "What he wanted to tell her but could not think quite how was that he did not propose country matters. He did not propose to press against her in an elevator. What he wanted was both more and less. He loved her. His heart melted. She was his sweetheart, his certain someone. He wanted to hold her charms in his arms. He wanted to go into a proper house and shower her with kisses in the old style" (*LG* 71). Coincidentally, Poppy Vaught is ready with a plan that would support Will's intentions. Saying that Will's mother and father are dead and that Will has no business in New York, Poppy offers Will a job, first as a chauffeur for the trip back to Birmingham (*LG* 78–86) and then as a companion for Jamie, in the Vaught home on number 6 fairway of the country club golf course, always a paradisiac place in Percy's fiction.

Such glowing prospects for success awaken other parents in the percept.[12] The next day Will meets Rita: "All at once he knew everything: she had come to get rid of him. She hoped he would take his telescope and go away" (*LG* 91). Having heard that Will is to go home with them (and therefore be a threat to her control over Kitty), Rita plans a diversion, requesting that Will stay in New York during an additional treatment for Jamie and then take Jamie anywhere he desires to go (*LG* 96). To sweeten her offer, she will sell "Ulysses," her camper, to Will for one dollar. When Will questions the camper's name, Rita replies, "He has meant to lead us beyond the borders of the Western world and bring us home" (*LG* 96). Rita is implying that Will will eventually reach Alabama to claim his bride, after a period of enjoyable wandering; but as Bad Mother she is really trying to tempt Will into accepting a fantasy in place of the reality that he could now claim.[13]

Then another parent appears, while Will is walking in his favorite place, Central Park, at night. The danger with which his fantasizing is fraught is implied by the fact that he is in the park at night, not exactly a brilliant idea even in the 1960s. That he is then accosted by a "damp young man" with an interest "in the Platonic philosophy" (*LG* 98) reinforces his danger and foreshadows the temptation to be posed by the new parent. Will is experiencing "old *déjà vus* of summertime" (*LG* 99), when a memory of his father intrudes. (Surely it is intentional that the scene of homosexual temptation is followed by the memory of the figure based on William Alexander Percy?) Strong enough to be an hallucination, the memory is of his father walking before their home, pacing as if a sentry, guarding the home from impurity, saying to his son, "Go to whores if you have to, but always remember the difference. Don't treat a lady like a whore or a whore like a lady" (*LG* 100). Such a dualism idealizes some women, apparently, and de-idealizes all the others—but it is based on the idea that a woman is a lady only because a man holds such an exalted conception of her; her real nature is to be of the tribe of whores. Laboring under that belief, one might well end up like the "damp young man." It is certainly no dualism for Will to be considering; he decides forthwith to pay court to Kitty in the mews in which she and Rita live.

Quite in her Bad Mother character, Rita eyes "him ironically, her head appearing to turn perpetually away" (*LG* 102), soon leaves the room. Yet Will pays suit unsuccessfully: only when he is defeated does Kitty respond, agree to go to Central Park with him, volunteer a "police special" so that he can protect them (sometimes a revolver is not just a revolver) (*LG* 106). Will takes her to a part of the park he knows as well as "his own back yard" "down a ravine choked with dogbane and whortleberry and over a tumble of rocks into a tiny amphitheater, a covert so densely shaded that its floor was as bare as cave's dirt" (*LG* 107). The Augustine metaphorics of the description suggest that the place is the locus of memory; the genital allusiveness of the topography suggests that the two are passing through the vagina; the description of the cave-place as an "amphitheater" recalls the womb-theater in *The Moviegoer* and anticipates the Lost Cove cave-theater in *The Second Coming:* "She moved away. As he traced a finger in the dust, drawing the old Northern Pacific yin-yang symbol, he heard the rustling of clothes and singing of zippers" (*LG* 108). Will's tracery of division-within-unity reveals that while he thinks that he is ecstatic that she is there, he is really thinking about the she who is ought to be there, the Good Mother.[14]

When Kitty returns, Will discovers the difference between the real and the idea. It is one thing to pursue a girl who represents the ideal, but it is another, when the girl thinks she is the real object of pursuit and takes off all her clothes; then there is the matter of "the astounding and terrific melon immediacy of nakedness" (*LG* 110). Kitty then utters the word that sons allegedly want to hear: "Lover." The arrested child in Will, like his Stone Age ancestor, concentrates primarily on the melons.[15] But it appears that melons are not in season for the arrested psyche in Will, for he, getting genital, is detumefacted by the parental distinction between the two types of women. Unlike Adam and Eve, Will and Kitty leave the park none the worse for wear.

The narrator has spent over a hundred pages telling of Will's attempt to reconstruct the Garden of Eden in Central Park—and of his failure and expulsion. It is only to be expected that the sequel will constitute a wandering that—although interrupted by distractions that seem important at the time—is always motivated by an unconscious desire to reach the Promised Land. Physically, the trip is to be from New York to the South and thence to the Southwest; temporally, the trip is to be into the past and thence into the future. Externally, the events experienced by Will Barrett are usually interesting, sometimes funny, sometimes sad; these events constitute the novel for many readers. What is proposed in this paper is that the external events act as a landscape of Will's mind, symbolizing the various psychic forces which affect his consciousness, rendering his direct experience of the wandering "gappy." Unable to recover his earlier experience through psychoanalysis, Will, still handicapped physically, had experienced the "gappy" events that he is now, many years later, recovering through creative narratization. It is laboring the obvious to point out that Walker Percy's own life to age thirty was a model for Will Barrett's to age twenty-five in many, many ways.[16]

Two days after the failed merger in Central Park, the Vaughts leave for home. Will is supposed to be with them, but is left behind, thanks to a stratagem by Rita (*LG* 155). Thus Will is forced into a sidetrack involving Forney Aiken, Mort Prince, and the Texas lady golfers (*LG* 152), before he catches up with the Vaughts in Williamsburg. There Will and Jamie use "Ulysses" as an outrider for the family Cadillac, rendezvousing in Wilmington and Charleston (*LG* 160). Will and Kitty have very little time together until the rendezvous at Folly Beach; there, despite Will's contradictory responses to women, he nearly merges with Kitty—until Rita opens the door (*LG* 168). At the Golden Isles of Georgia, Will and Kitty seclude themselves in "Ulysses"—an automotive Eden—until Rita braves a hurricane to knock at the door (*LG* 180).

Finally the Vaught home is reached, "in a beautiful green valley across a ridge from the city" (*LG* 189). Just how much the "beautiful green valley" recalls the Birmingham suburb of Mountain Brook, Percy's childhood home, may be seen by reading the chapter on Birmingham in George R. Leighton's *Five Cities: The Story of Their Youth and Old Age*. The prominence of the golf course around the Vaught "castle" suggests that this locale is the iconic Garden of Eden scene in Walker Percy's mental landscape; here it was still possible to dream of reconciliation with the mother and of reformation by the father, until the father's suicide.

Since the Vaught home becomes so heavily symbolic to Will Barrett, attention must be paid to Will's symbolization of Kitty and her siblings, Jamie, Val, and Sutter, all of whom grew up in that home and must have some relation to it and to the "beautiful green valley" in which it is located. Kitty is of course "his golden girl of summertime and old Carolina" (*LG* 213), first goddess and then mortal, always confusing. For Will, Jamie is "pure aching primary awareness" (*LG* 162), lacking the secondary awareness to reflect upon his alienation from the original object, arrested in a state that Will may envy but never recapture. The more Will learns about Val and Sutter, the more he must see them as opposite extremes in their reaction to the sense of loss that comes with the acquisition of language; although opposed and extreme, each provides a model for Will to emulate.

Val Vaught grew up at the country club swimming pool, but she has become Sister Johnette Mary Vianny (*LG* 212), after the "French country priest . . . whose holiness was exemplary" (James 243). As a student of the writings of Vilfredo Pareto (*LG* 299)—who sought a general law of sociology based upon "the Newtonian vision" (Powers 23–24)—Val came to herself in her misery, therefore welcoming conversion to Catholicism by a nun, who took her to her "mother house" (*LG* 300). At that point Val became a believer in the (W,w)ord. She took the Catholics "at their word" (*LG* 300), believing "the whole business" (*LG* 301), but being unable to reduce it to words. Before taking final vows as a nun, she was sent to a mission in Alabama by her superiors, who apparently did not know what else to do with her. There she works in linguistics, her field, she claims (*LG* 301), a very applied linguistics. The black children of the community can hardly speak because they have not been spoken to (*LG* 299); Val therefore acts as an Annie Sullivan, who taught another Alabama child to speak (*LG* 301). Underlying her pedagogy is the knowledge that the divine gift of language acquisition can be effectively accepted only if it is accompanied by maternal love (or an adequate substitute). Even so, at best, language acquisition necessarily entails the onset of alienation, necessitating the Word as the only reconciliation with the original Subject. Here Percy represents his paramount idea (drawing upon Christianity, object-relations psychoanalysis, and language theory) that the history of the (W,w)orded individual recapitulates the history of the (W,w)orded race—John 1: 1–5 offers a far more eloquent expression of this transcendent event than I can. In her nourishing action, appropriately feeding a chicken hawk (*LG* 297), Val is a newsbearer, who can feed anyone who understands that it is the human being's nature to be a peregrine.

Appropriately enough, it is the Vaught garden where Will has been dreaming of the Edenic bliss of high school necking in the library stacks (*LG* 205) that he first sees Sutter, who has been observing him from a balcony. Although Will is unaware of it, he quickly attributes aspects of his father's personality to Sutter and is soon drawn to ask him for answers to the questions raised by his father's rigid dualism. Sutter, for his part, seems already to know that Will's mental and sexual ailments result from his loss of his mother and his inability to gain his independence from his father (*LG* 220–21). At this time Sutter absolutely refuses to offer Will any advice, and it does not occur to Will that Sutter's refusal might be because he has enough mental and sexual ailments of his own with which to contend. Thus frustrated—being both in the home of his desire and yet prevented from satisfying it—Will is unconsciously controlled by his dreams and his sleepwalking (*LG* 237–40).

For all of his voluminous scientizing of sexuality in his journal, Sutter is utterly silent about the origin of his ideas—such a Cartesian split is the most obvious evidence of his absolute alienation. Thus Sutter's psychosexual development must be inferred from his later behavior. He records a crucial event in his notebook:

> The day before I left home I stood in a lewd wood by the golf links. . . . The wood was the lewd wood of my youth where lovers used to come and leave Merry Widow tins and where I dreamed the lewd dreams of youth. Therefrom I spied Jackie Randolph towing her cart up number 7 fairway sans caddy and sans partner. Invited her into the woods and spoke into her ear. She looked at her watch and said she had 20 minutes before her bridge luncheon. She spread her golf towel on the pine needles, kept her spiked shoes on, and cursed in my ear. (*LG* 349)

Sutter's description of leaving home is literal, but also symbolic of his exile from Eden. His disillusionment about the fact that the woods were used by lovers suggests that he was once a romantic idealist like Quentin Compson, whose yard was littered by at least one Merry Widow tin. To show his mature cynicism he lays Jackie Randolph right on iconic ground. As complaisant as any Merry Widow, she spreads her towel and curses like the whore that Sutter thinks her to be—for he thinks all women are whores. The first name of Sutter's partner and his sensitivity to those spikes on her shoes suggest that his masculinity might not be so absolute as his subsequent

154

sexual flagrancy might suggest. An observation by Karl Stern is helpful at this point: "The neurosis of Don Juan, the man who is fascinated by conquest, but unable to love, has been frequently made the subject of psychoanalytical studies. In such men the ambivalence towards the mother is so deep and the homosexual tie is so strong that they cannot commit themselves to woman other than by an ambivalent and sadistic relationship. And they are mysteriously compelled to go through this act of conquest and flight in an eternally repetitive experience" (221). To validate his neurotic behavior, Sutter has developed an elaborate theory that the loveless genital channel is the only one on which modern man can broadcast his desire for transcendence. The only trouble is that success in loveless genitalization guarantees failure: "post-orgasmic despair without remedy" (*LG* 345). It was after an encounter with a "winner of [the] Powder Puff Derby" (*LG* 373) that Sutter had attempted suicide. Thus his repetitive behavior is basically a drive toward Thanatos.

Since Will is unable to think clearly about his condition, he is subjected to competing "tugs" (*LG* 294), which are personified by Kitty, Val, and Sutter. Thus he vacillates between opposed decisions, depending upon the Vaught who is influencing him at the moment. It is a rare insight when he imagines himself and Kitty "as doll-like figures tumbling before the magic wand of an enchantress" (*LG* 277), in this case Rita. Within an hour, it could be yet another agent of enchantment.

When Sutter takes Jamie away, Kitty suddenly becomes very possessive of Will. Thus she shows him a G. E. Gold Medallion home— fit domicile for Aphrodite, "the golden one"—located by a "ferny dell and a plashy little brook with a rustic bridge" (*LG* 285), on "the last wrinkle of the Applachians [*sic*]" (*LG* 283), Percy's favorite Edenic acclivity. The place can be had at a special reduced price "to the family" (*LG* 285); indeed Kitty is so enthralled by real estate that she envisions a career as a real estate agent (*LG* 284); indeed she is suddenly so enthralled by the prospect of Will as husband that she envisions him "strolling up and down the bridge" of the good ship Matrimony "with his telescope under his arm" (*LG* 285). Her vision is more perceptive than she can know—if Will succumbed to domesticity, he would indeed still need his telescope/fantasy apparatus. Despite Kitty's sweetening of the deal by $100,000, no wonder that the narrator observes that "[a]lready the carnivorous ivy was stealing down the mountainside" (*LG* 287), as Will roared "down the gloomy Piedmont."

Despite such maternal temptations, Will feels a "huge tug forward" (*LG* 294), toward Sutter and Jamie, so that "Ulysses" starts out *away* from home. Like Ulysses' trip, Will's trip takes him by many places, stirring up many mystifying memories in the process. Approaching Val's mission, Will has a very vague flash of memory of a hunting trip that he may have taken with his father (*LG* 295), a memory that he will not be able to confront for years. This memory seems only to be an overture to the Brahms memories (*LG* 329) that he has when he reaches Ithaca, in the Mississippi Delta, his boyhood home; these memories are so dangerous, if fully addressed, that his unconscious offers an alternative "dread tug of the past not quite remembered" (*LG* 305), Kitty. But he does not turn back. Will actually is able to enter his boyhood home, even to enter the attic in which his father committed suicide (*LG* 331), even to recognize the futility of his father's act (*LG* 332), but the narrator seems to be implying that his young self had not been able at that time sufficiently to work through to an acceptance of what his father's selfish act had done to him. Without that bedrock realization, the subsequent past cannot be truly narratized so that as Will continues west he is tempted by the phony past of Shut Off, Louisiana (*LG* 337–47), and cannot, in regard to Senator Underwood, separate what he has heard from what he directly experienced (*LG* 347–51). So overwhelmed by pastness is he that he calls Kitty (*LG* 351–52), presumably for a comforting regression, but rather than being divine she is still domestic, promising a replacement for the $100,000 check that he has apparently lost. Rather than creeping, carnivorous ivy, "[e]vil low-flying clouds" pursue him; almost in a panic he uncouples "Ulysses'" "umbilical connections," roars for the Panhandle at eighty-five.

As he goes farther west, Will seems to increase his velocity, as if knowing that only increased force will tear him loose from the concrete South so that he can penetrate the abstract Southwest. At the Rio Grande he reaches absolute space: "Beside him a gold aspen rattled like foil in the sunlight. But there was no wind. He moved closer.

A single leaf danced on its pedicle, mysteriously dispensed from energy laws" (*LG* 355). By the time he gets to Sutter's ranch, the transition is complete: "The silence was disjunct. It ran concurrently with one and did not flow from the past. . . . The silence hushed everything up, the small trees were separated by a geometry of space. The sky was empty map space" (*LG* 356).

But, of course, the impact of the enormity of space only awakens his unconscious need for the original enclosure: "Under one bed he found a book of photographs of what appeared to him to be hindoo statuary in a jungle garden. The statues were of couples locked in erotic embraces. The lovers pressed together and their blind lozenge-eyes gazed past each other. The woman's neck arched gracefully. The man's hand sustained the globe of her breast; his pitted stone shaft pressed against the jungle ruin of her flank" (*LG* 357). The lovers' attempt to merge in the garden recalls Will's behavior first with Midge and then with Kitty, back in New York City. At that time Will had acted out his attempt to draw space closer by purchasing the telescope, so it is not surprising that he now mounts the telescope on the window of "Ulysses" (*LG* 358). But what he sees is cold comfort, so that he suddenly reverts to his need for the concrete (if smothering) South: "He shivered. I'm through with telescopes, he thought, and the vasty galaxies. What do I need with Andromeda? What I need is my Bama bride and my cozy camper, a match struck and the butane lit and a friendly square of light cast upon the neighbor earth, and a hot cup of Luzianne between us against the desert cold, and a warm bed and there lie dreaming in one another's arms while old Andromeda leans through the night" (*LG* 358). Will is, to labor the obvious, still torn between two opposed spheres, each first enticing and then dismaying him.

Neither sphere has banished death, of course: the reality that confronts Will in Santa Fe is that Jamie is dying. Will immediately throws himself into a frenzy of caring for the boy, even though he is still torn between "his umbilical connections" (*LG* 375) and Sutter's contention that "fornication is the sole channel to the real" (*LG* 372). He even has a dim realization that while the two "tugs" may have opposed effects on him, they originate from the same source; as he tells Sutter: "You know, Dr. Vaught, I have lived a rather abnormal and solitary life and have tended to get things backwards. My father was a proud and solitary man. I had no other family. For a long time I have had a consuming desire for girls, for the coarsest possible relations with them, without knowing how to treat them as human beings. No doubt, as you suggested, a good part of my nervous condition stems from this abnormal relationship—or lack of relationship—" (*LG* 385). Will should know better than to expect help from Sutter, for he has just described Sutter's own condition; while Will has been talking, Sutter has been "sighting [his] Cot at one after another of the passing women . . ." (*LG* 387). Sutter's fascination with the "little death" is only a preparation for the big (self-inflicted) death to which his philosophy will inevitably lead him. The narrator implies that his young self had somehow realized at that moment the ineffectuality of Sutter's behavior: "Perhaps this moment more than any other, the moment of his first astonishment, marked the beginning for the engineer of what is called a normal life. From that time forward it was possible to meet him and after a few minutes form a clear notion of what sort of fellow he was and how he would spend the rest of his life" (*LG* 389).

In effect Will here rejects a father figure, who has just offered him the same option offered by his real father, suicide. It is to be expected that Will will turn (through the agency of Val) to another father figure, Father Boomer (*LG* 396). This father figure will not—as had his predecessors—deny Will the door back to the Garden of Eden, but will on the contrary open the door for him.[17] His name booms out that he is a medium of the Word. He also offers Will a way of avoiding the subject/object split, spirit/flesh dualism personified by father Barrett/"father" Vaught: the Christian doctrine of incarnation. But Will has not reached the point of understanding the efficacy of the symbolic act. As Father Boomer baptizes Jamie (as God names Jamie as one of His Own), Will sees "a Holsum bread truck pass under the street light" (*LG* 404), but does not see that event as a symbol. Thus, when Jamie dies, Will is vaguely aware that something significant occurred through the baptism, but he does not know what. He has made a stand against death, even saved Sutter from it, but it will be years before he will understand that only love is the certain victor over death. Will will continue to yearn for the lost object and harbor suicidal tendencies, until he falls in love with Allison Hunicutt Huger, whose name indicates that she descends from both mother and mother-substitute, who is both mate and mother figure and also "a gift and therefore a sign of a giver" (*SC* 360). Here Percy repeats his paramount idea, that the Delta Phenomenon is the miraculous transposition from inescapable earthly loss (an awareness born in the birth of consciousness) to heavenly restitution.

Vestavia Temple (From the George B. Ward Collection, Birmingham Public Library, Birmingham)

Will Barrett and "the fat rosy temple of Juno"

In 1924 the LeRoy Percy family, of Birmingham, Alabama, moved from Five Points south over Red Mountain into a new development in Shades Valley. The family occupied a newly built, modernistic house on Fairway Drive, immediately adjacent to the new site of the Country Club, which opened in 1927. In that house Walker Percy spent his eighth through thirteenth year, until shortly after July 9, 1929; on that date LeRoy Percy shot himself to death in the attic and soon thereafter his widow Martha Susan took her three sons, Walker, LeRoy, and Phinizy, to live with her mother in Athens, Georgia. Within a year, Mrs. Percy and her three sons moved to Greenville, Mississippi, to live with her husband's first cousin, William Alexander Percy. Two years later, on April 2, 1932, Mrs. Percy drowned in an automobile wreck that may not have been an accident (Tolson 98–100). It may be fairly conjectured that she had not been able to cope with the loss of her husband back in Birmingham.

Also in 1924 George B. Ward, of Birmingham, Alabama, built himself a dark pink sandstone residence atop Shades Mountain, the next ridge south of Shades Valley.[1] Recently returned from a European vacation, the investment banker, clubman, and several times mayor of Birmingham designed his house as a replica of the Temple of Vesta, in the Forum Boarium, Rome. George Ross Leighton suggests why Ward's house quickly became a popular place to visit:

> [The] mansion, built in imitation of a Roman temple, is cylindrical in shape, made of bits of ore cemented together. By the steps of the mansion stand two black servants in white jackets. One has a felt hat under his arm, the other carries a cap in his hand. Each has pinned to his jacket a green felt label embroidered in yellow with the Roman standard, the letters SPQR, and his name; Lucullus for one, Caius Cassius for the other. Under a tree is an elaborate sort of Roman throne, tinted green and bronze. Above, swinging from a branch, is a radio concealed in a birdhouse. Nearby are two dog houses, built like miniature Parthenons, with classic porticoes and tiny pillars. One is labeled Villa Scipio. There is a pool filled with celluloid swans and miniature galleons and schooners. Scattered about are more benches, urns, and painted-plaster sculptures. (102–103)

Also nearby was a much smaller cylindrical building, the Temple of Sibyl, intended as the burial site of George B. Ward.[2]

Forty years later, as he wrote the novel that was published as *The Last Gentleman*, Walker Percy remembered both the house in the valley and the house on the mountain, when he reached Chapter Four, which describes Will Barrett's return to the South with the Vaught family. Tolson asserts that the house in the valley "provide[d] the model for the Vaughts' 'castle'" (37), himself providing several valuable pages characterizing the life lived there by the Percy family. The house on the mountain is introduced in the text itself with a specificity that leaves no doubt: "Directly opposite the castle, atop the next ridge to the south, there stood a round, rosy temple. It was the dwelling of a millionaire who had admired a Roman structure erected by the Emperor Vespasian . . ." (*LG* 189).

The novel does not begin with Chapter Four, of course, any more than life begins at the moment that one develops the capacity to reflect upon it. For that reason a short summary of the earlier part of the novel must be considered. In the beginning twenty-five year old Will Barrett is living in utter alienation, that is to say, New York City. Deprived of the psychological objects that he needs—his father is dead and his mother is literally unimaginable—Will has accepted Cartesianism as his saviour and embraced the material world as his object. He thinks of himself as an engineer and has recently brought an expensive telescope as an act of faith that technology will reconcile him to the objects that comprise his object.

Such mechanism merely masks a most messy mental life. Will suffers from a sense of depersonalization and derealization, from doubts about the reality of both himself and the external world. Since he was a child, he has experienced frequent *déjà vus*. His fugues have taken him to battlefields where the South was victorious, sites of early battles when the old order was not yet lost, and to greenhouses and parks. His hearing deficit seems to result from hysteria. He has been a patient of a psychiatrist for the past five years, but such is his resistance that he and the psychiatrist are just parting company, without ever having jointly addressed the cause of his distress.

The older Will Barrett who narrates the adventures of his younger self is obviously a close student of psychoanalysis.[3] Thus the case history of his younger self that he presents contains apparently disparate symptoms that fundamentally correlate: Will's existence has been shattered by the loss of his father and mother. The loss of the mother causes the worse trauma, so painful that Will cannot even personify her, but thinks symbolically of her as Eden, the South, a golf course, a park: thus he haunts Central Park. But his attempt to regain that lost object is impeded by the fact that when he is in the park, he hallucinates the image of the other lost object, the father, who confuses Will with his absolute distinction between ladies and whores. Not coincidentally a young man sidles up (*LG* 98–99) as a reminder to Will that one version of sexuality precludes the difficult distinction of ladies from whores.

Will's difficulties with the distinction are not sufficient to persuade him to follow the young student of Platonic philosophy, but it is undeniable that he knows absolutely nothing about the female tribe, and is therefore all the more curious. Through the magical efficacy of his telescope, he has fallen in love at first sight with Kitty Vaught, upon whom he immediately imposes the symbolic value of Good Mother. Harding could be describing Will Barrett when she writes: ". . . an individual who has not become conscious of himself as a separate person but is still enclosed in the father-mother world has no ability to see others as they really *are*. His *Umwelt* contains only mothers, fathers, and siblings" (63). The narrator (who is certainly now conscious of himself) refers to his young self's propensity to see everything in father-mother terms when he describes Will's final visit to his psychiatrist: "Once again he found himself alone in the world, cut adrift from Dr. Gamow, a father of sorts, and from his alma mater, sweet mother psychoanalysis" (*LG* 41). It turns out, though, that Will's Good Mother already has someone who wishes to have her, Rita, the ex-wife of Kitty's brother, Sutter. Thus Will's competitor for Kitty's affections, Rita, must therefore take on the role of Bad Mother in Will's *Umwelt*. Later, Will actually voices his identification: "Rita ran a hand through Jamie's hair (like my mother, thought the engineer in a sudden *déjà vu,* . . ." (*LG* 232).

Through his pursuit of Kitty, Will becomes involved with the other members of the Vaught family, several of whom assume roles in Will's symbolic world. Jamie is even more unconscious of himself—and dependent upon a Cartesian worldview—than Will is and therefore assumes the role of Will's younger brother. Val becomes his older sister, the one who has become so conscious that she has made a radical decision that Will cannot even understand yet, much less emulate. Sutter is destined to play the part of father for Will. Ironically, "[t]he Vaughts liked the engineer very much, each feeling that he was his or her special sort of person" (*LG* 64), but *he* is not cast in a family drama, as he casts them.

In his case history of Will Barrett, the narrator begins early and continues insistently to establish Will's experience of *déjà vu* as the salient symptom of his disorder. The experience had a very early origin:

> As a child he had had "spells," occurrences which were nameless and not to be thought of, let alone mentioned, and which he therefore thought of as lying at the secret and somehow shameful heart of childhood itself. There was a name for it, he discovered later, which gave it form and habitation. It was *déjà vu*, at least he reckoned it was. What happened anyhow was that even when he was a child and sitting in the kitchen watching D'lo snap beans or make beaten biscuits, there came over him as it might come over a sorrowful old man the strongest sense that it had all hap-

pened before and that something else was going to happen and when it did he would know the secret of his own life. Things seemed to turn white and dense and time itself became freighted with an unspeakable emotion. Sometimes he "fell out" and would wake up hours later, in his bed, refreshed but still haunted.[4] (*LG* 11)

Since there is very little general agreement about the nature of the *déjà vu* within the psychoanalytic community (Sno and Linszen 1587–1595), the narrator's vagueness—other than hinting that the experience was so shameful that it had to be repressed—is understandable. Since he offers no definition, then his meaning of the term must be sought in the contexts in which he subsequently uses the term.

In Chapters One through Three the narrator mentions Will's experiences of *déjà vu* ten times (*LG* 12, 14, 45, 68, 90, 99, 129, 128, 152, 161), referring either to his adolescence or to the present time of the narrative—following the initial childhood experience (*LG* 11), which sets some aspect, often a symbol, of home as the controlling theme of the subsequent references. But so completely is the central component of home—mother—directly ignored that Pacella's description of *déjà vu*, based upon object-relations theory, begs to be considered:

> The *déjà vu* thus involves a controlled regression in the service of the ego as a consequence of the defensive and frantic search of the ego for the symbiotic and the nonsymbiotic good, omnipotent mother, rapidly scanning the phases of life in a descent historically to the composite primal-preobject-early libidinal object-representations of mother. . . . This composite maternal representation, dressed in the cloak of only a familiar feeling (*déjà vu*) is superimposed upon the reality perception of the landscape of situation, and ultimately serves two purposes: (1) the recapture of the omnipotent and all-embracing mother (primal love-object), thereby achieving infantile gratification and protection; and (2) warding off castration anxiety through "encapsulation" with the love object, while at the same time insuring "distancing." (312)

In *The Interpretation of Dreams* Sigmund Freud offered the interpretation of *déjà vu* which has been the point of departure for subsequent psychoanalytic discussion of the phenomenon. Since the narrator is developing a narrative which relies upon the theory outlined

165

in that classic work, it is valuable to refer to Freud's comment upon the *déjà vu* of landscape, for many of Will's *déjà vus* are of this nature. Indeed both the Central Park setting of New York and the country club setting of Birmingham both assume the role of *Ur-déjà vu*, realizing Will's *Umwelt* as he must continually dream of it. Freud writes: "In some dreams of landscapes or other localities emphasis is laid in the dream itself on a convinced feeling of having been there once before. (Occurrences of '*déjà vu*' in dreams have a special meaning.) These places are invariably the genitals of the dreamer's mother; there is indeed no other place about which one can assert with such conviction that one has been there once before" (*SE* 5 399).

The maternality of Central Park is announced in the second sentence of the book: "[Will's] head was propped on his jacket, which had been folded twice so that the lining was outermost, and wedged into a seam of rock." Will's jacket would be a fine metonomy for the ego which desires enclosure within the "seam." But the third sentence suggests that Will's regressive "descent," as Pacella calls it, may not yet be all the way to the level of the genital (that descent may come in the cave in *The Second Coming*), but may be arrested at the level of the mammalial: "The rock jutted out of the ground in a section of the park known as the Great Meadow" (*LG* 3). With apologies to Freud, one has also leaned one's head against the rock jutting out before, though at the cost of one's blissfulness.[5]

The duplex pattern just described is repeated with amplification in Chapter Two. Will has now met all of the Vaughts who are in New York City. He fantasizes about hiding Kitty in Central Park (*LG* 64, 67), even before he avows his love to her (*LG* 71); these efforts to attain the Good Mother predictably arouse the activity of Bad Mother Rita, who intercepts his telephone calls (*LG* 89), who may spy on him as he dreamily goes back and forth (!) in a subway (*LG* 90), but who smooths "out her skirt until it [makes] a perfect membrane [!] across her thighs" (*LG* 93), as she entices him to go away, not come ahead. In such a state of frustration, Will goes into Central Park at night, there to be accosted by the "damp young man" (*LG* 98) and his father's ghost inveighing against fornicators (*LG* 99–101). Completely addled, Will calls upon Kitty, eventually persuading her to accompany him to the park. There they enter a "cleft" into a "covert" (*LG* 107). Quickly Kitty moves away, while Will traces "the old Northern Pacific yin-yang symbol" (*LG* 108) on the ground. When she returns, Will experiences "the astounding and terrific melon immediacy of [her] nakedness" (*LG* 110); lest there be any misunderstanding about the portion of her anatomy which is most prominent to Will, the narrator repeats his description of "Kitty as [a] great epithelial-warm pelvic-upcurving-melon-immediate Maja" (*LG* 111). As a child Will had had a *déjà vu* which he thought lay at the "secret and somehow shameful heart of childhood" (*LG* 11). Now he wonders if Kitty is offering him "the august secret of the Western world." Even if she is, he cannot accept, for his sinuses are blocked, so that "his head [is] caulked" (*LG* 110). He winds up talking about his noble kinsman who died, presumably a virgin, in the Crater at Petersburg (a locality can sometimes be not only a genital, but also a double *double-entendre*), while she speaks of her grandmother who "composed the official ATO waltz at Mercer" (*LG* 112). There is no need to ban them from Central Park, though the narrative is about Will's banishment from his park.

What has been going on here? Plenty, if this nighttime scene is enlightened by Harrison's explanation of awe. Harrison acknowledges Greenacre's primacy in the study of phallic awe, which is a response of reverential dread; his project is to show that in some cases what might be described as phallic awe might really be an awe aroused by the mother's body ("Maternal" 182), particularly the breast ("Maternal" 188), a response of wonder that occurs earlier in an infant's development than does phallic awe ("Maternal" 188). Harrison accepts Greenacre's argument that "awe is first experienced only after self-object differentiation has been accomplished, and it always—even in early childhood—involves regression" ("Maternal" 185). This awe experience is not unlike a *déjà* experience ("Maternal" 182, 192–93). Says Harrison:

> Presumably the infant's earliest fluctuating awareness of his own cold, wet, or hungry self alternates with a loss of self when a symbiotic merging occurs. Thus a complex situation normally evolves. During the developmental phase of the nursling, a gradual differentiation between self and breast regularly alternates with the loss of boundaries as the infant sinks into contented sleep, paradigmatically at the mother's breast. With

good mothering and other fortunate circumstances, the infant's needs do not rise to the point of trauma in this process. Later, usually in the early oedipal phase, the mother's body gains object meaning as potential receptacle or womb. I suggest that the initial recognition of mother's breast and, later, of her body customarily gives rise to wondrous awe. ("Maternal" 188)

Harrison continues that either form of awe, if affected by "very early trauma occurring well before self-object differentiation, and by other premature startling observations made by the infant or young child" ("Maternal" 188), will contain an element of anxiety or fear. When the fear- or anxiety-affected awe has been aroused by the "maternal element" the child (or regressed adult) experiences smothering or engulfment, "the primal distress of suffocation" that Freud linguistically identified as "a primary source of anxiety" ("Maternal" 191). Harrison argues that the symbols of the breast, as well as the phallus, revealed in "many cultural shrines and comparable stimuli to awe are remarkable in that they have an impact upon the individual as a member of a group and at the same time revivify the early awe-arousing experiences which they symbolize" ("Maternal" 193–94). He concludes that much more work must be done on the phenomenon of awe, for he accepts Freud's contention that religious feelings "arise from awe feelings in childhood" ("Maternal" 189), although Freud limited the object of awe to the father, whereas Harrison accepts the presence, indeed the primacy, of the mother as the object of awe.

As the representation of Paradise or Eden, Central Park is the most persistent symbol of "mother" for Will, who does not visualize that figure throughout the narration.[6] In Central Park, at a point identified in the New York *Times* as "ground zero" (*LG* 48) for a possible attack of "some kind of nerve gas," Will has observed Kitty Vaught, who occasions his regression to his personal "ground zero," the mother, the site at which he suffered an assault upon his "nerves." As Tolson points out (304–5), Percy had originally entitled the novel-in-progress *Ground Zero;* thus he hinted that the *germ* of his conception was maternal, while the actual title suggests that his inspiration was paternal. Despite the immediate opposition of the internalized father-figure (whom he sees very clearly) and of the representation of the Bad Mother, Will succeeds in restoring the Good Mother—the one with the breast—to "ground zero" by taking her into the womb-like enclosure in Central Park. There his creation of the yin-yang, symbol of "symbiotic merging," occurs, assertion that his project is to reexperience wondrous awe, as his response to "the astounding and terrific" (*LG* 110) melons indicates. It is as if Kitty understands her maternal role in Will's fantasy, for three times (*LG* 107, 110) she strokes his cheek, an action which activates a newborn baby's reflex to suck.[7]

But the very act of focusing on the "part-object" awakens the anxious experience of suffocation. (Literalists will object that Will's nose had begun to stop up back at the apartment, ostensibly from "[d]ander from the old blankets" (*LG* 104) on which Will and Kitty recline, but he is said to experience the dander just at the moment that he is asking her to take off the "quexquemetl" that covers her bosom: "He hadn't meant to undress her but only to get her out of these prickly homespuns and back into decent Alabama cotton" (*LG* 104). His apparent intention merely anticipates his desire to incorporate her into his fantasy.) Thus, in the park, as far as stuffiness goes, as above, so below. There can be no connection, not oscular and certainly not genital, so he trails off into a revery of chivalric chastity that ought to delight his father's ghost.

When the Vaughts invite Will to take a job as Jamie's companion, he accepts, for he genuinely likes the boy. He also continues to think that he, an adult, loves Kitty, an adult, although said second adult is often confused by the perverse courting behavior of said first adult. Will's continued pursuit of Kitty ensures that Rita will continue to baffle him. The course of true love never did run smooth—even through Virginia, North Carolina, South Carolina, and Georgia.

When the Vaught "castle" is finally reached, Will must indeed feel certain that he is about to fulfill his dreams. The house is right on the country club golf course, on which Will thinks "his grandfather had played an exhibition round with the great Bobby Jones in 1925 or thereabouts" (*LG* 188).[8] Thus "[i]t was an ancient sort of links, dating from the golden age of country clubs, ..." This "golden age" links (or Paradisal symbol of mother) does not appear to be tunneled by the old mole, the father, like the links in *The Second Coming.* Yet soon Sutter, the *souterre,* shows up (*LG* 188).

On the next ridge south is the "round, rosy temple." But in the transition from fact to fiction, a remarkable change has occurred: George B. Ward had been inspired by and named his building the Temple of Vesta, but the narrator renames the building the Temple of Juno. While Vesta was the deity of the fire on the hearth, whose temple was tended by virgins, Juno was the deity of motherhood and childbirth, whose milk created the Milky Way.[9] Thus the narrator formally designates the "temple" as a symbol of motherhood, while his description of it as "round" and "rosy" designates it as a "part-object," the breast. There is a psychoanalytic literature to support the narrator's assignment of such symbolic values to a temple. In reference to the class *house* in dreams, Harding writes:

> But this does not cover every possible meaning of "house." For the house may be church or temple, namely the "house of God," when, as in the theme of parent and child, the individual is led over to an attitude that transcends the personally oriented one. He is brought to the realization that he is in the presence of God, of a transcendent reality, and that some service or ritual is about to be performed which will have as its purpose the establishment of a relation between the ego, that is, himself, his "I," and the tremendum that men call God, that is, the "not-I." So that again the symbol of an object leads over into the archetype of a situation. (173)

And Harrison writes, in connection with another temple, sacred to a goddess, on a hill: ". . . the temple, which so regularly represents the mother's body (and, in fact, so often reawakens awe of her body) . . ." ("On Freud" 405). The temple to which Harrison refers is the Parthenon, dedicated to the worship of Athena, on the Acropolis; Niederland reminds us that this temple also "appears bathed in a peculiar, singularly rosy-pink light," concluding: "Indeed, the unique quality of the temple on the Acropolis lies precisely in the fact that the ruins do not appear as ruins, but look very much alive, "amber-colored," as Freud has it, or almost the color of pink human flesh" (376).

It should be recalled that the narrator, at the point in his life that he is describing, had just concluded five years (*LG* 32) of psychoanalysis and that he reveals a close reading of Freud, especially *The*

Interpretation of Dreams, with its discussion of *déjà vu*. Freud continued to be curious about that phenomenon, mentioning it in passing and finally personally and at length in "A Disturbance of Memory on the Acropolis: An Open Letter to Romain Rolland on the Occasion of his Seventieth Birthday."[10] There is a strong likelihood that the narrator is alluding to Freud's experience on the Acropolis as he describes his younger self in the vicinity of the temple of Juno.

In the beginning of the letter Freud congratulates Rolland on his having reached such an advanced age, but then says that he is eighty and that his "powers of production are at an end" (239). Thus all that he has to offer Rolland is a story of an experience that had occurred to him in 1904, when he was forty-eight. Freud and his younger brother had, somewhat reluctantly, taken a short trip to Athens. When the brothers climbed the Acropolis, Freud was overwhelmed by "a momentary feeling: '*What I see here is not real*'" (244). Now, thirty-two years later, Freud analyzes that moment of "derealization," which, he says, is intimately related to "depersonalization": "There is another set of phenomena which may be regarded as their positive counterparts—what are known as '*fausse reconnaissance*,' '*déjà vu*,' '*déjà raconté*,' etc., illusions in which we seek to accept something as belonging to our ego, just as in the derealizations we are anxious to keep something out of us" (245). There are "two general characteristics of the phenomena of derealization": "The first is that they serve the purpose of defence; they aim at keeping something away from the ego, at disavowing it" (245); "The second general characteristic of the derealizations—their dependence upon the past, upon the ego's store of memories and upon earlier distressing experiences which have since perhaps fallen victim to repression—is not accepted without dispute" (246).

Freud then rather hastily applies his model to his own experience. He concludes that he had been reluctant to visit Athens—even though he had dreamed of such a visit all his life—because he felt guilty that he would be doing what his father had never gotten to do.[11] Thus when he actually got to the Acropolis, he had to deny that the event was really real. With his firm dedication to the primacy of the oedipal relation as the origin of all subsequent psychic behavior, Freud does not—or at least does not allow himself to—speculate that

171

the visualized object that he was rejecting as "unreal" might be a symbol of the mother, whose earlier loss is the primary wound of the self.

There is an extensive recent psychoanalytical literature which argues that Freud, because of his own personal involvement, was unable to distance himself from his Athens experience sufficiently to analyze it fully. In a way he is silently admitting to Rolland the overwhelming power of the "oceanic experience," which, elsewhere, he avowed that he had never felt. It is enough for my purpose here to say that the narrator is implying that Will Barrett at twenty-five was, like Freud at forty-eight—perhaps like Percy himself at forty-eight—unable to allow himself to respond to his maternal awe, elicited by the Temple of Juno, and thus to come to grips with his fundamental source of distress, even as the Temple continues to impress itself on him (191).[12]

Correspondingly, Will begins to withdraw his interest in Kitty as a Good Mother figure; when he sees her in a "cashmere sweater with a tiny gold sorority dagger pinned over her breast" (*LG* 228), it may be inferred that the part-object is not the "melon" that it had been in Central Park and that even the slightest acknowledgement of it evokes the "dagger," the castration anxiety that Pacella and others associate with *déjà vu*. Rather he is in the presence of far stronger evocations of the Good Mother: the golf course, the garden, and the South in general.[13] All of these phenomena coalesce in a gorgeous October scene, when Kitty, Jamie, and Will have returned from their day at the university (*LG* 200). In the garden Will takes a nap (*LG* 202), regresses to an "examination dream," associated with birth-trauma fantasies (Ferenczi 47), then dreams of kissing Alice Bocock in the library stacks (*LG* 205), a permissible erotic substitute for the original object. But at the same time, half awake, he hears Bad Mother Rita call Kitty "Hebe," the goddess youth, in effect telling him that Kitty will not be his Junosubstitute. As Will becomes fully awake—goes from preoedipal to oedipal awareness—he notices that Sutter is standing on a ledge, god-like, "looking down into the garden" (*LG* 206), evoking in Will a "Lilliputian fantasy" also associated with "examination dreams" and birth-trauma fantasies (Ferenczi 47).

172

In the next sequence of the narrator's story Will becomes preoccupied with Sutter's vaunted sexual shenanigans and his fiddling
with his pistol—both traits activating Will's phallic awe, further di-
minishing any possibility that he will allow himself to experience
maternal awe. Will tries to read his *R. E. Lee* (225), hoping that somehow he can prevent the "horrific Confederate foul-ups"—especially
the one at Sharpsburg ("Antietam" to Yankees), which was as fatal
to the Southern cause as Gettysburg or Vicksburg—thus to hang on
to an image of original perfection or the unLost Cause. But he is
drawn ever more deeply into a relationship with Sutter, even to becoming a voyeur (*LG* 214–15), a behavior that Harrison associates
with the onset of oedipal rivalry ("Reconsideration" 522). One night,
after talking with Sutter, Will dreams a screen-memory of the events
that immediately preceded his father's suicide (*LG* 237), an experience no doubt incited by the "fruity steel smell of Hoppe's gun oil"
(*LG* 217) that Sutter had been using on his pistol during their talk.

Awakened by the dream, Will goes outside "into the moonlight."
"The golf links was as pale as lake water" (*LG* 238). But neither of
these immemorial feminine images is to induce him to acknowledge
the maternal aspect of what he next sees:

> To the south Juno's temple hung low in the sky like a great fiery star. The
> shrubbery, now grown tall as trees, cast inky shadows which seemed to
> walk in the moonlight.
>
> For a long time he gazed at the temple. What was it? It alone was not
> refracted and transformed by the prism of dreams and memory. But now
> he remembered. It was fiery old Canopus, the great red star of the south
> which once a year reared up and hung low in the sky over the cottonfields
> and canebrakes. (*LG* 238–39)

Here Juno's temple seems to want to be regarded with awe, to be
perceived as a maternal symbol. And Will's hesitation suggests that
he is on the verge of allowing it to be "refracted and transformed by
the prism of dreams and memory." But then he decides that he is
looking at the star Canopus, although Canopus is actually yellow-
white. Ironically, the early Egyptians worshipped the star, aligning
some of their religious buildings by it.

Thus while Will cannot allow himself to respond to the building as
a maternal image he can transform it into a star, an object which,

from here on, becomes a very persistent paternal image. This symbolic appearance should have been expected: why else does anyone buy a telescope—as Will had done when he abandoned psychoanalysis—but to look at stars? On the night under discussion, Will turns away from the prospect of the Temple, to go into the house, there to seek the attic, with its star-like "row of bulbs in the peak of the roof" (*LG* 239)—but he is prevented from visualizing the place as the scene of his father's suicide by the timely arrival of Kitty, who seems to have just enough residual symbolic value to keep Will from identifying totally with the image of father and the lure of death.

Will's conflicted quest for parental objects continues for the remainder of the story. The narrator offers, from Will's point of view, a prologue to the remainder: "How can one take seriously the Theory of Large Numbers, living in this queer not-new-not-old place haunted by the goddess Juno and the spirit of the great Bobby Jones [i.e., mother and father]? But it was more than that. *Something is going to happen,* he suddenly perceived that he knew all along. He shivered. It is for me to wait. Waiting is the thing. Wait and watch" (*LG* 241). Shivering is the appropriate physiological accompaniment for the experience of awe, but the object of the awe must be recognized, if one is to gain any relief from the distress which the object is causing.

The fatally ill Jamie is so desperate that he wishes to escape Birmingham, to go to New Mexico, where he had before been with Sutter. Will agrees that they will leave immediately, to the displeasure of Kitty. Of course they will take the telescope and the "Freylinghausen star charts" (*LG* 253), the better to locate the star that they seek. Before *they* can leave, though, Sutter takes Jamie off (*LG* 273), first, presumably, to visit Val, then on to New Mexico. Will quickly decides to follow (as a result of a post-hypnotic suggestion implanted by Sutter [*LG* 294]), even halfheartedly asks Kitty to accompany him. But she is under the dominion of Bad Mother Rita, as Will notes: "Then, registering as he did a fine glint of appraisal in Rita's eye, he saw the two of them, Kitty and Billy, as doll-like figures tumbling before the magic wand of an enchantress. Nor, and here was the strangest part of it, did he really mind" (*LG* 277).

Having lost her charm as a priestess of Juno, Kitty tries to insure that Will return to "Miss Katherine Gibbs Vaught," whose wedding photograph would appear in the *Commercial Appeal* (*LG* 261). She takes him to see the house that she wants them to live in: it is on "South Ridge" (*LG* 382), thus replaces the Temple of Juno in Will's building symbolism. But her picture of Will as a "lovable eccentric who spied through his telescope at the buzzards and crows which circled above this doleful plain" (*LG* 285–86) inspires nausea, not awe. Thus, thanks to a convenient chaos, he is able to pursue Sutter, going backward through a memoryscape of experience with his father even as he goes forward through Alabama, Mississippi, Louisiana, and Texas.

In Ithaca, Mississippi, there is a "dread tug of the past not quite remembered" (*LG* 305), so he attempts to call Kitty "in the purple castle beside the gold links and under the rosy temple of Juno" (*LG* 313), but the new divinity of domesticity is not at home. Without hindrance, then, Will runs under Scorpio (*LG* 327)—the sign of "the Mystery of Sex and the secret of Ancient phallic rites" (Zolar 233)—to the house in which his father had killed himself. There Will confronts the sidewalk on which his "father took a stroll and spoke to a stranger of the good life and the loneliness of the galaxies" (*LG* 330). Then he sneaks up to the attic, in which an "old clear-glass 25-watt bulb shed a yellow mizzling light, a light of rays, actual striae" (*LG* 333). In the presence of death, handling the very shotgun, which has not been cleaned and thus invites further use, he seems to wait and watch, "while his eyes followed the yellow drizzle of light into every corner of the attic room" (*LG* 334).

But nothing happens, so he is pulled farther west. There is still a feeble attraction from Birmingham, for he calls Kitty from Dallas. But she speaks only of the Mickle house atop the doleful plain. No wonder that when he at last falls asleep, he awakens immediately to think that he is in Birmingham: "Evil low-flying clouds reflected a red furnace-glow from the city. . . . Wasting no time, he uncoupled his umbilical connections . . ." (*LG* 352). By the time he reaches New Mexico, he is aware that he is in a land radically unlike the South: "The country there is peopled, a handful of soil strikes a pang to the heart, *déjà vus* fly up like a shower of sparks. Even in the Southern wilderness there is ever the sense of someone close by, watching

175

from the woods. Here one was not watched. There was no one. The silence hushed everything up, the small trees were separated by a geometry of silence. The sky was empty silence. The sky was empty map space" (*LG* 356).

This site, Will seems to feel, is truly the place for a revelation. He picks up a *Life* magazine on which Sutter has written something, but can make no sense of the message, for "the script ran off into the brown stipple of a girl's thigh and he could make out no more" (*LG* 357). Then he finds another message, though probably not intentionally left by Sutter: "Under one bed he found a book of photographs of what appeared to him to be hindoo statuary in a jungle garden. The statues were of couples locked in erotic embraces. The lovers pressed together and their blind lozenge-eyes gazed past each other. The woman's neck arched gracefully. The man's hand sustained the globe of her breast; his pitted stone shaft pressed against the jungle ruin of her flank" (*LG* 357). These photographs are exactly like those to which Ernest Jones refers, in his essay "The Psychology of Religion," in which he offers the psychoanalytic theory that religious practices originated in the deification of the father as God:

> In India and elsewhere the original source of [religious] worship has broken through to the surface by a process akin to what in psychoanalysis is called "the return of the repressed." I refer to the widely distributed phallic worship of the East. It is certain that this is not the lewd performance it seems to Western eyes, but is a solemn adoration of the sorce [sic] of power which in the child's unconscious is the starting-point of the feelings of awe, respect, fear, and admiration he entertains towards the father. It can be shown that the symbols commonly used there to represent the phallus, the serpent, erect stones, etc., are symbols not of the phallus *per se*, but specifically of the father's phallus.[14] (321)

Again Will practices waiting and watching. Fittingly "[d]ark fell suddenly and the stars came out" (*LG* 357), as the paternal sky is charged with the paternal awe Will feels for the "pitted stone shaft." Appropriately Will suddenly remembers his telescope, the objectification of his quest, to look at Pegasus, the winged horse sprung from Medusa, the monster mother who was later described as "coldly and calmly beautiful" (Rose 30). The starry sky as paternal object evokes a shiver (*LG* 358) of awe.[15]

But such is his ambivalence that Will immediately creates images to the contrary: since awe threatens to overwhelm the ego, the ego must escape succumbing: "I'm through with telescopes, he thought, and the vasty galaxies. What do I need with Andromeda? What I need is my Bama bride and my cozy camper, a match struck and the butane lit and a friendly square of light cast upon the neighbor earth, and a hot cup of Luzianne between us against the desert cold, and a warm bed and there lie dreaming in one another's arms while old Andromeda leans through the night" (*LG* 358).

Yet the attempt to identify with Dixie domesticity is undercut by the narrator's description of Will's ensuing behavior. Returning to Santa Fe, he has to settle for Cream of Wheat instead of grits, an unthinkable substitution for any idealistic Southerner. Worse yet, he views the site of a Confederate defeat without exercising body English to reverse the outcome of the battle.

Thus apparently free of the mother's hold, Will is eligible to find the object of his quest, Sutter, who informs him that Jamie is in the hospital, fatally ill. Will's days are now busy with caring for Jamie, but not so completely that he is unbothered by his vacillation toward parental objects. His obsessive reading of Sutter's notebook is sufficient to propel him back to the mother-figure, who appears in her customary disguise as a *déjà vu* of landscape:

> He recalled everything, even a single perception years ago, one of a thousand billion, so trivial that it was not even remembered then, five minutes later: on a college field trip through the mangy Jersey woods look for spirogyra, he had crossed a utility right-of-way. When he reached the farther woods, he had paused and looked over his shoulder. There was nothing to see: the terrain dipped, making a little swale which was overgrown by the special forlorn plants of rights-of-way, not small trees or bushes or even weeds exactly but just the unclassified plants which grow up in electric-light-and-power places. That was all. He turned and went on. (*LG* 374–75)

This is what Eden would have looked like, if Adam had bothered to look back. The narrator uses an image of Southern particularity to describe the impact of this *déjà vu* on Will: "Desolate places like Appomattox and cut-over woods [national and ecological deterioration] were ever the occasion of storms of sexual passion" (*LG* 375). Psychoanalysis attributes Don Juanism to a futile attempt of the son to reach the mother through the flesh of another woman, which is exactly what Will intends, though he cannot attend to his purpose without inciting its opposite: "Yet now when he rushed out into the abstract afternoon to find a maid (but who?) he forgot again and instead found himself picking through the ashes of the trashburner" (*LG* 375) for Sutter's notebook.

Will is now frantic with discomfort. The notebook is destroyed, so he jumps "into the cab of the G.M.C., [tearing] out of the poplar grove, forgetting his umbilical connections until he heard the snappings of cords . . ." (*LG* 375). He *thinks* that he is going to Albuquerque to find a girl, any girl, but within the same instant he decides to call Kitty, even as he clings to a paternal telephone pole, "buffeted by an abstract, lustful molecular wind . . . ," acting out responses to both parental objects simultaneously. No wonder an observing Hoosier is so astounded that he takes refuge in his "deluxe Sun-Liner."

Will talks to Kitty for two hours (*LG* 380), agreeing to return to her, to share the Mickle place on South Ridge and the "same church home" (*LG* 383), as Kitty puts it. Things have changed: Bad Mother Rita has left, there evidently being no more business for her, now that Kitty is no longer Good Mother. As Will tells this information to Sutter, the narrator describes "the empty sky, which instead of turning rosy with sunset was simply going out like a light" (*LG* 386). The rosy breast has been vanquished by the starry phallus, for Sutter immediately begins to sight "the Colt at one after another of the passing women" (*LG* 387).

Now that the phallus is ascendant, Will expects an answer from it, namely whether or not to fornicate (*LG* 381). Sutter declines to answer that question, but does tell Will that he will not have any more "fugues" (*LG* 384), those flights in quest of the landscape of the ideal mother. He has no cosmic answer to give Will—unless it is the unintended message, *Christ*, which punctuates his discourse (*LG* 381, 386, 389). His only disclosure is that he will kill himself, if not before, then immediately after Jamie's death.

For Will, that disclosure destroys Sutter's godlike image as a paternal figure. Will thus turns back to a woman, Val, for direction. With authority she tells him that his responsibility is simple: see that Jamie is baptized (*LG* 392). This Will does, thus assuring that Jamie achieves blessedness, but the narrator indicates that Will does not know what the baptism has accomplished: Will sees "a Holsum bread truck pass under the street light" (*LG* 404), without attaching any significance to it.

Since Will comes to no realization, there is no closure for the story. At one time the narrator may have shared Walker Percy's idea that Will would return to marry Kitty. But the narrator now knows that Will, despite the discrediting of Kitty and Sutter as parental figures, is not free of a susceptibility to maternal and paternal awe, of a susceptibility to regress to a psychological level that renders him an alienated human being. Will will continue to be in awe of golf courses and shotguns (and Lugers), until he achieves through conversion a restitution of the original unity: then his experience of awe will be replaced by a sense of blessedness.

Will Barrett's Psychoanalysis

In Walker Percy's novel *The Last Gentleman* (1966) the narrator, Will Barrett, tells the story of a crisis in his life when he was twenty-five (*LG* 41). A sparse background for this crisis is given in Chapter One, though it is not given in strict chronological order, as it will be reconstructed here. Here is the earliest memory given:

> As a child he had had "spells," occurrences which were nameless and not to be thought of, let alone mentioned, and which he therefore thought of as lying at the secret and somehow shameful heart of childhood itself. There was a name for it, he discovered later, which gave it form and habitation. It was *déjà vu*, at least he reckoned it was. What happened anyhow was that even when he was a child and was sitting in the kitchen watching D'lo snap beans or make beaten biscuits, there came over him as it might come over a sorrowful old man the strongest sense that it had all happened before and that something else was going to happen and when it did he would know the secret of his own life. (*LG* 11)

There are two memories "when he was a boy," but there is no way to determine which is earlier. The first is: "Once when he was a boy, a man next door had gone crazy and had sat out in his back yard pitching gravel around and hollering out to his enemies in a loud angry voice. The boy watched him all day, squatted down and watched him, his mouth open and drying. It seemed to him that if he could figure out what was wrong with the man he would learn the secret of life" (*LG* 10). The second is: "Once when he was a boy his father and stepmother put him in a summer camp and went to Europe" (*LG* 13). Already having difficulty with group activities, Will left the camp to return home.

There appear to be two memories from early adolescence, though neither can be dated or given precedence, albeit the first could imply the second. The first is: "When he was a youth he had lived his life in a state of the liveliest expectation, thinking to himself: what a fine thing it will be to become a man and to know what to do—like an Apache youth who at the right time goes out into the plains alone, dreams dreams, sees visions, returns and knows he is a man" (*LG* 11). The second is: "He took to wandering. He had a way of turning up at unlikely places such as a bakery in Cincinnati or a greenhouse in Memphis, where he might work for several weeks assaulted by the *déjà vus* of hot growing green plants" (*LG* 12).

Later events may be roughly dated by working backward from the present. Probably he was sixteen when he was sent to Princeton, where "[o]ne beautiful fall afternoon of his junior year, as he sat in his dormitory room, he was assaulted by stupefying *déjà vus*. An immense melancholy overtook him" (*LG* 14). Consequently he abandoned school to live in the Manhattan Y.M.C.A. The following summer, probably when he was nineteen, he went home, at the request of his father, to clerk in the family law firm, but "[a]t the end of summer his father died" (*LG* 16). Then he was drafted into the army, serving two years before "he was honorably and medically discharged when he was discovered totally amnesic and wandering about the Shenandoah Valley between Cross Keys and Port Republic, sites of notable victories of General Stonewall Jackson" (*LG* 18).

Returning to the Manhattan Y.M.C.A. Will engaged a psychiatrist. After a six-month preparatory course at Long Island University, he got a job as a humidification engineer. He also worked as a paid companion to "lonely and unhappy adolescents" (*LG* 19). To improve his behavior in groups, he joined an interracial group and an expatriate

Southerners group, but he unintentionally offended both groups. After about three years he got a job at Macy's, spending his leisure time with a group of his fellow employees, but their companionship so exacerbated his condition "that he lapsed into a fugue state which was worse than the last" (*LG* 22). In the summer before the present "he had fallen into a fugue state and wandered around northern Virginia for three weeks, where he sat sunk in thought on old battlegrounds, hardly aware of his own name" (*LG* 12). It may have been at this time that he voluntarily committed himself for three months, for "an episode of amnesia" (*LG* 56).

In the very recent past Will has been unusually active. Some weeks before, he had seen a telescope in "the window of an optical store on Columbus Circle" (*LG* 29). Perhaps the location made him think that he might discover a new world, for "[t]he conviction grew upon him that his very life would be changed if he owned the telescope." The next morning he decided to buy the telescope, even though its purchase depleted his bank account. As Will had hoped, the telescope "penetrated to the heart of things" (*LG* 29), so he decided that, since he had the telescope, he no longer needed the services of his psychoanalyst, Dr. Gamow:

> For the thousandth time Dr. Gamow looked at his patient—who sat as usual, alert and pleasant—and felt a small spasm of irritation. . . . For the first year the analyst had been charmed—never had he had a more responsive patient. Never had his own theories found a readier confirmation than in the free (they seemed to be free) associations and the copious dreams which this one spread out at his feet like so many trophies. The next year or so left him pleased but still baffled. This one was a little too good to be true. At last the suspicion awoke that he, the doctor, was being *entertained*, royally it is true and getting paid for the privilege besides, but entertained nevertheless. . . . Charged accordingly, the patient of course made an equally charming confession, exhibited heroic sweats and contortions to overcome his bad habits, . . .
>
> The last year of the analysis the doctor had grown positively disgruntled. This one was a Southern belle, he decided[,] a good dancing partner, light on his feet and giving away nothing. He did not know how not to give away nothing. (*LG* 33)

Then the narrator summarizes: "The doctor didn't like his patient much, to tell the truth." Then he employs a nice contrast: "The engineer, on the other hand, had a high opinion of his analyst and especially liked hearing him speak":

> Though Dr. Gamow was a native of Jackson Heights, his speech was exotic. . . . The engineer liked to hear him say *neu-wosis,* drawing out the second syllable with a musical clinical Viennese sound. Unlike most Americans, who speak as if they were sipping gruel, he chose his words like bonbons, so that his patients, whose lives were a poor meager business, received the pleasantest sense of the richness and delectability of such everyday things as words. Unlike some analysts, he did not use big words or technical words; but the small ordinary words he did use were invested with a peculiar luster. "I think you are pretty unhappy after all," he might say, pronouncing *prĕtty* as it is spelled. His patient would nod gratefully. (*LG* 33)

The narrator, again noting that Will savors the analyst's words (*LG* 34), again emphasizes the analyst's most prominent trait: ". . . he served his patients best as artificer and shaper, receiving the raw stuff of their misery and handing it back in a public and acceptable form. 'It does sound to me as if you've had a prĕtty bad time. Tell me about it.' And the unspeakable could be spoken of" (*LG* 35).

The last session between Will and Dr. Gamow is like all the others. Dr. Gamow's office is decorated "in a Bahama theme, with a fiber rug and prints of hummingbirds and Negresses walking with baskets on their heads, . . ." (*LG* 33). Something of a semioticist, Dr. Gamow had explained that the hummingbirds "symbolized ideas, . . . happy ideas which he hoped would fly into the heads of his patients" (*LG* 36–37). But it is likely that Will makes a different interpretation: a hummingbird may evoke the sound of humming to him. Just before Will looks at the hummingbirds, he is listening to his analyst: "'Hnhnhn,' said Dr. Gamow. It was an ancient and familiar sound, so used between them, so close in the ear, as hardly to be a sound at all" (*LG* 36). Then Will notes: "One bird's gorget did not quite fit: the print had been jogged in the making and the gorget had slipped and stuck out like a bib. For years the patient had gazed at this little patch of red, making a slight mental effort each time to put it back in place" (*LG* 37). Will may liken the bird to himself; just as the bird has something wrong with its throat, so must Will, for Dr. Gamow does not appear to hear him very well, chasing after imagined Freudian slips (*LG* 34–36) and taking Will's descriptions of his condition literally

(*LG* 36). Toward the end of the session the narrator describes Will: "The patient took a last look at the dusty hummingbird which had been buzzing away at the same trumpet vine for five years. The little bird seemed dejected" (*LG* 40). A little earlier the narrator had indicated the source of Will's dejection: "[h]e meant to signify that he wished to say something that should be listened to and not gotten at" (*LG* 36). Will, the little hummingbird, has not penetrated the trumpet flower, Dr. Gamow.

Will tries to be diplomatic when he tells Dr. Gamow that he is terminating his analysis. But Dr. Gamow has seen the telescope in the reception room and thinks it proof that Will is deteriorating, rather than cured:

> "So now it seems you have spent your money on an instrument which will enable you to see the truth once and for all?"
> The patient shrugged affably.
> "It would be prĕtty nice if we could find a short cut and get around all this hard work. Do you remember, the last time you left you stood up and said: 'Look here now, this analysis is all very well but how about telling me the truth just between ourselves, off the record, that is, what am I *really* supposed to do?' Do you remember that?"
> . . . .
> The patient nodded.
> "You also recall that this great thirst for the 'answer,' the key which will unlock everything, always overtakes you just before the onset of one of your fugue states?"
> "Not always."
> "Always in the past."
> "Not this time." (*LG* 37–38)

Their session having reached an impasse, Dr. Gamow gets clinical: "May I review for you one or two facts. Number one, you have had previous fugue states. Number two, you give every indication of having another. You always quit the analysis and you always buy something expensive before taking off. The last time it was a Corvette. You still have a defective ego structure, number three. Number four, you develop ideas of reference. This time it is hollow men, noxious particles, and ultimate truths" (*LG* 38).

But Will, convinced of the "magical means" of his telescope, persists in his decision to terminate his analysis. It will be assumed that Will has told Dr. Gamow everything that the narrator reveals about Will's past, but that Will has not told Dr. Gamow certain things because he is repressing them: "Although they had spent a thousand hours together in the most intimate converse, they were no more than acquaintances. Less than acquaintances. A laborer digging in a ditch would know more about his partner in a week than the doctor learned about this patient in a year" (*LG* 33). From the available data Dr. Gamow emphasizes three "facts" (?) about Will's condition: that he has a history of "fugue states," a "defective ego structure," and "ideas of reference"—all symptoms which are very general and significantly overlap. Perhaps Dr. Gamow has spoken to Will about his condition with a degree of specificity which he does not use here, or perhaps he has deferred such explicity until such time as Will is prepared to respond emotionally, rather than intellectually, to his guidance—a time which is not reached, or perhaps the narrator knows now that at the time these were the only data (however superficial) to which Will could attend. At any rate, Will's relations to Dr. Gamow and Dr. Gamow's responding diagnosis can be dredged for much more specific information about Will's condition.

What must be mentioned first, though, is the significant information which is omitted from the narrator's account. There is no reference to Will's birth mother or to the fact that Will's father killed himself when Will was just reaching adolescence. Surely Dr. Gamow must have investigated these essential formative factors, so their absence in Chapter One probably indicates that he was silent about them because he knew that Will was not emotionally ready to attend to them and that the narrator is silent about them because at the time Will was repressing such knowledge from his consciousness. Both these "facts" are essential to an understanding of Will's subsequent behavior, both in the remainder of *The Last Gentleman* and in *The Second Coming* (1980), which treats a crisis in Will's life when he is about fifty. But the omission of any mention of his mother is immediately important for a discussion of the mental condition which led Will to seek analysis in the first place.

First, Dr. Gamow mentions Will's "fugue states." There are several amnesic flights from reality recalled in the brief history of Will that is provided. But no attention is paid to where the fugues lodge. The actual places—a bakery in Cincinnati, a greenhouse in Memphis, battlefields in the Shenandoah, battlefields in northern Virginia— are varied, but they suggest either generation or landscape; eventually the two aspects suggested coalesce into a paradisal image, epitomized as Central Park, in which Will lies thinking, when *The Last Gentleman* opens.

Second, Dr. Gamow mentions "defective ego structure," but without adducing any symptoms. Perhaps he refers to Will's frequent experience of *déjà vu*. Indeed, the earliest memory given for Will is his experience of a *déjà vu* "[a]s a child." Since no incitement for the *déjà vu* is given and since, considering Will's age, the range of possible incitements would be severely limited, it is tempting to attribute to this instance of *déjà vu* the maternal significance that Freud placed upon certain *déjà vus* (SE 5 399). In a subsequent memory the *déjà vu* is elicited by the Memphis greenhouse. And in yet another memory, at Princeton, "he was assaulted by stupefying *déjà vus*. An immense melancholy overtook him" (*LG* 14). Again, since no cause for the melancholy is offered, it is tempting to assign to this series of *déjà vus* the meaning of original melancholy offered by Rado:

> . . . drinking at the mother's breast remains the radiant image of unremitting, forgiving love. It is certainly no mere chance that the Madonna nursing the Child has become the emblem of a mighty religion and thereby the emblem of a whole epoch of our Western civilization. I think that if we trace the chain of ideas, *guilt—atonement—forgiveness*, back to the sequence of experiences of early infancy: *rage, hunger, drinking at the mother's breast*, we have the explanation of the problem why the hope of absolution and love is perhaps the most powerful conception which we meet with in the higher strata of the mental life of mankind.
>
> According to this argument, the deepest fixation-point in the melancholic (depressive) disposition is to be found in the "situation of threatened loss of love" (Freud [7]), more precisely, in the hunger-situation of the infant. (427)

The literature on *déjà vu* frequently notes that *déjà vu* experiences afflict children and adolescents, especially those weakened "by states of fatigue, stress, illness . . . , etc. (factors which presumably favor regression or the emergence of repressed material)" (Arlow 611).

The event of *déjà vu* itself is thought to occur when "[t]he ego does not want to be reminded of something that has been repressed, and the feeling of *déjà vu* consists of its being reminded of it against its will" (Fenichel, quoted in Arlow 613). Thus, in his "spells," Will would lose consciousness. In a sense, then, in its amnesic characteristic, the *déjà vu* is a stationary fugue.

Third, Dr. Gamow offers "ideas of reference," supporting this diagnosis with three symptoms, "hollow men, noxious particles, and ultimate truths." An explanation of "ultimate truths" will be developed later in this essay. The other two symptoms strongly suggest that Will suffers from alienation (as it is considered in psychoanalysis). Will's reference to "hollow men" argues that he is trying to convey his sense of depersonalization to Dr. Gamow, who obviously understands, for he suggests that Will join a group session, rather than abandon treatment completely, tempting Will by describing other members: "They are people like yourself who are having difficulty relating to other people in a meaningful way. Like yourself they find themselves in some phase or other of an identity crisis. There is—let me see—a novelist who is blocked, an engineer like yourself who works with digital computers and who feels somewhat depersonalized" (*LG* 39). Will's reference to "noxious particles" argues that he also suffers from the related condition of derealization. Both are considered to be defense mechanisms against the reality that the ego is forced to endure (Harrison "On Freud" 399). A full treatment of these and other "exceptional states" that Will later evinces may be found in Fliess (1973).

A fairly comprehensive description of Will's presenting behaviors has been established, but their ultimate cause has only been inferred. What must still be examined is the telescope, whose purchase annoys Dr. Gamow, who, however, apparently sees no psychological significance in it. The telescope points to the narrator's use of Freud's model of the telescope (Chapter 7 *Interpretation*) to structure and verbalize his story; the telescope also points to the subjective interference of fantasy in Will's actual visualization. But there is yet another significant role for the telescope, as "the transformational object"; for an explanation of this role Christopher Bollas' essay of that title must be introduced.

Following Winnicott, Bollas emphasizes the infant's absolute dependence upon the mother (or the mothering agent) for survival. Such is the closeness of the infant-mother relationship that the infant experiences the mother as "the environment," "less identifiable as an object than as a *process* that is identified with cumulative internal and external gratifications":

> As the mother integrates the infant's being (instinctual, cognitive, affective, environmental) the rhythms of this process, from unintegration(s) to integration(s), informs [sic] the nature of this "object" relation rather than the qualities of the object *qua* object. The mother is not yet identified as an object but is experienced as a process of transformation, and this feature remains in the trace of this object-seeking in adult life, where . . . the object is sought for its function as signifier of the process of transformation of being. Thus, in adult life, the quest is not to possess the object; it is sought in order to surrender to it as a process that alters the self, . . . (97)

Bollas notes the wide-ranging search "for an object that is identified with the metamorphosis of the self" (98), that is, an object that, it is hoped, will substitute for the lost original (transformational) object. This "is an object-seeking that recurrently enacts a pre-verbal ego memory" (98), for the original experience occurred before the infant was verbal. This concern with a process, rather than an object, explains Will's inability to visualize his mother and his compensatory search for transformational environments. Bollas notes the transformational efficacy that many people attribute to a divine power. He also notes that many people invest their faith in "a new job, a move to another country, a vacation, a change of relationship" as "both a request for a transformational experience and, at the same time, a continual 'relationship' to an object that signifies the experience of transformation" (98). One of his most interesting assertions is that such object-seeking must be a primary impulse to the aesthetic experience:

> It is usually on the occasion of what I have called the aesthetic moment (Bollas, 1978) when an individual feels a deep subjective rapport with an object—a painting, a poem, during an opera or symphony, before a landscape—that the person experiences an uncanny fusion with the object, an

event that recalls the kind of ego experience which constituted his earliest experiences. But such occasions, as meaningful as they might be, are less noteworthy as transformational accomplishments than they are for their uncanny quality: the sense of being reminded of something never cognitively apprehended, but existentially known, the memory of the ontogenetic process rather than thought or fantasies that occur once the self is established. That is, such aesthetic moments do not sponsor memories of a specific event or relationship, they evoke a total psychosomatic sense of fusion—an ego experience—that is the subject's recollection of the transformational object. This anticipation of being transformed by an object— itself an ego memory of the ontogenetic process—inspires the subject with a reverential attitude toward the object, so that, even as the transformation of the self will not take place on the scale it did during early life, the adult subject tends to nominate the object as sacred. (98–99)

The anticipation of a "psychosomatic sense of fusion" explains Will's "drawing the old Northern Pacific yin-yang symbol" (*LG* 108) in the dirt, as he waits for Kitty, his substitute mother object, to turn to him when they are secluded in a womb-like place in Central Park, the landscape which most deeply conveys the experience of fusion to him. The uncanniness that he feels toward the "melon immediacy" (*LG* 11) of her breasts then and that he feels toward "the fat rosy temple of Juno" later is also explained by Bollas' analysis of the aesthetic moment.[1]

After experiencing the fugue which caused him to be discharged from the army, Will engaged Dr. Gamow. Anyone in his right mind would do the same, but Will also has an unconscious reason: ". . . the search for the transformational object, in both the narcissistic and schizoid character, is in fact an internal recognition of the need for ego repair and, as such, is a somewhat manic search for health" (Bollas 101). Will's anticipation of the relief that he will receive from analysis can be expressed more precisely: ". . . the patient's identification with the analyst as the transformational object is not dissimilar to the infant's identification of the mother with such processes" (Bollas 102).

But such a regressional goal necessarily dictates the particularities of Will's analytic situation. Will's fascination with Dr. Gamow's voice and with the hummingbird prints can thus be explained:

189

. . . one of the features of such patients [i.e., manic searchers for health] is their comparative unavailability for relating to the actual other—their obtuseness or excessive withdrawness [sic]—but I think such characteristics, reflective of psychodevelopmental arrests, also point towards the patient's need to assert the region of illness as a plea for the arrival of the regressive object relation that is identified with basic ego repair. In analysis this can result in the patient's almost total inability to relate to the analyst as a real person, while at the same time maintaining an intense relation to the analyst as a transformational object. . . . such patients seek to live within a special ambience with the analyst, where the analyst's interpretations are far less important for their content, and more significant for what is experienced as a maternal sound—a kind of verbal humming. Indeed, so-called analytic neutrality of expression—ostensibly to mitigate the hysterical or obsessional patients' dread of feeling criticized and to facilitate the analysand's freedom of association—actually works in a different way for the narcissistic or schizoid patient; they become *enchanted* by it, and can appear oblivious to the actual content of the interpretation so long as the song of the analytic voice remains constant. (Bollas 101–2)

When Bollas describes one of his patients—

[h]e was convinced I knew how to take care of him, and even if it was only for an hour a day, he wanted me to soothe him. Analysis proper was regarded as an intellectual intrusion into his tranquil experience of me, and I was for him a kind of advanced computer storing his information, processing his needs into my memory banks, all this towards an eventual session when I would suddenly emerge with the proper solution for him and in an instant remedy his life. I have come to regard this part of his analysis as that kind of regression which is a re-enactment of the earliest object experience, and I think it is folly for a therapist to deny that the culture of the analytic space does not facilitate such recollections (Bollas 102)—

he is accounting for Will's response to Dr. Gamow's appearance: "Dr. Gamow put his knees exactly together, put his head to one side, and sighted down into the kneehole of his desk. He might have been examining a bank of instruments" (*LG* 34). The foregoing statement by Bollas also explains Will's abrupt declaration at the end of his penultimate session: "Look here now, this analysis is all very well but how about telling me the truth just between ourselves, off the record, that is, what am I *really* supposed to do?" (*LG* 38). It also explains Dr.

Gamow's expression of frustration: "It would be prĕtty nice if we could find a short cut and get around all this hard work" (*LG* 37). But Will possesses another attitude observed by Bollas:

> . . . the patient's regression is to the level of relating to the transformational object, that is, experiencing the analyst as the environment-mother, a pre-verbal memory that cannot be cognized into speech that recalls the experience, but only speech that demands its terms be met: unintrusiveness, "holding," "provision", insistence on a kind of symbiotic or telepathic knowing, facilitation from thought to thought, or from affect to thought, that means many of these sessions are in the form of *clarifications* which the patient experiences as transformative events. Interpretations which require reflective thought, or which analyse the self, are felt to be precocious demands on the patient's psychic capacity, and such patients may react with acute rage or express a sudden sense of futility. (103)

Will has talked, entertained, offered "trophies to put [Dr. Gamow] off the scent while the patient got clean away" (*LG* 32), but the realization that gradually dawns upon Dr. Gamow can be paraphrased by Bollas: ". . . in the analyses of such patients, psychic material was readily forthcoming and one could be relatively pleased that there was considerable grist for the analytic mill, but treatment often continued endlessly with no apparent character change, or was suddenly intruded upon by archaic or primitive material" (103). It is then that Dr. Gamow dances with Will "the strangest dance in history, each attuned to the other and awaiting his pleasure, and so off they went crabwise and nowhere at all" (*LG* 32–33). Meanwhile Will has reached a recurrent "sense of futility," so that he is susceptible to "archaic or primitive material," the fantasy of the telescope as transformative object.

The narrator now knows of himself at the time: "He did not know how not to give away nothing" (*LG* 32). What, apparently, Dr. Gamow did not know is stated by Bollas:

> In such cases I believe the analyst was unaware that the failure of the patient to experience the analytic situation as a regressive invitation was— if we will—a resistance; indeed, the analytic process, with premium on the mechanics of free association and interpretation of patient's defences, could often result in denial of the very object relation that was "offered" to the patient. If the analyst cannot acknowledge that in fact he is offering

a regressive space to the patient (that is, a space that encourages the patient to relive his infantile life in the transference), if he insists that in the face of the "invitation" *work* must be carried out, it is not surprising that in such analyses patient and analyst may either carry on in a kind of mutual dissociation that leads nowhere (obsessional collusion), or in a sudden blow up on the part of the patient, often termed "acting out." (103)

Bollas' "mutual dissociation that leads nowhere" is an apt paraphrase for "the strangest dance in history, . . ." The reason for Dr. Gamow's blindness probably results not from his ineptitude but from a glaring weakness that Bollas detects in the metapsychology that Dr. Gamow follows:

> . . . I believe that much of the time a patient's passivity, or wordlessness, or expectation that the analyst either knows what to do or should do something is not a resistance to any particular conscious or preconscious thought, but is a recollection of the early pre-verbal world of the infant being with the mother. Unless we recognize that psychoanalysts share in the construction of this pre-verbal world, through the analyst's silence, the total asbence of didactic instruction, and empathic thought, we are being unfair to the patient and they may have reason to be perplexed and irritated.
>
> I have taken this diversion into (hopefully) excusable oversimplification of clinical issues, in order to clarify my belief that the transference relation rests on the paradigm of the first-transformational-object relation. Freud tacitly recognized this when he set up the analytic space and process and, though, there is comparatively little about the mother-child relation within Freud's theory, we might say that Freud acted out his non-verbal and unconscious recognition of it in the creation of the analytic ecology. Indeed, the construction of psychoanalytic process rests itself on the memory of this primary relation, and the psychoanalyst's collective unconscious re-enactment (a professional counter-transference) is to recollect by enactment the transformational object situation. What Freud could not analyse in himself—his relation to his own mother—was acted out in his choice of the ecology of psychoanalytic technique. And unless we can grasp that as psychoanalysts we *are* enacting this early paradigm, we continue to act out in the countertransference Freud's one, and eminently excusable, area of blindness.[2] (103–4)

Thus Will, who has fled analysis before, to seek the landscape which promises the experience of fusion, now finding that Dr. Gamow cannot offer regression, attributes to the telescope all of the potentialities that he seeks in a transformational object:

> These lenses did not transmit light merely. They penetrated to the heart of things.
>
> The conviction grew upon him that his very life would be changed if he owned the telescope. (*LG* 29)

Then he has his last session with Dr. Gamow. The narrator now realizes that Will had unconsciously expected Dr. Gamow's treatment to be a transformational object, an "alma mater, sweet mother psychoanalysis" (*LG* 41), but that it had failed.

The new candidate for transformational efficacy seems to work splendidly at first. When Will sets up the telescope in Central Park, he catches sight of a woman holding a tabloid that announces ". . . parley fails" (*LG* 5). Will must take the sighting as a sign: parley, psychoanalytic parley, has failed him, but the telescope is already succeeding. The woman hides a note, so Will waits to see for whom the note is intended:

> His heart gave a leap. He fell in love, at first sight and at a distance of two thousand feet. It was not so much her good looks, her smooth brushed brow and firm round neck bowed so that two or three vertebrae surfaced in the soft flesh, as a certain bemused and dry-eyed expression in which he seemed to recognize—himself! She was a beautiful girl but she also slouched and was watchful and dry-eyed and musing like a thirteen-year-old boy. She was his better half. (*LG* 7–8)

Will immediately transfers his transformational desires from the telescope to the girl in the park who embodies basic unity. He pursues the girl, Kitty Vaught, throughout the remainder of *The Last Gentleman*. In the sequel, *The Second Coming*, the narrator reveals that Kitty had proved not to be the transformational object, for he had torn loose his "umbilical connection" (*LG* 352, 375) in going to New Mexico. Will became a successful lawyer and married a rich woman whom he did not love. Central Park became only a place where he took his dog to defecate. His secret life is captured by Bollas:

193

In adult life, therefore, to seek the transformational object is really to recollect an early object experience, to remember not cognitively, but existentially through intense affective experience, a relationship that was identified with cumulative transformational experiences of the self. Its intensity as an object relation is not due to the fact that the object was desired, but because the object is identified with such considerable metamorphoses of being. In the aesthetic moment, the subject briefly reexperiences through ego fusion with the aesthetic object, the sense of the subjective attitude towards the transformational object, but such experiences are only memories, not actual recreations. The search, however, for such symbolic equations of the transformational object and the experience with which it is identified continues in adult life. Man develops faith in a deity whose absence, ironically, is held to be as important a test of man's being as his presence. We go to the theatre, to the museum, to the landscapes of our choice, where we search for aesthetic experiences. We may *imagine* the self as the transformational facilitator, and we may invest ourselves with capacities to alter the environment that are not only impossible but downright embarrassing on reflexion. In such daydreams the self as transformational object lies somewhere in the future tense, and even ruminative planning about the future (what to do, where to go, etc.) however it may yield practical plans is often a kind of psychic prayer for the arrival of the transformational object: a secular second coming of an object relation experienced in the earliest life. (99)

Although Will's life seems to have been nearly dead, his haunting of golf courses, the Edenic landscape, asserts that he had not given up the fantasy. Then the dream comes true: he strays off the links, to meet Allie Huger, Kitty Vaught Huger's twenty-something daughter, to find love in the ruins of a greenhouse. His journey into her sacred landscape through a cave marks his successful regression to the womb and to a romantic object who satisfies his maternal needs and achieves Bollas' "secular second coming," as Percy's title suggests. Their sexual relationship offers Will a literal second coming, when Allie returns his lost (golf) balls. And during his ordeal in the cave he becomes convinced that God has manifested His presence (through a providential toothache), so that a divine second coming occurs. If *The Last Gentleman* was Percy's *Paradise Lost, The Second Coming* is certainly his *Paradise Regained.*[3]

Tom More's "Nobel Prize Complex"

In *Love in the Ruins* (1971), a Louisiana highway intersection orients the world mediated through Dr. Thomas More's consciousness. Tom's narration of immediate sensory data is presented for brief parts of two days. The first day is July 4, 1983, when Tom responds to his environment from 5 p.m. (*LR* 3) to a few minutes past 7 (*LR* 56), when he falls into a "catnap" (*LR* 58), and then when Tom wakes up at 7:15 to recount his experience at a golf tournament for perhaps two hours. The second day reveals selected moments of Tom's awareness of Christmas Eve, five years later (*LR* 379), from 9 a.m. until shortly after midnight mass.

By far, the bulk of the novel consists of Tom's dream, primarily of the events of the past four days, July 1 through July 4, and much less frequently of events that range all the way back to his childhood. Such a narrative structure forces the reader to attend not to a "public" reality, but to Tom's conscious and unconscious responses, the images of which are influenced much more by the psychological dynamics of his entire life than by his interpersonal involvement during the immediate past.[1]

Immediately after Tom begins to dictate what he sees, he says: "Either I am right and a catastrophe will occur, or it won't and I'm crazy" (*LR* 3). He does not really believe that he might be crazy. Thus he believes that a catastrophe will result from the misuse of his own invention, the lapsometer, a magical machine that can influence a person's thought. The word *influence* is deliberately introduced, for the properties that Tom alleges the lapsometer to have are the same properties that a certain type of disturbed person attributes to a mysterious machine which, he is convinced, influences, even controls his own behavior.[2]

Indeed, in his dream Tom recalls that the Devil, Art Immelmann—the Original Bad Influence—had used the machine on him on July 3, to stimulate Brodmann 11, the locus of the "musical-erotic" mindset, in which "the abstract is experienced concretely and the concrete abstractly" (*LR* 213). That is to say, concepts are experienced as percepts and percepts as concepts, without symbolic activity as mediation, thus eliminating the Cartesian split. Thus possessed by the Devil, Tom had been able to use his lapsometer to confound his detractors in the Pit by demonstrating that Mr. Ives was perfectly sane. But in the aftermath, the Devil had distributed dozens of lapsometers which were used to influence the audience of faculty and students to act demoniacally. Or to be alienated—for to experience the abstract concretely and the concrete abstractly would roughly approximate derealization and depersonalization, respectively, the chief symptoms of alienation as it is understood in psychotherapy.

The following day, Tom had influenced himself with a succession of lapsometric shots (*LR* 245, 386) before taking up his vigil in the "southwest cusp" of the interstate cloverleaf. Tom had intended the machine to be used to achieve universal tranquilization of spirit—surely at least a mild version of the "world savior" delusion. But the lapsometers taken by Immelmann promise universal "dystranquiliation"—hence Tom is now affected by a "world destruction" delusion.

The world will not be destroyed physically, but psychically. Demoniacally used, the lapsometer will "inflame and worsen the secret ills of the spirit and rive the very self from itself" (*LR* 5), complete the riving that begins in infancy. All the while failing to recognize that he is himself possessed, Tom envisions global possession, thinking that only he and three young women, Moira Schaffner, Lola Rhoades, and Ellen Oglethorpe, all of whom he has inoculated with his personal machine, are immune.

Tom can do nothing but wait, so that his comment ranges widely, from observation of specific detail to revelation of highly personal matters. He soon announces the hierarchy of values by which he lives: ". . . I love women best, music and science next, whiskey next, God fourth, and my fellowman hardly at all" (LR 6). The fact that he alternates sleeping with Moira and Lola—each of whom he sees as a love goddess, Moira as Aphrodite, Lola as Venus[3]—validates his statement that worship of women is his highest priority. His second ranking, music and science—as confirmed by his obsession with Don Giovanni (LR 138, 154, 165)—reveals his indebtedness to Kierkegaard for the concept "musical-erotic," for it was in Kierkegaard's analysis of Mozart's famous opera that the idea first appeared.[4] His first two rankings are not really discrete: his elevation of Woman/women very likely comes from his confusion about a woman; and his identification with Kierkegaard—whose philosophy of spirit/flesh rested on "the schism between the paternal and the maternal in his own origins" (Stern 223)—leads to his own obsession with a bifurcated reality.

Tom, like Binx Bolling, Will Barrett, and Lance Lamar, displays certain symptoms of Don Juanism, a syndrome arising "from a deeply-lying fear of impotence, which is in turn frequently traced to a heavily repressed mother-attachment" (Hunt 280). That Tom might harbor a fear of impotence is given additional credence by Tausk's assertion that the "influencing machine" is always "a symbol of the entire body conceived as a penis, and hence a representative of the pregenital epoch" (555), that is, the epoch of basic unity with the maternal object.

If Tom's invention and manipulation of the lapsometer is primarily an attempt to restore his world to a condition of basic unity, then his profession of indifference to his fellowman does not constitute a contradiction. While he may say and even think that he wishes to return the world to a Utopian condition for everyone, he is really driven by a highly personal motive. He reveals that he is still unconsciously drawn toward his sixty-something mother's loins: "She sits bolt upright, handsome legs crossed, nylon swishing against nylon, one hand pressed deep into her waist to emphasize her good figure" (*LR* 176). Indeed, her very name may echo his infant attempts to win her attention: "Marva." But Tom had had to seek in his romantic object what he had been denied by the crossed legs of his original object. Thus he married Doris, whose name evokes a goddess resident in the central locality of Doris in ancient Greece. Doris More's celebrity as the "Apple Queen of the Apple Blossom Festival" (*LR* 13) hints that Tom saw in her Eve, the original object mythologized: together they had lived in Paradise Estates, near the gold course, until the death of their daughter caused Doris to depart.

The highly personal nature of Tom's scientific quest also has a bearing on another of his quests, which he introduces just after announcing his hierarchy of values. He asks: "which prospect is more unpleasant, the destruction of the world, or that the destruction may come before my achievement is made known? The latter I must confess, because I keep imagining the scene in the Director's office the day the Nobel Prize is awarded" (*LR* 7). This is the Nobel Prize that he is sure he will win for his invention of the lapsometer, which, he is positive, will be made known to the world through the article that he plans to submit to the influential journal *Brain*.

Tom soon returns to his hierarchy of values: "My life is a longing, longings for women, for the Nobel Prize, for the hot bosky bite of bourbon whiskey, and other great heart-wrenching longings that have no name" (*LR* 23). Only this time his priorities sound more like symptoms of deprivation. His longing for women masks his longing for the first woman; his longing for the Nobel is his longing to give her a prize that will recapture her love. At that point, Tom searches the past for the answer to the present: "When I was a young man, the question at the time was: where are the Catholic Einsteins, Salks, Oppenheimers? And the answer came, at least from my family: well, here comes one, namely me." Since all these men have the stature equivalent to that of Nobel Prize winners, it is a fairly safe inference that Tom early became a potential victim of the Nobel Prize Complex.

Dr. Helen H. Tartakoff was the identifier of this "new nosological entity," in her paper "The Normal Personality in Our Culture and the Nobel Prize Complex." But it was Dr. Michael A. Sperber who amply confirmed her findings and theories in two valuable papers, "Freud, Tausk, and the Nobel Prize Complex" and "Symbiotic Psychosis and the Need for Fame." From these three papers a psychological profile may be drawn. The afflicted person is likely to be a male, often the first-born and frequently the only child. Such a situation fosters a precocious ego development that often contains two abiding fantasies, (1) an active, omnipotent, grandiose conviction of being the "powerful one," and (2) a passive confidence in being destined to be the "special one." The maturing male does not appear aberrant: such are the values of our society that a single-minded, mechanistic, *driven* person is admired as the Toyota of life's freeway. The trouble begins with the experience of failure and frustration. The male has not been able to resolve his Oedipal conflict, nor has he been able to accept subsequent social restraints to his desire. Thus when—typically in middle age—he is denied what he thinks is his rightful recognition or is stymied in his projects or is stunned by the loss of a romantic object whom he had not valued, but upon whom he now realizes he had depended, he often develops psychosomatic symptoms, experiences depression, and threatens or even commits suicide. If he seeks psychological treatment, he unconsciously expects it to be not a working-through to adjustment but a magic cure which will reinforce his self-image and restore him to the omnipotent position that he had held in the symbiosis with his mother. The "Nobel Prize Complex" seems to be one form of what Sydney Smith identifies as "the Golden Fantasy," "a regressive reaction to separation anxiety."

It is useful to evaluate Tom's recollection of his life against this "complex"/fantasy, for such a contrast helps us see him not as he sees himself—as a "special case"—but as a "typical case." If we accept Tom's early contention that he is a "genius" (*LR* 11), we may be persuaded to accept "the ideology of genius" which argues that "*humanity needs genius to rescue it from alienation*" (Currie 9). But if we see that, for all his talk about his singularity, Tom is still one of a type, then we can be more dispassionate about him. Like the rest of the human race Tom is alienated from the time that his mother gave him language which gave him consciousness of separateness.

Thus, beneath Tom's announced program for perfecting the entire human race lies his pursuit of a singularly personal program

199

for retrieving the perfect mother-figure and vanquishing the intrusive father-figure. Apparently an only child, Tom had been reared to great expectations in a milieu of a strong mother and a weak father. He had become a psychiatrist, married Doris, and moved to Paradise Estates; at the age of twenty-six (*LR* 23) he had "stumbled onto an extraordinary medical discovery" (*LR* 24), "More's Paradoxical Sodium Radiation Syndrome" (*LR* 26), first published in *J.A.M.A.* (*LR* 27) and then immortalized in the appropriate textbooks (*LR* 26).[5]

But then Tom had gone into "twenty years of silence and decline" (*LR* 24), which culminated in the death of his daughter and then the defection and subsequent death of his wife. His life appeared but a repetition of his physician father's life of drunkenness (*LR* 22) and longing (*LR* 21).[6] In such a state Tom experiences "simultaneous depression and exaltation" (*LR* 90). As a result of an exaltation he conceives of his theory of lapsometric diagnosis (*LR* 90) and writes up his explanation for the scientific world. That same night, Christmas Eve, he copulates with Lola on a golf course (*LR* 83), thus unconsciously acting out his desire to return to the original object, whispering "Doris" (*LR* 95) in Lola's ear, though fortunately he is inaudible. After wandering on "18 fairway" he returns to "lie at Lola's breast, a blind babe" (*LR* 96), before making love to her again.[7] His description of himself as a blind babe at breast suggests that his motive is more pregenital than genital. His inaudibility and blindness are the result of anaphylactic shock caused by consuming albumen, to which he is allergic. His frequent erection may be caused by priapism, for after the second set-to Lola has to save his life, according to his ambiguous description: "She could have gone, left me to die in the bunker, swell up and die and be found stiff as a poker in the foggy dew" (*LR* 96). Having conceived of an influencing machine, which, according to Tausk is "a symbol of the entire body conceived as a penis, and hence a representative of the pregenital epoch," Tom is suitably influenced by its symbolism. But epinephrine restores his fall-ability; at home he suffers depression, following the "Nobel Prize Complex" profile, though his is probably post-coital, for he attempts suicide by cutting his wrists. Then he has sense enough to commit himself to an asylum (*LR* 97).

Soon after checking himself in, Tom grandly imagines the global impact that the lapsometer could have. He therefore leaves the hospital, although he is never officially discharged, to work feverishly to get the lapsometer into production. Six months later, when he applies to the Director for support of his draft article and of his request for a twenty-five million dollar grant (*LR* 203) from N.I.M.H., the Director—himself a Nobel laureate for his experiments with the Skinner box—thinks Tom's proposals so far-fetched that he urges Tom to acknowledge his insanity by returning to his ward. Thus spurned, Tom has a powerful motive for proving the Director wrong about both his condition and his contribution, to transcend the Director's work with work that will also win a Nobel Prize, to dream of the Director's public acknowledgement of Tom's superiority—in other words to get down and Oedipal with him.

The competition in the Pit—aptly named—over which the Director presides, will offer Tom his opportunity. On his way to the Pit, Tom allows Art to influence him with the lapsometer (*LR* 212). As the source of the magical activities of the machine, Art has the same symbolic value as it does, evoking Tom's yearning for "the pregenital epoch." As if aware that he is symbolic, Art never thereafter misses an opportunity to tell Tom that he will certainly win the Nobel Prize. The message is first conveyed through Ellen: "He also said to tell you . . . that he's been in touch with the Nobel Prize committee in Stockholm . . ." (*LR* 320). Later, when Tom sees him, "Art waves cheerily": "Don't worry about a thing, Doc! . . . Don't worry about the Nobel Prize either. You're in" (*LR* 329). With such seduction, Tom may be pardoned for beginning to dream of his "second Nobel" (*LR* 339).

In the Pit, Tom achieves a great victory, for he demonstrates that Dr. Buddy Brown, using the theories of behaviorism, has completely erred in diagnosing the patient, Mr. Ives. Since both the Director and the other Nobel laureate on the staff, Dr. Kenneth Stryker, are behaviorists, Tom's demonstration discredits their professional position. Indeed, influenced by Art's lapsometer, both the Director and Dr. Stryker lose their scientific detachment as they pursue their own psychosexual needs. But Tom misses the point that Mr. Ives illustrates: Mr. Ives has located intersubjectivity in symbolism, the Delta phenomenon, by which one subject communicates with another subject through the mediating sign. Tom is still wedded to his idea that consciousness is amenable to technology, when he should see all around him in the Pit the demonism unleashed when human relationship is not grounded in words. Instead, his behavior has to be moderated by a sedative injected by Max Gottleib (*LR* 242), and he is put to bed by his nurse, Ellen, who seems always to be, in Tom's words, "wet[ting] her thumb with her tongue and smooth[ing] my eyebrows with firm smoothings like a mother" (*LR* 155, 325, 377).

The next day, July 4, appropriately enough, is the day that Tom expects to reunite the United States with technology. As the day progresses, he is on a manic roll, bemused by memories of primal Doris, protecting Paradise Estates with Colonel Ringo (*LR* 281), bringing about his own symbolic rebirth out of the church (*LR* 307), "feet-first born again" (*LR* 311), sleeping first with Moira (*LR* 259) and then with Lola (*LR* 338), his priapism once again stoked by Ramos gin fizzes, his cheek once "again against the warm slump of her biceps" (*LR* 339). Both professionally and psychosexually, he seems to have unity in his grasp. But then the news turns bad, and he can only retreat to the cloverleaf to await the cataclysm by going to sleep.

But when he awakens, Tom discovers that nothing remarkable has happened. The golf course to which he staggers is not the paradise of which he had dreamed, but more like the inferno, with the Devil fanning the flames. Indeed, Art is now determined to drag Tom to his lair, "Denmark" (*LR* 375). When Tom asks, "Why Denmark?" Art replies: "Number one, it is my home base. Number two, it is close to the Nobel Prize committee. Number three, it is the vanguard of civilization. Number four, I can get you a job there." Momentarily tempted, Tom asks, "What kind of a job?" Replies the Devil, "Of course after the Nobel you can write your own ticket. Meanwhile you've been offered the position of chief encephalographer at the Royal University."

Just to make sure of his conquest, Art administers a booster shot to Tom's musical erotic locus, reinforcing Tom's nostalgia for the merging of sensation with cognition, that is to say, basic unity, that is to say, mother, even as Tom is once more being tempted to seek the Nobel Prize, whose attainment would finally please Marva. Understandably Tom watches Art "dreamily" (*LR* 375). At that point Ellen offers a mother's sacrifice, to go to Denmark in Tom's place. Such a maternal gesture spurs Tom to action, as he prays to his patron saint, Sir Thomas More, to banish Art. As the Devil "disappears into the smoke" (*LR* 377), Ellen triumphantly moistens her thumb, smooths Tom's eyebrows, and takes him home for good.

Five years later, on Christmas Eve: If Tom remembers his dichotomy of five years past, he would have to conclude that since the catastrophe did not occur, then he had been crazy. Now he is married to Ellen and is the father of two children. Although he is poor, he is happy. He is still trying to perfect the lapsometer, though he sees it only as a diagnostic flashlight, not as a metaphysical welding torch. Rather, having returned to the church, he finds unity in the Incarnation, as it is memorialized in the Mass. Restored to modesty, he seeks answers, not fame: "What I want is no longer the Nobel, screw prizes, but just to figure out what I've hit on" (*LR* 383). He no longer suffers from the Nobel Prize Complex, from the compulsion so to please the mother that she will offer him basic unity. He accepts the exile that language imposes on the human, but he has learned of the consolation of the other that language bestows on us. Thus his goal on Christmas Eve is not love on the eighteenth hole with a goddess, but Holy Communion and then with a mate-who-can-mother in a new king-size Sears Best, surely the best of all earthly repetitions.

Moviemaking
in *Lancelot*

In 1976[1] as he recalls the previous year for Father John, Lancelot Lamar pictures a world dominated by moviemaking. His Louisiana estate, Belle Isle, had been invaded by his "wife's friend's film company" (*L* 25), to make a movie "about some people who seek shelter in the great house during a hurricane, a young Cajun trapper, a black sharecropper, a white sharecropper, a Christlike hippy, a Klan type, a beautiful halfcaste but also half-wit swamp girl, a degenerate river rat, and the son and daughter of the house . . ." (*L* 25–26). Absent from the cast of what would have been the worst Southern movie of all times is the drunken owner of the great house, Lipscomb: that much of the movie parallels life.

On a certain day, during a test of the "thunderstorm machine" (*L* 27), a drinking Lance discovers that he had not sired his wife's six-year-old daughter and conjectures that his wife's friend, Robert Merlin, had (*L* 32). In that moment Lance becomes rather more interested in the activities of the film company, which takes its meals at Belle Isle and its lodging at the Holiday Inn. At supper that night he realizes that he is held in contempt by the company (*L* 50–51); sober at night for the first time in years, he waits up for his wife to return from viewing "the week's rushes" (*L* 86) at the Holiday. When she does not return until the next morning, he plans to have the after-hours activities of the company watched by Elgin, his faithful retainer (L 97).

At supper that night Lance notes that Margot is sexually attracted to Janos Jacoby (*L* 110), who seems to be the actual director of the movie. In his recital to Father John, Lance asserts that he had scorned Jacoby's talk about "cinematographic language," "the semiotics of film," "Griffith as master of denotative language," and "Metz as the only critic who understands the connotative film" (*L* 110–11). Presumably Jacoby had been reading the just translated *Film Language*, which contains such locutions. Nevertheless, Lance admits that he had wanted to be noticed by Jacoby, to impress him (*L* 114). That may be, but it may also be that Lance had envied Jacoby's role as director, as one who creates a world. For when Elgin reports the next morning, Monday, that Margot had spent over two hours in Jacoby's room (*L* 124–25), Lance immediately announces that he will make a "cinéma vérité" (*L* 128). His plot (in both senses of the word) requires that the film company sleep (in both senses of the word) at Belle Isle, with each bedroom to be monitored by a TV system installed by Elgin on Wednesday and Thursday (*L* 144).

It seems that Lance had read *Film Language* as well, particularly the essay "Mirror Construction in Fellini's *8½*," for he uses an idea from Metz to catch the Metz-quoter. In the essay Fellini's movie is placed in the category of self-referential artworks, "the category of works of art that are divided and doubled, thus reflecting on themselves" (Metz 228). Lance thus decides to make a "home movie" that reveals what the professional moviemakers would want to conceal. Metz terms such a structure "*construction en abŷme*" (literally, "inescutcheon construction"), that is, as the translator explains, the placing in the center of a large heraldic shield a smaller shield which reproduces it in every detail. Lance hints that his movie is related to the other movie. When he first sends Elgin to spy on the film company, he notes that Elgin is wearing "his guide jacket with the Belle Isle coat of arms on the breast pocket" (*L* 91). When Elgin brings the videotapes of the "little film company resting from their labors" Elgin is reminded to put on his "tour-guide coat" (*L* 180). The small shield has been put on the large one.

On Thursday night Elgin had activated his system. Having gone this far, though, Lance seems to have had second thoughts, for on Friday morning—before seeing "the rushes"—Lance asks Margot to leave with him, before a real hurricane, not the movie version, strikes. She replies that she cannot leave, for she and Jacoby are to write a screen treatment of *A Doll's House*, a movie which she will finance and Jacoby direct and in which she will play Nora. At the same time, she parrots Jacoby: "Jan's theory is that by the very nature of the medium cinema should have nothing to do with ideas. The meaning of a film derives from the narrative itself. Narrative and person are everything" (*L* 173). Jacoby's avowal of Metzian theory is as phony as his name probably is, for he depends upon a trendy liberal allegory to assign meaning to each character (for example, the sadistic southern sheriff with homosexual tendencies) in his incoherent narrative. Using Jacoby's theory against him, Lance plans to catch him in the very narrative.

Spurned both as a husband and as a layman, Lance spends "FRIDAY AFTERNOON AT THE MOVIES" (*L* 185–92). What he sees is the copulation of Margot and Jacoby and an orgy in which Troy Dana and Raine Robinette, two other members of the film company, consort with his daughter Lucy. That the scenes occur *flagrante delicto* is confirmed by Lance's many references to the redness of the scenes (*L* 185, 186, 191). Later that night he murders Jacoby and causes an explosion in which Margot, Troy, and Raine are killed. In effect, Lance proves himself a better actor than any of the others, for he actually leaps from spectatorship into participation in his movie, killing Jacoby beside Margot's bed. And, too, he proves a better director than Jacoby, for—leaving Jacoby on the cutting room floor—he completes his "cinéma vérité" (which becomes very vérité), whereas Jacoby will never finish his movie—even if he had survived, his "Christlike hippy," "beautiful half-caste but . . . ," and Sarah the liberated librarian are on location elsewhere.

There are yet a third and fourth movie to be viewed in the novel—the entire novel. It is a commonplace of film criticism to say that a certain kind of movie is an attempt to make visible the thinking process of an individual. Lance decides to make a narration that is like such a movie. From the narrow window of his room in the hospital can be seen what used to be the old Majestic Theater (life before the Fall), in which he and his visitor (then Harry Percy) had seen such innocent movies as *The 49ers* (*L* 22) in their youthful past. Now the theater is Adult Cinema 16, showing *The 69ers*. Lance thus chooses movies as the model of the psychic apparatus. The Sodomic nature of the contemporary consciousness is illustrated for Lance by such sexual perversions as that implied by the title now showing. The hatred that Lance reveals toward the film people with whom Margot had become so infatuated must derive from his belief that they as moviemakers are responsible for the world of *The 69ers*. Since all the world's a dirty movie, he will construct his narration *à la cinéma*, using the film technique of montage, rather than writing, for transition from scene to scene.

Thus his "movie" (narration) is structured as a series of scenes toward (it has to be said) the climax, when his "home movie" links art and reality, the copulating actors of *The 69ers* with those of the film company. Lance takes care to repeat his conceit that his narration is a "movie." When Elgin starts to leave, after bringing him the videotapes, Lance tells him to wait: "He stood in the doorway, freeze-framed, waiting for me to push a button and set him going" (*L* 180). And when Lance describes the scene in which he murders Jacoby, after art has become reality; he says that the room was lighted every "eight or ten seconds" (*L* 237), by lightning, each stroke "a short bright burst like a camera flashbulb" (*L* 238).

It is should be added that Lance has, in his "movie" narration, used Metz's *"construction en abŷme"* almost into infinity: the behavior depicted in the "movie" narration is like the behavior presented in *The 69ers*, which is like the behavior of the "home movie," which is like (no, *is*) the behavior of the film company. Technique has held the mirror up to nature.

There is yet another "movie" in the narration, the making of which Lance is unaware. What is not so commonplace is to say that the thinking process of the human being is like the cinematographical apparatus, that "mind screen" is like film screen. But it has been done, brilliantly, in Ernst Kretschmer's *Textbook of Medical Psy-*

chology. When Kretchmer's thesis is applied to the images of Lance's narration, they become a "movie" about a mind sinking into schizophrenia.[2]

Kretschmer's basic argument is that "underneath the psychic imagery of civilized man and behind the predominant modern psychological mechanisms we can observe other types of psychic functions" (Kretschmer 85). Sharing common characteristics and probably phylogenetically regressive, these psychic functions include dreams, hypnosis, hysterical twilight-states, and schizophrenic thinking. At times these "hyponoic mechanisms" (or "under thoughts") intrude into ordinary thinking.

What is most striking about the most elementary of these mechanisms, dreaming and hypnosis, is their intense visuality. No doubt everyone has felt the impact of an especially vivid dream; Kretschmer builds upon such an experience to describe the hypnotic state:

> If we direct the attention of the hypnotized person whose eyes are closed to what is taking place in his visual field, . . . as hypnosis deepens, he frequently becomes aware of unformed coloured or black-and-white materials, blotches, veils, lines, silhouettes, lattices, rings, &c. . . . This brief and relatively amorphous stage is followed by one of "visualized thought", . . . In it there is a retranslation of the abstract ordered flow of thought into pictorial imaginal series. The psychic apparatus is set to work again at a lower level where it can only deliver sensory images and can no longer produce higher abstract syntheses. What the hypnotized person ordinarily thinks is now experienced imaginally; episodes from his past life are actually relived in orderly scenes which correspond with his memory of the events. The psychic experience is reeled off before him like a cinema film. The experience is passive as in a dream; he retains the feelings of being a spectator. (Kretschmer 97)

In a second stage of hypnosis, "the still fairly orderly 'thinking in picture strips' becomes more and more asyntactical and gives way to a stage of bizarre experiences of fantastic forms and colours which no longer exhibit a directly intelligible or logical character" (Kretschmer 98).

Kretschmer then discusses "the usual course of an hysterical twilight-state": "A nervous, affectively labile person has an experience which violently upsets his emotional equilibrium, e.g. the breaking off of an engagement of marriage, sexual infidelity, rape, bitter family 'scenes', severe fright, escape from death, &c. Directly following such an experience or possibly some time after, he falls into a twilight state which lasts for minutes, hours, or days, is of sudden onset and equally suddenly gives way to normal consciousness" (98).

Such states are distinguished from dreams by being more violent and dramatic; unlike the passive dreamer, the hysteric feels a striking immediacy: "Thus, the hysterical twilight-state often represents nothing more than a living picture, a dramatic scene in which the events are as it were cinematographically replayed, each time with grotesquely exaggerated affective expression" (Kretschmer 98).

Such twilight-states also have the two-stage mechanism: "The imaginal processes closely approximate to those occurring in dream and hypnosis. They either unwind scenically in orderly pictorial series in natural time and place sequence, or with increasing regression they are split up into catathymic imaginal agglutinations in which symbolization, condensation, displacement, and substitution play their part as in dreams" (Kretschmer 99). But the difference is, that with the hysteric the images "are far more frequently projected into the outside world and perceived with hallucinatory vividness" (Kretschmer 99).

As Kretschmer explains, schizophrenic thinking is even more complicated: ". . . the imaginal processes are often broken up in such a regressive way that not only isolated mechanisms but large cohesive features of the primitive world-pictures are made to live again before our eyes, although the primitive mechanisms are complicated by the interference of great complexes of developed cultural thought which remain in the picture" (100–101). Thus the schizophrenic may speak "brilliantly" for shorter or longer periods before regressing to fantastic imaginings.

Kretschmer was one of the first psychologists to assert that genuine expressionistic painting opens a window on the "hyponoic mechanism":

Anyone who has studied expressionistic pictures knows that condensation and symbolism play a predominant role in that form of art. Attention should also be directed to the strong formalist tendencies, here called Cubism, which crop at the same time and again reveal a part of the primitive world-picture. The tendency to approximate the outlines of concrete objects to geometrical figures, squares, triangles, circles, or to split objects up into such figures, or to reject forms and express sensations and ideas only in lines, curves, and spots with the help of strong colour effects, is widely met with in expressionistic art and in the analogous productions of schizophrenics. (103–4)

Kretschmer stresses the fact, though, that such reduction to the geometrical is not restricted to concrete objects: ". . . we find this tendency towards naked stylization (i.e. to bare schematization almost devoid of real form) at the higher levels of apperceptive thought in the works of schizophrenic and schizoid philosophers, . . . Rigid, mechanical thought-patterns are imposed athwart the rich diversity of the world of reality; and the final product of such abstractions which are poor in real imagery is then readily fitted into a written or printed schema exhibiting optical symmetry" (106). Thus Kretschmer has traced the earlier forms of the "hyponoic mechanism" to reach schizophrenia: ". . . in the case of schizothymes we find, on the other hand, a symbolical, completely mystical and irrational view of the world, and on the other hand, a dry and exact, strictly logical and systematized philosophy of life. In schizothymic thought (this applies both to the insane catatonic person and to great schizothymic philosophers) these two contrasted forms cut across each other and combine in the most amazing way" (110).

Any discussion of *Lancelot* must consider the layering of time, that is, the intrusion of the "hyponoic mechanisms" into Lance's consciousness of the present. Having been isolated for an indeterminate period of time, Lance now speaks to someone who does not audibly respond. (I) From time to time, Lance notes the present, which takes place during five days, Monday through Friday, November 1–5, in a Center for Aberrant Behavior, in New Orleans, most likely in 1977 ("Perpetual Calendar" 472). (II) Lance spends most of his time describing the few days of the previous year, most likely 1976 (*L* 157, 200), when he had made his home movie. Since his auditor, Father John, had been a very close friend until after college, Lance also refers to more distant past times with which Father John would already be somewhat familiar.

210

(III) There is a past that is paradisiac: Lance recalls the legendary exploits of his male ancestors and remembers in vivid detail the blissful moments of his first marriage, to Lucy Cobb, and of his second marriage, to Margot Reilly. (IV) There is also a past that is antiparadisiac: Lance recalls discovering that his father was a bribe taker and constructs a story that his mother had committed adultery, with the tacit acknowledgement of his father.

(V) And there is, finally, an intrauterine past that Lance fantasizes. The clue to this layer of past time is a dream that on Tuesday, November 2, Lance recalls having had "the other night" and cannot forget (*L* 36):

> It was not about Belle Isle or my past life at all but about my *future* life. I'm sure of it. I was living in an abandoned house in a desert place, a ghost town which looked like one of those outlying Los Angeles neighborhoods Raymond Chandler describes.
>
> I was in a room and strangely immobilized. I don't know why but I could not move. Outside there were trees and other houses and cars but nothing moved. There was perfect quiet. Yet I was not alone in the house. There was someone else in the next room. A woman. There was the unmistakable sense of her presence. How did I know it was a woman? I cannot tell you except that I knew. Perhaps it was the way she moved around the room. Do you know the way a woman moves around a room whether she is cleaning it or just passing time? It is different from the way a man moves. She is at home in a room. The room is an extension of her.
>
> She came out of the house. We were having a picnic, sitting on the tailgate of a truck. It was not the desert now. The land plunged almost straight down into the blue ocean. A breeze had sprung up and there was a tinkle of wind chimes. We had been working hard and were very hungry. We ate in silence, looking at each other. There was much to be done. We were making a new life. It was not the Old West and there was no frontier but we were making a new life, starting from scratch. There was no thought of "romance" or "sex" but only of making a new life. We knew what we were doing. (*L* 35–36)

The first full paragraph argues that Lance is recalling a womb dream: the enclosing room is an extension of a woman. The second paragraph—with an appropriate reversal, "She came out of the house"—is a scene of basic unity, symbolized by the first nursing: "We had been working hard and were very hungry. We ate in silence, looking at each other. . . . We were making a new life . . . starting from scratch. There was no thought of 'romance' or 'sex' but only of making a new life. We knew what we were doing." That recurrent mutual pronoun, that silent eating and looking, that conviction of shared consciousness! When the theme of the ancestral estate is remembered, Belle Isle—the fetus surrounded by water—an argument is tenable that Lance's actions leading up to the explosion, (II), amount to a regression through the house-mother back to the room-womb, in which the preOedipal mother is recaptured and the intruding Oedipal father is dismembered. If this interpretation is plausible, unless there is evidence that Lance undergoes a radical change in the succeeding three days, then there is no question but that he is profoundly mentally disturbed when last we see him on November 5.

All the layers constitute a narration which is divided into at least fifty dissociated segments, ranging from less than five minutes to an hour in lapsed time, with indeterminate gaps of silence between. Lance loses no time in getting to his story. He had been reading a Raymond Chandler novel, an act Percyites recognize as an extreme form of alienation.[3] But it is also extremely appropriate here, for his idealistic tradition has made Lance conceive of consciousness as a private eye (private I). As he describes that past scene, Lance had reacted like

> . . . a scientist, an astronomer say, who routinely examines photographic plates of sectors of the heavens and sees the usual random scattering of dots of light. He is about to file away one such plate, has already done so, when a tiny little something clicks in his head. *Hold on. Hm. Whoa. What's this? Something is wrong. Let's have a look.* So he takes another look. Yes, sure enough, one dot, not even a bright dot, one of the lesser dots, is a bit out of place. You've seen the photos in the newspapers, random star dots and four arrows pointing to a single dot. To make sure, the astronomer compares this plate with the last he took of the same tiny sector of the heavens. Sure enough, the dot is out of place. It has moved. What of it, thinks the layman, one insignificant dot out of a billion dots slightly out of place? The astronomer knows better: the dot is one millisecond out of place, click click goes the computer, and from the most insignificant observation the astronomer calculates with absolute certainty and finality

that a comet is on a collision course with the earth and will arrive in two and a half months. In eight weeks the dot will have grown to the size of the sun, the oceans risen forty feet, New York will be under water, sky-scrapers toppling, U.N. meeting on Mount Washington, etc. (*L* 19)

Lance's simile is significant for several reasons. For one thing, although he is dealing with a most human phenomenon, infidelity, he thinks of himself as a scientist, that modern form of Platonist: thus he is already imagining the type Woman, not Margot, his wife. Second, there is a direct line between discovery and world destruction, from cool detachment to the *Weltuntergang* fantasy found in schizo-phrenia. Third, it is certainly a strained and excessive comparison, to say that one sexual act is like the end of the world—a psychic vio-lence is hidden beneath the apparently disinterested behavior. The equation is true only in the sense that a discovery means the end of Lance's world—this could be an instance of a cryptic truth hiding in an extravagant, "schizophrenic" statement.[4] Finally, Lance later mentions that his father was a star watcher (*L* 56) and a cuckold (*L* 96)—regression has already become one thread of Lance's con-sciousness. He will dwell in the past, but he seems determined not to repeat it.

The time of discovery was 5:01 p.m., as Lance says three times (*L* 18, 19, 26), implying by such specifics just how sane he was then and is now. But is it literally twilight time, and he has just had one of the experiences that Kretschmer instances as a cause of the "hysteri-cal twilight-state." Thus every effort by Lance to establish his equa-nimity is undercut by some slip. There is, for example, a persistent attempt to substitute a letter or a number for a word or group of words; Lance seems to recognize that words link humans together, enable two people to share a world. Thus he reduces the entire act of infidelity to the letter O (*L* 20, 21, 27, 29, 30); but it is not beyond conjecture that the O does not conceal the act, but rather suggests other, more violent images. An O is close to ♀, as Lance must ac-knowledge, when he uses the latter symbol (*L* 129); an O is a hole, which is what Lance comes to believe all women are; an O becomes part of the geometric figures that hide a human in the second after-noon movie (*L* 192); and an "Oh" is what Raine becomes when

Lance prepares to sodomize her (*L* 235)—an O is the hole out of which the whole world leaks. No longer does "$♀ = ∝$" (*L* 129).[5]

Having imagined himself as one who looks, Lance uses the theme of visual detection to give momentum to his story; having shut his mind to the rich diversity of ordinary experience, to think exclusively about his wife's infidelity, which occurred over seven years before, he becomes the moviegoer whom Kretschmer describes. Later Lance returns to the astronomer image, when he alludes to the Michelson-Morley experiment that only Einstein understood (*L* 42). By which he means that while he has proved Margot a whore by deduction (after all, he found the proof in "a manila folder neatly lettered "DEDUCTIONS, 1968" [*L* 31], he nevertheless wants "ocular proof" to convince him that the bell-shaped curve (*L* 33) has not thrown him one—his allusions to *Othello* in his later narration may hint that he now knows just how obsessed he had been at the time.

Scientific proof—replication of the series—will be provided by his experiment, the "home movie." When Elgin delivers the tape, he tells Lance that there is a great deal of distortion in the images, but it becomes clear that there is distortion on the "mind screen," as well as on the TV screen. "FIRST FEATURE: MISS MARGOT'S ROOM" begins: "The figures, tiny figurines, were reddish, like people in a film darkroom, and seemed to meet, merge, and flow through each other. Lights and darks were reversed like a negative, mouths opened on light, eyes were white sockets. The actors looked naked clothed, clothed naked. The figures seemed to be blown in an electronic wind. Bodies bent, pieces blew off. Hair danced atop heads like a candle flame" (*L* 185–86). Lance's visual consciousness is responding to full schizophrenic distortion. And the audio is no better than the video: "The voices were scratchy and seemed to come not from the room but from the sky like the blackbirds rattling and rising and falling. When they turned, their voices went away. Half sentences blew away like their bodies" (*L* 186). Speaking of "voices" as a classic schizophrenic does, Lance experiences language as a truncated medium.

Unable to accept Margot and Merlin as humans, Lance sees them as stick figures, describing their embrace as a Y (*L* 186). There follows a lengthy conversation between them which is nearly inaudible. But

Lance thinks that he hears the words "fucking triangle" and is prompted to "approximate," as Kretschmer would say, the human figures to a geometric figure:

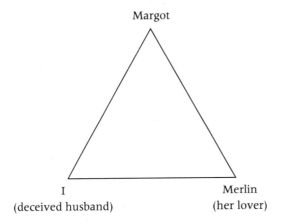

I see they are not talking about me at all, that it is a different triangle:

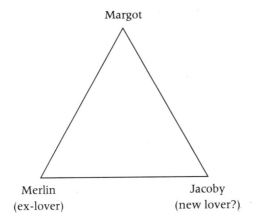

Since the thought of Jacoby has occurred, it is appropriate that he appear: "Another figure materializes (they don't seem to use doors). It is Jacoby" (*L* 189). He and Margot also make a Y (*L* 190), but soon an H and then the O that lurks in Margot's name:

> They dress, putting dark on light. No, it is undressing, for dark is light and light is dark. They are shedding light clothes for dark skin.

215

They approach each other. Sections of their bodies detach and fly off. Other sections extend pseudopods.

They turn, their hair blowing sideways in an electronic wind. There are two sockets of light on Margot's back. They are, I recognize, the two dimples on either side of her sacrum.

Margot lies across the bed and pulls him onto her. He is gazing down at her. Her head comes off the bed and bends back until her face is looking upside down at the camera. Her eyes close on light, but her mouth opens letting out light.

Still there is no conversation but presently a voice says, at first I think from my room or even from the sky with the blackbirds: *Oh oh oh ah ah aaah, oh my Jesus oh ah ah sh-sh-sh-* (*L* 190)

Kretschmer's comments are particularly helpful at this point, for Lance is never more the spectator reliving a picture-strip series. The repetition of "They" for the first three paragraphs emphasizes the ordered sequence of shots and contrasts beautifully with the reversed, erratic, and blotchy images within each frame.

Lance then provides an "INTERMISSION" (*L* 190), remembering that he had gone outside, apparently for respite. If all the distortion of the videotape were mechanical, then unfiltered consciousness should not occur. The memory is so vivid that Lance has been using the present tense throughout: "I sit on my porch and watch the blackbirds rising and settling and the clouds hurrying toward the hurricane like latecomers to the kickoff" (*L* 191). He is attempting to describe a consciousness at rest, simply capable of making such picturesque patter as would grace *Readers Digest*. What he does reveal is a mind so shaken that it can only deal with exteriority as a frieze of geometric figures:

The clouds straighten out and form a line. The sky becomes flat and yellow. The view from the porch is very simple. There are six parallel horizontal lines, the bottom rail of the iron fence, the top rail, the near edge of the River Road, the far edge, the top of the levee, the straight bottom line of the clouds. There are many short vertical lines, the iron spikes of the fence. There is a single oblique line, a gravel road leading from the River Road over the levee. Atop the levee are the triangles of the bonfires. The slanting boom of a ship intersects with the triangle of the bonfires, making trapezoids and smaller triangles. (*L* 191)

216

The orderliness implied by the succession of "There" sentences is undercut by the concluding repetition of "triangles," so recently imagined as a substitute for the figures on the bed.

Then Lance describes the "SECOND FEATURE: MISS RAINE'S ROOM" (*L* 191). The content of this "movie" makes clear what he sees when he looks out his narrow window to the theater showing *The 69ers* (which has been replaced by *Deep Throat,* on the last day[*L* 255]):

There are three red figures on the pink bed. Pieces of bodies, ribs, thighs, torsos, fly off one body and join another body. Hair blows in a magnetic wind. Mouths and eyes open on light. Light pubic triangles turn like mobiles, now narrowing, now widening, changing from equilateral triangles to isosceles triangles to lines of light. The posters of the bed make a frame.

Lucy is lying lengthwise in the middle of the bed. She is recognizable by the flame-curl of hair under her ears, by her big breasts, and by the still slightly immature not wholly incurved line between calf and knee. Lucy is like a patient. Certain operations are being performed on her. The other two figures handle her as efficiently as nurses. Raine is slim and swift, moving so fast her body leaves ectoplasm behind. Dana stands naked and musing beside the bed, one hand browsing over his shoulder like an athlete in a locker room.

The three lie together. Their bodies fuse but their arms move like a six-arm Shiva.

Now they are doing something else. Dana kneels in a horizontal plane, takes Lucy's head in both hands, and guides it toward him. Raine moves much more quickly. Her sleek head flies off and burrows into Lucy's stomach.

The figures make a rough swastikaed triangle:

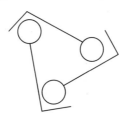

Elgin is right. The sound track is poor. No words are audible except near the end an unrecognizable voice which is neither clearly male nor female seems to come from nowhere and everywhere—and only fragments at that: *Oh Christ dear sweet Jesus oh oh*— (*L* 191–92)

Again the immediacy of "reliving," the sense of the helpless spectator, the orderly series of shots containing reversals, blotches, trunca-
tions, geometric figures—especially triangles, stick figures (though it
should be noted that they are neither the female nor the male biol-
ogy symbols) and the incessant O.

The "dirty movie" has confirmed Lance's suspicion of his wife
and her friends. He can, therefore, proceed with a plan for punishment. As if planning a most ordinary chore, he compiles a "shop-
ping list" for items needed to blow up his house (*L* 194). At the
same time, the hurricane is approaching, and Lance has a handy
excuse for sending away those whom he will save. Surprisingly,
Merlin is spared, presumably because Lance now knows from the
videotape that he is impotent (therefore a "safe" angle in this triangle) and now unsuitable to play the Oedipal role in the movie that is
to be shot.

As twilight time parallels the twilight state, Lance swallows two
"downers" that Raine gives him (*L* 207). Lance says that he took the
drug to get some distance from his pain, and that may indeed be the
reason. But his confession could just as well be a ploy to get Father
John to believe that any distorted consciousness in the remainder of
the story is the result of narcotic hallucination, not schizophrenia.
Almost immediately Lance describes the visit of "OUR LADY OF THE
CAMELLIAS" (*L* 210–13); in this dreamlike experience a mysterious
whorish figure tells Lance that his mother had been an adulteress.
There is a sharp cut between many of the short scenes that follow, of
anti-paradisiac past and prophecy, as Lance unwittingly demonstrates that his entire life is dominated by a sense of the Fall, for him
personified by his father's bribe-taking and weakness and by his
mother's unfaithfulness. Then Lance continues his narration of the
dream: the woman has become his mother, who offers him a
"sword"—so he identifies it for Father John, then quickly corrects
himself to say, "Bowie knife." Lance must realize that he had allowed
his fantasy to break into the open—with which he is to kill Margot's
lover (*L* 225–26).

There is yet another triangle in Lance's imagination: Uncle Harry,
Lance's father, and Lance's mother. Lance cannot redeem his moth-

er's honor by killing Uncle Harry, but, in his regression, if he identifies Margot with his mother, then killing Jacoby will restore his mother to an honorable state. There is an Oedipal drama occurring in Lance's consciousness, but Erich Fromm's interpretation of that event is more appropriate here than Freud's: ". . . it is not the sexual desire which makes the relationship to mother so intense and vital and the figure of the mother so important, not only in childhood but maybe for a person's entire life. Rather, this intensity is based on the need for the paradisiacal state . . ." (29).

Quickly the regressive attempt to rescue the mother is played out. Lance mines his house so that it will soon explode, thus culminating his end-of-the-world fantasy. Then he enters Raine's bedroom, to sodomize her as a punishment for her seduction of his daughter Lucy (*L* 235). And then into Margot's bedroom, to expose Margot and Jacoby—and save his mother. Lance's description of the scene indicates that what he sees is distorted by the apparatus through which he sees it: seen through the triangular bracing of the great bed, a family heirloom, is "the strangest of all beasts, two-backed and pied, light-skinned and dark-skinned, striving against itself in prayers and curses" (*L* 239).

At that point, Lance's regression is absolute: "I ran my thumbnail along my teeth" (*L* 239). Sucking his thumb, in other words, he has the sense of "floating over them." Now magic replaces cause-and-effect. They fight, until Lance is able to twist Jacoby around to cut his throat (*L* 242–43), re-enacting a technique which he earlier claims that his great-great-grandfather had used on someone who had defamed *his* mother (*L* 154–55). (Thus the story grows in Lance's hysterical retelling: when he first tells it, the hero is Jim Bowie [*L* 18]).

Then, still following the legend that he seems to have developed for his own psychic needs, he mutilates the body. John Vernon notes that "[d]ismemberment is a common hallucination in schizophrenia . . ." (24),[6] but it is particularly appropriate for Lance to employ such activity. It is not beyond conjecture that he dismembered Jacoby, especially that he cut off the member which occupied the space that had once been his O. Once Lance refers to Margot's genitals as his only source of transcendence:

She was like a feast. She was a feast. I wanted to eat her. I ate her.

That was my communion, Father—no offense intended, that sweet dark sanctuary guarded by the heavy gold columns of her thighs, the ark of her covenant. (*L* 171)

Thus to have been robbed of such an object meant for Lance not merely the awakening of jealousy or even wrath, but of a horrified sense of alienation. In describing their first copulation, Lance says: "she infallibly knew where the vector of desire converged" (*L* 81). Using that astronomical term, *vector*, he identifies himself as a body drawn toward a greater body, his penis as an "arrow of interest" (*L* 235) toward the $\wedge$ that must always hide in his imagination of a triangle. Sexual incarnation in Margot was his adult fantasy of his paradisiac intrauterine incarnation. Now, having destroyed the foreign element in his world, he plans to take Margot away to the Shenandoah Valley—Virginia being a fit place for a woman restored to the virgin state, as in his dream of the future (*L* 36–37). It is then that the actual house, not the house-mother, blows up—in perfect accord with Lance's complete breakdown.

Although Lance has refused to talk to anyone (before Father John) about his actions the previous year, it is obvious that he has thought about them a great deal. He would be justified in thinking that his survival of an explosion which killed everyone else in the house was a miracle. Since he had constructed the explosion as the manifestation of his world-destruction fantasy, he must believe that, since he alone survived, he is destined to play a role of cosmic leadership. To that end, he has given much thought to the philosophy which will motivate his actions. This philosophy is characterized by the "completely mystical and irrational view of the world" and the "strictly logical and systematized philosophy of life" described by Kretschmer.

Lance soon announces his "sexual theory of history":

First there was a Romantic Period when one "fell in love."

Next follows a sexual period such as we live in now where men and women cohabit as indiscriminately as in a baboon colony—or in a soap opera.

Next follows catastrophe of some sort. I can feel it in my bones. Perhaps it has already happened. Has it? (*L* 35–36)

Lance's question masks his conviction that it has happened.

Lance alone has discovered the *logos* that motivates history. It is not Christ, the Christian love that Father John keeps asking about. It is hatred: "The great secret of the ages is that man has evolved, is born, lives, and dies for one end and one end only: to commit a sexual assault on another human or to submit to such an assault" (*L* 222). Since men are the stronger and more violent sex, they will obviously be the rapists. If women are not to deserve such hatred, then they must change: "Freedom? The New Woman will have perfect freedom. She will be free to be a lady or a whore" (*L* 179).

There is a patient, Anna, in the room next to Lance. As she lies there, she must resemble Margot at the moment the house exploded, although Lance says that she reminds him of his first wife (*L* 62). Lance has decided that she is the New Woman whom he will take to the Shenandoah Valley. Probably she initially appeals to Lance because she is mute and because he can attempt to communicate with her merely by coding letters on the wall (*L* 34). Thus he does not have to use his voice or words, both of which are treacherous instruments, he must feel. She is qualified as an image. At one point Lance informs Father John that he saw her yesterday, lying on her cot in a fetal position: "Her brown boylike arms make a perfect V, hands pressed palms together between her thighs" (*L* 109). In an attitude of prayer, she guards her genitals, **X,** making a safe angle. Thus he can give her Hershey kisses, reward her for being a good girl. She is also qualified to be the New Woman by the same reason that he is qualified to be the New Man: "The New Woman is the survivor of the catastrophe and the death of old worlds—like the woman in the next room. The worst thing that can happen to her has happened. The worst thing that can happen to me has happened. We are both survivors" (*L* 37).

So Lance will take her off to Virginia ". . . where it will begin. And it is where there are men who will do it. Just as it was Virginia where it all began in the beginning, or at least where the men were to conceive it, the great Revolution, fought it, won it, and saw it on its way. They began the Second Revolution and we lost it. Perhaps the Third Revolution will end differently" (*L* 219). Thus Lance envisions himself in the company of Washington, and Jefferson, and

Madison, and Monroe, and Lee; thus Lance reveals his delusion of grandeur.

Thus, too, he reaches his world-reconstruction fantasy, frequently a late stage in schizophrenia (Fenichel 424–25). Although Anna refuses to go with him to Virginia, she lends him a homestead: "Oh, one last thing she said. She held my hand for a while after shaking hands goodbye. 'When you get up there in Virginia,' she told me, 'you'll find a fallen-down house but a small solid two-hundred-year-old barn. One side is a corn crib and a tack room with a loft. It would make a lovely cozy place to live in the winter and big enough for three.' Christ, do you think this is another woman trying to fix me up in a pigeonnier?" (*L* 252). His choice of expletive betrays him: a new religion born in a barn will save the two-hundred-year-old fallen-down country.

Since Anna surprisingly refuses to accompany him, however, Lance is left once again mystified by Woman, as he has been all his life: "What happened to Anna? Really it's incredible. I shall never understand women. We were going to have a new life together . . . we were qualified as the new Adam and Eve of the new world. If we couldn't invent a new world and a new dignity between man and woman, surely nobody could" (*L* 251).

After all his talk, Lance is left without a New Eden, as mystified by Woman and as numbed and chilled (*L* 253) as he had been last year when his discovery of Margot's betrayal had reawakened his hysteria over losing his mother.[7] Yet because of his talk he has made some progress toward recovery. During Father John's first visit, Lance notes "a sign" which can be seen from his window (*L* 4):

Free &
Ma
B

Lance must realize what the "sign" signifies, that alone he can see only partially, as though "through a glass darkly," as St. Paul puts it. Cartesian consciousness (of which we are unconscionably proud) is curtailed consciousness. We need the confirmation of another to enjoy completeness; we need to see our self in the eyes of another.[8]

Thus from the very beginning Lance stresses another idea from his reading of Metz's essay. After introducing the "*construction en abŷme,*" the translator writes: "At the risk of losing some of the accuracy of the original term, the translator has preferred to substitute the term 'mirror construction,' which is less unfamiliar, certainly less awk-ward-sounding, and therefore perhaps more suggestive than 'ines-cutcheon construction.' The image is that of a double mirror reflect-ing itself." Lance's use of the mirror construction is essential to his purpose. If the images he saw (camera shots) reveal his past deter-mination, his arrangement of them into film sequences and thus into narrative by using a recurrent image of looking at/looking in (itself a mirror image!) hints at his on-going recovery.

Lance understands at once that he and Father John could stand as mirrors for each other, for he says, ". . .whom I saw you yesterday, it was like seeing myself" (*L* 5). But Father John prefers to look out the window (*L* 3, 9, 22), so Lance has no choice but to become a disem-bodied voice, desperately seeking a resonance. Since his eyes are not permitted to meet Father John's, he feels that his eyes are not focus-ing properly (*L* 6, 60, 95).

As he talks, Lance frequently refers to mirrors—and to their op-posite, transparent glass. The latter is more noticeable—such instru-ments as microscopes, telescopes, cameras—for Lance uses this im-age to describe his successful detective work. But it is the very success of his past effort that has left him so in need of confirmation. Thus he uses two kinds of mirror images, one to describe the past and the other the present.

His reference to mirrors in the past reveals he had ignored their possible beneficial effects. He notes that Margot had used mirrors to satisfy her vanity and arouse his desire (L 170, 171). He himself had used mirrors to spy (*L* 49, 237). Even when he had seen himself in a mirror (*L* 63–64), he had not recognized himself for what he was. Even when he deliberately looked in a mirror, he could see only his external appearance (*L* 64). He must have thought that the possibil-ity of looking or even the need to look was ludicrous, for he had noted Lucy's lament that she as "an adult human being, a person" had never seen her own cervix and Merlin's rejoinder that he had never seen his own asshole: "What's the big deal?" (*L* 182). If he had felt that mirrors could accomplish only such reflections as those,

223

then no wonder that he had continued to focus his 'scopes (even though—as Kretschmer's analysis of imagery shows—there is some reflection of the individual in the 'scope glass which inevitably distorts the distant phenomena being observed).

In the present, though, Lance continues to look to Father John. Thus he projects his images against the mirror, allowing them to escape his mind in order to see them, really, for the first time. Seeing Father John, Lance confesses, was an awakening: "I had the sense of being overtaken by something, by the past, by myself" (*L* 5). Father John becomes an accessory to focusing (*L* 13). And gradually he seems to be responding to Lance's overtures for eye contact, perhaps even vocal response. By the end of the third day, deeply disturbed by Lance's threats, Father John gives him a "stricken" look (*L* 160). In the two days following, he is much more attentive.

On the last day, Lance informs Father John that he is to be released and that he feels nothing about the events of the previous year. This confession prompts the priest to look at Lance in sadness and ask yet again about love (*L* 254). At that point Lance analyzes the "mirror construction" that they have developed: "You know, something has changed in you. I have the feeling that while I was talking and changing, you were listening and changing" (*L* 254). Lance thinks that his focus on hatred has defeated Father John's focus on love, and so he takes him to the window (like the Devil tempting Jesus, Lance says [*L* 254]), to show him modern love, the poster at Cinema 16 announcing *Deep Throat* (*L* 255): he believes that his "movie" is proved by that "sign" and that he can impose his view on Father John. Such pride threatens any progress Lance has made, so Father John for the last time serves as a mirror for him: "At last you're looking straight at me, but how strangely! Ah, all at once I understand you. I read you as instantly as I used to when we were close. All of a sudden we understand each other perfectly, don't we?" (*L* 256).

Then follows the only sustained dialogue between the two men. On the first day, Lance had claimed that he had no use for words and guessed that Father John shared his feeling (*L* 5). By now he has come to understand that what another speaks can be more truthful than what the auditor himself sees. Lance accepts the openness of

Father John's glimpse of the future: "I can see it in your eyes" (*L* 256). No longer the moviemaker or moviegoer, Lance will trust the face as the mirror of truth, probably for the first time since he lost the mother's face as mirror in infancy, often a disaster, as Winnicott points out (110–18).[9]

CHAPTER 1

1. It should be noted, however, that there is an awful consequence to the attainment of language. Language makes possible consciousness, which informs the child of his physical separation from the mother-object, informs the child of his alienation. The only transcendence of alienation is through love, love of the human—especially of the complementary Other, with whom one manifests love through sexuality—and love of the divine. Sexuality in Percy's work, then, is never the ultimate act (that is, biologically driven), but the penultimate act (psychologically driven) that prefigures a spiritual relationship. Physical love, blessed as a sacrament, is symbolic of spiritual love. We cannot know as the angels know, directly; as embodied creatures, we can know only through symbols.

2. Simone Vauthier was the first to perceive the significance of "triangulation" in Percy's thought, in "Narrative Triangle and Triple Alliance: A Look at *The Moviegoer*" (Johnson and Johnson 71–93) and "Narrative Triangulation in *The Last Gentleman*" (Broughton 69–95). For these essays, and other essays as well, Percy critics in general and I in particular owe a great debt of gratitude to Professor Vauthier.

3. Since I first offered this speculation I have found confirmation for it in the thought of Margaret Little, a British psychoanalyst who argues that the experience of "basic unity," "primary total undifferentiatedness" [of infant with mother] must be understood as the key to psychological development:

> I am postulating that a universal idea exists, as normal and essential as is the oedipus complex (which cannot develop without it), an idea of absolute identity with the mother upon which survival depends. The presence of this idea is the foundation of mental health, development of the whole person, and the capacity for

holistic thinking. It is to be found not only in the delusions of the mentally sick, where it takes the form of transference psychosis, but also in the sane and healthy.

The most obvious and immediate example is here, right now. You and I can only understand each other insofar as we possess an area of unity which is a psychic reality, to which temporarily we unconsciously regress. This is how empathy works. The finding of agreement, or consensus of opinion between individuals or in any group, depends upon it; in turn agreement strengthens unconscious belief in survival and so provides the necessary security for tolerating differences and disagreement elsewhere.

. . . .

Contact or communication between the artist and his public depends upon the presence of, and regression to, this unconscious delusion in both. To the artist his creation is his work, is his feeling, is himself; to the hearer or the viewer what is heard or seen is *his* feeling, is his response, is himself. So each psychicality *is* the work of art, and *is* the other, in the area where they overlap. (123–24)

Mrs. Little's idea of the aesthetic transaction is very similar to Susanne Langer's assertion that "the form which is created represents, *symbolizes*—not just the thousand and one subject matters of the various arts but rather the *feelings*, the *felt life* of the artist and so of the observer" (Percy "Symbol as Need" 288), a key element of Percy's aesthetics. Since Percy's work represents and embodies the need for "regression in the service of the transcendent," it is particularly magnetic for any reader who unconsciously or consciously is aware of his own "universal idea" of "basic unity."

CHAPTER 2

1. Percy remembers staying "in the car reading a Raymond Chandler novel" (Chandler 96)—the first of which, *The Big Sleep*, was not published until 1939. He probably had a false memory because he volunteered it just after *Lancelot* was published (see fn. 3).

2. Percy certainly understood that "moodishness" overlies the response to the present, even if the response is only boredom or indifference or alienation. See his essay "The Man on the Train" for his treatment of "rotation" and "aesthetic repetition" as inauthentic evasions of the alienating present and of "existential repetition" or conversion as the authentic defense against the alienating present.

3. In "'Spiritually in Los Angeles': California Noir in *Lancelot*," I argue that Chandler's *The Big Sleep* is the appropriate sub-text for *Lancelot*, since it too is a detective story by an author obsessed with the lost mother-object.

4. Faber's references suggest the growing awareness of the inadequacy of

the scientific attitude as an existential stance. See also Suttie (71): ". . . in all his social activities—Art, Science, and Religion included—man is seeking a restoration of or substitute for that *love for mother* which was lost in infancy."

5. The confession that Percy makes through his fiction is that his experience of maternal deprivation originated in very early childhood, probably even before he could separate the mother figure from the total environment.

CHAPTER 3

1. In *Feeling and Form* Langer speaks of the likeness of cinema to dream and of the "virtual present" (412), both ideas essential to the technique of *The Moviegoer*. That Percy had closely read *Feeling and Form* is apparent from his review of it, "Symbol as Need," *The Message in the Bottle*.

2. See " 'The Parent in the Percept' in *The Last Gentleman*," which follows, for a discussion of psychically-impaired visualization in Percy's second published novel.

3. Percy's essay "The Man on the Train," with its discussion of moviegoing and of a psychology of alienation, was an essential preparation for the writing of and is an essential preparation for the reading of *The Moviegoer*.

4. See my "Walker Percy's *The Moviegoer:* the Cinema as Cave," for a discussion of Binx Bolling's scientistic education.

5. See Firestone: "When deprived of love-food, an infant experiences considerable anxiety and pain and attempts to compensate by sucking its thumb and by providing self-nourishment in various ways. At this point in its development, a baby is able to create the illusion of the breast. An infant who feels empty and starved emotionally relies increasingly on this fantasy for gratification. And, indeed, this process provides partial relief. In working with regressed schizophrenic patients, my colleagues and I observed that some had visions and dreams of white hazes, snow, and the like, sometimes representing the wish for milk and nourishment. One patient described to me a white breast that he saw, and when I asked what came out of it, he said, 'Pictures.' Thus, fantasy may eventually become 'more real' to the seriously disturbed person than does experience in the 'real' environment" (37–38). Firestone's findings closely link the psychoanalytic research by Lewin et al with Percy's regressive creativity.

6. See Esman: First he offers an account of a session: "About three months after he began psychotherapy, Tommy reported that he had gone with his father to a baseball game the previous Sunday. They had little to say to one another, their principal communication consisting of Tommy's request for ice cream and his father's peremptory refusal to buy it for him. That night the child had the following dream: "I was sitting in a movie theater, or some-

place. There was a sort of screen, and baseballs were coming out of it toward me. There was a man there who was catching the balls and deflecting them to everyone else, so I couldn't get any." Esman makes this interpretation: "The dream reported here appears to exemplify the dream screen concept in all respects. The day residue is an experience of oral deprivation in a profoundly orally fixated boy, in whom depression and overreating represent desperate attempts at restitution for gross early deprivations. The frustrating person in the dream is a direct representation of the reality figure. Aside from its obvious transference implications, the latent content of the dream appears to be: 'My father repeatedly deprives me of the breast and milk that I so desperately want. Only by directly representing the breast and its longed-for solace can I remain asleep.' Thus, the dream is seen to have oedipal and preoedipal content; it serves the oral regression that is the principal defensive measure at this boy's disposal against the intense rage evoked by the experience of deprivation" (250–51).

7. See Boyer: "Rycroft's patient (personal communication 1959) 'was in a state of "narcissistic identification" since (1) he had withdrawn interest from external objects, (2) he was preoccupied with an introject, and (3) he identified himself with this introject.' The analysand presented dream screen phenomena at a time when an object relationship was developing. Rycroft considered the most significant aspect of the appearance of the screen phenomenon to be that it marked a shift from narcissistic identification with the internal object to turning toward an external object. He concluded that the phenomenon of the dream screen represents, in addition to the fulfillment of the wish to sleep at the mother's breast, an attempt in the course of the analysis to reestablish an object relationship with the mother via the transference" (48). Through his self-analysis (i.e. his narrative) Binx is describing his success in shifting from an internal object to an external object.

8. It is tempting to think that Binx alludes to Rorschach Plate VII, which, as Booth—Percy's second psychoanalyst—acknowledges, many Rorschach psychologists interpret as the "mother card" (97).

9. This scene reflects a very important aspect of Walker Percy's psychodrama. The character "Aunt Emily" is based on Percy's adoptive father (his father's first cousin) William Alexander Percy, an unmarried man who seems never to have had a close feminine relationship. Thus his validity as a father-figure may have been undercut in Percy's mind, as the gender change of the character might suggest. Percy's biographer Tolson cites the paper by Janet Rioch, Percy's first psychoanalyst, which, he believes, discusses Percy's aborted analysis (140–43) and which, I believe, supports my inferences. I

suggest that it was the aborted analyses which destined Percy to work through his self-analysis in fiction.

CHAPTER 4

1. The author greatly appreciates the help of Ms. Lola Norris, Editorial Assistant for *The Southern Quarterly*, in which this essay originally appeared, who untiringly applied for permission to print the illustrations, and the help of Dr. Stephen Young, the Editor, whose layout tied the illustrations to the text. The author also greatly appreciates the help of Associate Dean Charles Rutherford and Dean Robert Griffith, College of Arts and Humanities, University of Maryland, College Park, who funded the printing of the illustrations. Additional support for research on this article was provided by the Mississippi Humanities Council.

2. Interestingly, in the spring of 1955, Stanley Kauffman, who was later to be Percy's editor for *The Moviegoer*, met Marilyn Monroe in her bedroom, to think of her as "the globe's Aphrodite" (567).

3. Wendy Lesser (210) cites Tom Ewell's observation in her discussion of Marilyn Monroe.

4. Jean Shinoda Bolen (234) speaks of "Venus on the Half-Shell." Edward E. Barthell, Jr. (32fn.) refers to the peep show at Chicago. Percy says there was a "Venus in marble" in "Uncle Will's House," which is reprinted in *Signposts in a Strange Land* (63–66). Uncle Will himself was ambivalent about representations of the love goddess; on a trip to Europe he admired the *Venus de Milo*, missed the *Birth of Venus*, and loathed the *Crouching Venus* of Syracuse as "nasty" (WA Percy 110–11).

5. Christine Dowling (204) writes to Aphrodite: "It is only recently that I have learned [from Karoly Kerenyi, *Goddesses of Sun and Moon* 2] that the Greeks perceived in you a 'joy-creating *sun-like* Magic' . . ." Percy told Gilbert Schricke (247) just how much he admired *Der Rosenkavalier* and implied just how heavy was his emotional investment in Lotte Lehman's farewell role as the Marschallin, the older woman who gives up the love of the young man Octavian, allowing him to seek love from a woman of his own age.

6. Percy told Bradley R. Dewey (107) of his introduction to "The Diary of a Seducer." Tolson suggests that an early fragment entitled "Confessions of a Moviegoer (from the Diary of the Last Romantic)" is a preliminary sketch for *The Moviegoer* (262).

7. See Kierkegaard *Either/Or* I 327, 429, 460 fn. 60.

8. The rather more discreet Swensons say that she was worshipped for her "beautiful back" (*Either/Or* I 460, fn.60).

9. Simone Signoret confirms that Ms Monroe retained her fresh, Renoir quality: "Without makeup or false eyelashes, her feet bare, which made her quite short, she looked like the most beautiful peasant girl imaginable from the Ile-de-France, as the type has been celebrated for centuries" (Faust 55).

10. In an early, Jungian reading Ted Spivey provides a similar explication of the Chicago theater scene:

> Bolling's movement from anima possession to anima encounter is seen in his relationship with the one woman in his life who is not totally connected with those fantasies of endless pleasure that always surround the anima-possessed psyche. He flees to Chicago to lose himself in the movie palace that he calls the great Urwomb, symbol of his desire for total immersion in the feminine, which is the goal of the journey of the anima possessed; but he is at the same time taking a journey of encounter with the woman that he will marry. (280)

12. Robert Graves speculates that Icarus—Binx's father's mythological counterpart—was one of those figures who "was invested with a single-day royalty and then burned to death" (320) as a sacrifice to the Great Mother, of whom Aphrodite was one representation.

CHAPTER 5

1. Despite the basic differences of genre between the two texts, there are at least two aspects of similar influence in the thought of Michael Washburn and Walker Percy, the existential and the psychoanalytic. The following authors listed in Washburn's bibliography are referred to in Percy's essays and interviews: Sigmund Freud, Martin Heidegger, Edmund Husserl, Carl Jung, Soren Kierkegaard, R. D. Laing, Blaise Pascal, Jean-Paul Sartre, and Ernest Schachtel.

CHAPTER 6

1. Reiss (363–73) offers a very helpful description of Freud's use of the image of the telescope.

2. In the same place, Percy states that his new regime of reading at Saranac Lake began with Dostoevsky. In an earlier interview (*Conversations* 75) he indicates that "the last two pages of *The Moviegoer* were meant as a conscious salute to Dostoevsky, in particular to the last few pages of *The Brothers Karamazov*."

3. Sacks (125–42) has an excellent discussion of the strong musical sensitivity of epileptics.

4. Alfred Knopf, an old friend of William Alexander Percy, published both

Spengler and Percy; it is likely that William Alexander Percy was an early and appreciative reader of Spengler when he was translated.

5. Sacks (149–53) has an excellent discussion of the heightened sense of smell possessed by epileptics.

6. There is another nasal memory on p. 85, which probably refers to Will Barrett's hallucination of Senator Oscar Underwood and to Walker Percy's memory of Senator LeRoy Percy.

7. See *Civilization and Its Discontents*, SE 21, 61, 99n., and 106. See also Sulloway (198–204), "Repression and the Sense of Smell."

CHAPTER 7

1. In many respects, what Freud (1911, p. 222) said about fantasy in the world of reality may be said about love relationships. He compared fantasy to a natural preserve, like Yellowstone Park—"a bit of the pristine wilderness preserved within the confines of civilization" (Arlow 142). Arlow's linkage between general fantasy and the specific fantasy quest for the ideal love object is particularly pertinent to the thesis that I pursue in this essay.

2. Mario Jacoby shows the linkage between the racial myth of the original paradise and the individual dream of the original object, mother. Jacoby was anticipated by, among others, Erich Fromm: ". . . it is not the sexual desire which makes the relationship to mother so intense and vital and the figure of the mother so important, not only in childhood but maybe for a person's entire life. Rather, this intensity is based on the need for a paradisiacal state" (29).

3. In *The Message in the Bottle* Percy credits Charles Sanders Peirce with the original formulation of the language model that he, ignorant of Peirce, had developed as "the delta factor." It is probable that Percy had also learned of Peirce's model of thinking, which he traced back to Plato: "the inward dialogue carried on by the mind with itself without spoken sound" (Fisch 358). Only the conceptualization of consciousness as dialogic (". . . consciousness, one suddenly realizes, means a knowing-with," [*MB* 274]) could support Percy's implication throughout his work that narratization is the therapeutic technique inherent in psychoanalysis, religious experience, and belletristic authorship, "regression in the service of transcendence," as Washburn calls it.

4. In Plato's *Symposium*, Aristophanes asserts that in the beginning each human was double, with two heads, four arms, and four legs. Some of these creatures were male and female joined, others were the same sex joined. Fearing such powerful creatures, Zeus cut them in two; thus each half-creature is born with a desire to be rejoined with its matching half. Inter-

estingly Gaylin, after relating Plato's story, acknowledges its recent application in psychoanalysis: "The concept of originally being one with another and of the birth of the self by cleaving from another, the poetic myth of Aristophanes, finds renewal in the psychological theory of a modern-day psychoanalyst, Dr. Margaret Mahler" (99–100).

5. Faber (20–25) credits Dr. Margaret Mahler's work as one of the foundations for his theory, which is described in this essay.

6. For example, Friedrich Nietzsche: "Every man keeps in himself an image of the woman deriving from that of his mother, and according to that image he will be prone to respect or despise women" (quoted by Ellenberger 708).

7. Faber: ". . . philosophy's deepest unconscious aim—its 'secret longing' as Husserl expressed it—has not been simply the attainment of 'objectivity' but the accomplishment of a new or renewed sight of the world in which the internalized object no longer rules our perception, killing wonder and joy, and breeding the stressful delusions of projective awareness. Descartes, Hume, Kant, Hegel, Husserl, Merleau-Ponty—all these philosophers have sought not only 'truth' but release from 'passion,' from what Spinoza called 'human bondage,' from the anxiety and tension of the 'parent in the percept'" (157–58). Storr bases his study of Newton on Manuel's biography, then amplifies Faber's list of thinkers having an "absence of close personal ties": Descartes, Locke, Hobbes, Hume, Pascal, Spinoza, Kant, Leibniz, Schopenhauer, Nietzsche, Kierkegaard, and Wittgenstein (101). Almost all of these thinkers are alluded to or directly referred to by Will Barrett or the other narrators of the Percy canon (including Percy in his own voice).

8. Faber: "What occurs as the infant undergoes separation has been described as a 'life-long mourning process,' a process that triggers an endless search for 'replacement' which is tied integrally to our participation in the symbolic realm . . ." (29). Faber later speaks of psychoanalytic theory "as it understands and discloses the word as an avenue back to the parental figure and language as originating in the defensive reply to the fear of separation and loss" (180). This theory begs to be applied to the problem of Percy's language theory and may explain why so many of Percy's neurotic characters are "speechless."

9. From the very beginning of *The Last Gentleman,* the bench in Central Park on which the mother-figure first sits is also "exactly at ground zero" for a possible explosion of nerve gas (48). Thereafter, numerous details evoke Will's sense of disintegration as he moves toward "ground zero" at Trinity site in the starry New Mexico desert. At one point the working title of the novel was "Ground Zero" (Tolson 305). In Percy's mind object-loss is world-

234

loss. Washburn's description of the "*zero point*" (169) or nadir is applicable to the metaphorics of "ground zero."

10. Perhaps it will be a comfort to some readers to learn that the reason they bungled an early sexual relationship was because it was a twelve-step process.

11. Bergmann: "In my 1971 paper, I suggest that the symbiotic phase leaves a psychic residue in the form of a longing for merger and this state of longing is reevoked when one falls in love. It was this longing that Plato described so well over 2500 years ago. Bak's (1973) views on this subject are similar to mine. He writes: 'Being in love is an uniquely human, exceptional emotional state, which is based on undoing the separation between mother and child' (p. 6)" (240–41). See, also, Person: "Successful lovers establish a union, characterized by ongoing warmth, commitment, intimacy, reciprocity, and some degree of mutual identification. But although the lovers may strive for complete merger (what we might then describe as fusion) they cannot sustain it. Instead, if they are lucky enough to enjoy a *passionate* love, their feelings of union will be interspersed with ecstatic moments of merger" (126–27). Will's lovemaking may be a case of putting the cart before the horse, psychologically speaking.

12. It must be remembered that this story is being recreated by an older Will Barrett, who—long after the fact—is attributing the identification of Good Mother to Kitty and Bad Mother to Rita. When Will thinks, "she hoped he would take his telescope and go away," it is with the awareness of the telescope as symbol reflecting his quest for the Good Mother.

13. Bergmann sees *The Odyssey* as a grand illustration of what he calls "the rapprochement subphase": "Odysseus represents a mythical tale of a child enjoying life's adventures on the way home" (25). See also: "When the rapprochement subphase [in childhood] has not been navigated successfully, lovers will repeat the need to leave and return only to leave again, subjecting their partner to an infinite number of waiting tests" (241).

14. The yin-yang is Percy's symbol of the original duality in unity, that state of consciousness *before* consciousness becomes alienated from the original object, the mother figure. Basically the yin-yang symbolizes the "two polar energies that, by their fluctuation and interaction, are the cause of the universe. Yin and yang are polar manifestations of the Tao of the supreme ultimate (—*t'ai-chi*), their concrete manifestations being Earth and Heaven" (Schumacher and Woerner 428–29). The yin-yang thus becomes one of the symbol group that Neumann identifies as "the Self-Contained" (8). Such a symbol group, in Jung's system, constitutes an archetype. As Neumann defines them, archetypes "are the pictorial forms of the instincts, for the un-

conscious reveals itself to the conscious mind in images which, as in dreams and fantasies, initiate the process of conscious reaction and assimilation" (xv). So frequently has this symbol group been represented by the uroboros, the serpent biting its tail, that Neumann entitles his examination of the creation myth "The Uroboros."

15. Neumann attributes a breast-fixation to the infancy of consciousness by lengthy examination of the emphasis upon breasts in the prehistoric art work representing the Great Mother (32 ff).

16. Rochlin stresses the need for restitution as an enormous stimulus to creativity (165–224).

17. Rochlin, following Mircea Eliade, discusses Christianity as offering restitution for the lost paradise of infancy (134–42). Jacoby also quotes Eliade: ". . . paradisiac symbolism is attested in the rites of baptism . . ." (207)—hence the appropriateness of Jamie's baptism to close the story.

CHAPTER 8

1. An informative account of Vestavia, which mentions Percy's use of it in *The Last Gentleman,* is provided by Glenn Eskew, whose article I did not discover until after I had published my study.

2. Tolson's account (98–100) of Mrs. Percy's drowning is dispassionate, but leaves no doubt that she could have caused the wreck that resulted in her death.

3. I am indebted to Ms Anne F. Knight, Birmingham Public Library, for providing me with newspaper clippings on Vestavia Temple. After Ward's death in 1940, the "temple" was abandoned until 1947, when it was renovated and operated as a restaurant. In 1957 it was purchased by the Vestavia Hills Baptist Church, serving as its sanctuary until it was razed in 1971. The Temple of Sibyl was moved to a new location in 1976.

4. The "unspeakable emotion" is probably maternal awe, about which more later.

5. When Walker Percy was fifteen months old, his brother LeRoy was born. Will Barrett's sporadic flight behavior may be explained by Little: "We are accustomed to think of truanting in children as meaning a search for the lost 'good' mother, but I would say that the loss in these cases is often the loss by the devaluation through the mother's pregnancy" (26).

6. The narrator is of an age to remember himself in a sequence of events when he was twenty-five. Sometimes he remembers past times when he remembered events from an even more distant past. When or why Will's biological mother disappeared is not remembered, though he remembers that while still a "boy" he had a stepmother (*LG* 13). With perhaps the ex-

ception of the *déjà vu* (*LG* 232) in which Will likens an action of Bad Mother Rita to an action of his mother (assuming that he is thinking of his biological mother), Will does not see his mother in his *déjà vus*, for the class *déjà vu* is a regression to an age when the infant can perceive only a "part-object," the breast (see Guntrip 226–30). The entire visual content of most of Will's *déjà vus* is the symbol of, ultimately, the breast, to which Will reacts with awe tinged by anxiety. Bloom-Feshbach and Bloom-Feshbach cited fascinating studies showing that at eighteen months, infants in a study could all identify a photograph of their father, while only a few could identify a photograph of their mother (11–13). The point of trauma for Will (and, therefore, the level of his regression during a *déjà vu* or a fantasy experience) is probably shortly after his fifteenth month. Harding points out that "[i]n the creation story in Genesis we are not told of any mother-image—the Garden itself was the mother, while God acted in the role of father-creator" (22). Her insight about the mythic-consciousness of an ancient tradition is being validated by empirical evidence about infant consciousness.

7. Brazelton and Cramer: "When a breast is offered and touches a newborn's cheek, the infant will search for it by a few head turns, then almost gobble to mouth the nipple. An awake, hungry newborn exhibits active search movements in response to any stimulation in the region around the mouth. This reflex is set off by touch as far out on the face as the cheek and sides of the jaw and head" (51–52). Recall that when Binx invites Sharon to the fishing camp of his mother—she of the forbidden big breasts—he notes this change: "She has become tender toward me and now and then presses my cheek with her hand" (*M* 136).

8. Tolson records that in 1927 LeRoy Percy played a round on the newly opened country club course with his friend Bobby Jones (44). Walker Percy would have reason to picture this course as Paradise, for the Fall was still two years away.

9. I am indebted to my colleague Vincent Carretta, for pointing out that *Lempriere's Classical Dictionary* records that Juno's milk was traditionally said to be the source of the Milky Way. Since Will is frequently aware of particular stars or planets—indeed he likens the Temple of Juno to Canopus—he might be subconsciously responding to Juno as the Great Giver of the Milky Way.

10. If for no other reason, Percy would have been drawn to this essay because of its dedication to Romain Rolland, who inspired Freud to coin the term "oceanic feeling" to describe the brief experience of the oneness of allness that must replicate the experience of "basic unity," as Little calls it. Percy was deeply impressed by Rolland's novel *Jean Cristophe* (*Conversations*

5, 260; *More Conversations* 25). Niederland also indicates that interest in "A Disturbance of Memory" greatly increased "after the Freud Centennial in 1956 and the publication of Jones' biography" (373)—just the years when Percy would have been mulling the story of his young manhood.

11. William Alexander Percy, Walker's adoptive father, probably was not guilty of ever reading a page of Freud, certainly not "A Disturbance of Memory," which was not published in English until 1941, the year that *Lanterns on the Levee* was published. Had he known of Freud's letter, Percy might have left out this anecdote: he and his father arrived late in the evening in Athens, so Will planned to get up early to climb the Acropolis, thus to crow over his father, only to discover when he stepped into the Parthenon that his father had beaten him to it: "The curative morning was flooding over him, and he laughed when he saw me" (155). More than one analyst of William Alexander Percy has suggested that his whole life was governed by his feeling that his father had beaten him to it.

12. By indirection, too, the narrator is probably offering the reason for Will's unsatisfactory analysis, so recently terminated in New York. The *author* might even be saying something about his own unsuccessful analysis, for Tolson's description of it (137–42) allows a reconstruction of Percy's distress that is somewhat similar to my description of Will's distress. Tolson emphasizes the loss of the father as the source of the greater distress, but acknowledges that the distant posture of the mother was certainly an aspect of the total condition of loss.

13. Gedo shows how the Athens of "A Disturbance of Memory" was just one aspect of Freud's symbol of the "classical South," which "stood for magic, beauty, fantasy and happiness . . . , [with] feminine connotations" (102). He quotes Freud's statement "I hate Vienna almost like a person," a statement which Bernfeld had used "in support of the hypothesis that statues, vases, buildings and towns were symbolic representations of loved and hated persons from Freud's childhood past." I contend that Percy associates similar connotations with his South, that he here has the older Will Barrett symbolize mother with a building (Tolson relates that Percy used Vulcan, the other famous Birmingham mountaintop edifice, in *The Charterhouse*, Percy's first unpublished novel [214]), and that his discomfort with Birmingham (Tolson 115) is certainly validated by Will Barrett's behavior while under its influence.

14. Both Lewin ("The Train Ride") and Harrison ("On Freud") ground their discussion of awe in Jones' essay.

15. Washburn accounts for the shiver of awe by saying that "[a]we is breathless astonishment that mixes both perspiration and chill, palpitation

and horripilation" (207); his description aptly characterizes Will before the Naked Mama (*LG* 111). This paper relies upon the scheme *awe to blessedness* provided by Washburn (208).

CHAPTER 9

1. Bollas' statement that an individual can experience a deep subjective rapport (that amounts to a fleeting unconscious experience of fusion) before a painting is illustrated by Will's response in Central Park to a naked Kitty as a painting: "great epithelial-warm-pelvic-upcurving-melon-immediate Maja" (*LG* 111).

2. Tolson (142) quotes an article by Walker Percy's first analyst which he believes refers to Percy, an opinion I share. The following statement by Dr. Janet Rioch bears directly on Bollas' conclusion: "At that point, he developed very disturbing feelings regarding the analyst, believing that she was untrustworthy and hostile, although prior to this, he had succeeded in establishing a realistically positive relationship to her. The feelings of untrustworthiness precisely reproduced an ancient pattern with his mother." What Dr. Rioch reveals here is "the intrusion of archaic or primitive material" (Bollas 103), the "sudden blow up on the part of the patient" (Bollas 103) that marks the failure of an analysis. Dr. Rioch implies that reaching "that point" marked a crucial development in the analysis, but it is worth noting that Percy abandoned it, to submit himself to a male analyst, Dr. Gotthard Booth, for another year (Tolson 151, 153).

3. In effect the narrator of *The Last Gentleman* and *The Second Coming*, failing to achieve relief from psychoanalysis, eventually gains spiritual and mental health through faith (enabled by God's grace) and fiction (that is, by narratizing his life). Walker Percy follows the same route: he unsuccessfully consulted two psychoanalysts in his early twenties (Tolson [151] records that Percy told his friend Shelby Foote, "I could never effect a transference"; Percy also told Dr. Gentry Harris, "In my own experience the most valuable lesson of psychoanalysis was learning what it could not do" [Tolson 333]), then found relief through marriage, conversion to Catholicism, and the creation of a body of fiction that amounts to a self-analysis.

CHAPTER 10

1. In "Tom More: Cartesian Physician" I discuss aspects of the philosophical and scientific background of the novel.

2. The classic paper on this phenomenon is by Tausk.

3. The original name of Aphrodite was Moira (Otto 94). Moira has her Venusian aspect, for she almost never leaves home without her Cupid's

239

quiver (*LR* 135). Lola is identified as the Roman counterpart of Aphrodite by Tom himself: "A big lovely girl, big and white and cool-warm, a marble Venus with a warm horned hand" (*LR* 95).

4. Swenson and Swenson I 43–134.

5. In keeping with the Nobel Prize Complex profile is the Oedipal rivalry that Tom, the psychiatrist, betrays toward Dr. Freud. See my "Tom More and Sigmund Freud."

6. The locus of paradisiac longing in Percy's fiction is frequently the golf course, as in this novel: "When I was ten years old I woke one summer morning to a sensation of longing. Besides the longing I was in love with a girl named Louise, and so the same morning I went out to this same sand trap where I hoped chance would bring us together" (*LR* 21).

7. Tom's choice of the eighteenth hole for his assignation is symbolic of his paradisiac longing, for the last hole on the course is known as the "home hole" (Copeland 216).

CHAPTER 11

1. ". . . in this two hundredth anniversary year of the First Revolution . . ." (*L* 250).

2. About the time that he was writing *Lancelot*, Percy referred to Arthur Koestler's *The Ghost in the Machine* (Smith 140). Koestler cites Kretschmer, and in an earlier book that Percy probably read, *The Act of Creation* (1964), relies on Kretschmer extensively, praising him as "that excellent German psychiatrist—whose work, comparable in importance to Jung's, is far too little known to the English-speaking public" (322). Admittedly, I have not demonstrated that Percy knew Kretschmer's model of mind. But three factors suggest his familiarity: (1) Percy's wide reading in psychiatry generally and in his special field, schizophrenia (Tolson 311), specifically makes it hard to believe that he would not have read a classic in the field (if he knew Freud's *The Interpretation of Dreams* well enough to use Freud's model of the psychic apparatus, the telescope, as a method of narrative structure in *The Last Gentleman*, he could be expected to repeat his strategy); (2) the references in Koestler, if Percy had already known Kretschmer, would have been too tempting to ignore; (3) the points of congruence between Percy's model and Kretschmer's are too many and too close to be coincidental.

3. My essay " 'Spiritually in Los Angeles': California Noir in *Lancelot*" examines Percy's use of Raymond Chandler's *The Big Sleep*.

4. Kretschmer: "Schizophrenic symbols, like primitive and dream symbols, are the products of uncompleted thought; they are the pictorial antecedents of concepts and are not developed beyond that stage. The imaginal

240

syntheses antecedent to abstract thinking which in the case of the normal man are completed in the 'sphaira', i.e. in the nebulous periphery of consciousness, in schizophrenic thought occupy the central point of the psychic field of vision in place of the abstract. A schizophrenic sees real fire and has a vivid experience of being physically burned, when a normal person would say: 'I have love thoughts and feelings' " (102). Thus there is a direct route from Lance's imagination of Margot's Big O, orgasm (*L* 16, 21), to "woman? She is your omega point" (*L* 223). If the microcosm is evil, then the macrocosm shall be destroyed.

5. Here Lance's verbal statement ". . . a human female creature . . . an infinity" is contradicted by his symbol statement. The symbol $\propto$ means "varies as"; the symbol ∞ means "infinity." Lance's formula is thus incoherent, as is his entire discourse.

6. There are suggestions that Percy may have found John Vernon's *The Garden and the Map* particularly interesting as he worked on *Lancelot*, especially its reading of Conrad's *Heart of Darkness.*

7. Fenichel: "Open manifestations of the Oedipus complex [in schizophrenia] are so conspicuous that they attracted the first attention of psychoanalysts . . ." (436–37).

8. I have profited greatly from my conversations with Ms. Elizabeth Johnson, who shares my interest in Percy and in the Patmos group. She deserves credit for pointing out that Father John could tell Lance what the sign says. In effect he holds the piece that must be joined to Lance's piece in order to create a symbol. Until that occurs, Lance's response is schizophrenic thought, according to Kretschmer, uncompleted thought.

9. See Rinsley (89–93) for a summary of the concept of a mirroring stage of infant development, which "was put forward by the French psychoanalyst Jacques Lacan" in 1949 (89).

WORKS CITED

Arlow, Jacob A. "Object Concept and Object Choice." *Essential Papers on Object Relations.* Ed. Peter Buckley. New York: New York UP, 1986.

———. "The Structure of the *Déjà Vu* Experience." *Journal of the American Psychoanalytic Association* 7 (1959): 611–31.

Atlas, James. "An Interview with Walker Percy." *Conversations with Walker Percy.* Eds. Lewis A. Lawson and Victor A. Kramer. Jackson: UP of Mississippi, 1985.

Badcock, C. R. *Madness and Modernity.* London: Basil Blackwell, 1983.

Bak, Robert C. "Being in Love and Object Loss." *International Journal of Psycho-Analysis* 54 (1973): 1–7.

Balint, Michael. *Primary Love and Psycho-Analytic Technique.* London: Hogarth, 1952.

Barrett, George. "Visit with Aphrodite." *The New York Times Magazine,* September 14, 1958. Pp. 28, 79.

Barthell, Edward E., Jr. *Gods and Goddesses of Ancient Greece.* Coral Gables: U of Miami P, 1971.

Becker, Ernest. *The Revolution in Psychiatry.* New York: Free P of Glencoe, 1964.

Bergmann, Martin S. *The Anatomy of Loving.* New York: Columbia UP, 1987.

Bernfeld, Suzanne C. "Freud and Archeology." *American Imago* 8 (1951): 107–28.

Bloom-Feshbach, Jonathan, and Sally Bloom-Feshbach. *The Psychology of Separation and Loss.* San Francisco: Jossey-Bass, 1987.

Bolen, Jean Shinoda. *Goddesses in Everywoman.* New York: Harper, 1984.

Bollas, Christopher. "The Transformational Object." *International Journal of Psycho-Analysis* 60 (1979): 97–107.

Booth, Gotthard. *The Cancer Epidemic.* New York: Edwin Mellen, 1979.

Works Cited

Boyer, L. Bryce. *The Regressed Patient.* New York: Jason Aronson, 1983.

Brazelton, T. Berry, and Bertrand G. Cramer. *The Earliest Relationship.* Reading, MA: Addison-Wesley, 1989.

Brinkerhoff, Derickson Morgan. *Hellenistic Statues of Aphrodite.* New York: Garland, 1978.

Brown, Ashley. "An Interview with Walker Percy." *Conversations with Walker Percy.*

Calvin, William H. *The River That Flows Uphill.* New York: MacMillan, 1986.

Campbell, Joseph. *The Hero with a Thousand Faces.* New York: Meredian, 1956.

Casey, Edward S. *Remembering: A Phenomenological Study.* Bloomington: Indiana UP, 1987.

Chandler, David. "Walker Percy's Southern Novel Has a Lunatic Hero and Other Gothic Touches." *People* 7 (May 2, 1977): 95–96.

Cheney, Brainard. "To Restore a Fragmented Image." *Sewanee Review* 69 (1961): 693.

Ciuba, Gary M. "Walker Percy's Enchanted Mountain." *Walker Percy: Novelist and Philosopher.* Eds. Jan Nordby Gretlund and Karl-Heinz Westarp. Jackson: UP of Mississippi, 1991.

Copeland, Robert. Ed. *Webster's Sports Dictionary.* Springfield, MA: Merriam, 1976.

Cowan, P. A. *Piaget with Feeling.* New York: Holt, 1978.

Currie, Robert. *Genius.* New York: Shocken, 1974.

Dewey, Bradley R. "Walker Percy Talks about Kierkegaard." *Conversations with Walker Percy.*

Dilman, Ilham. *Love and Human Separateness.* London: Blackwell, 1987.

Dowling, Christine. *The Goddess.* New York: Crossroad, 1981.

Eberwein, Robert T. *Film and the Dream Screen.* Princeton: Princeton UP, 1984.

Ellenberger, H. F. *The Discovery of the Unconscious.* New York: Basic, 1970.

Eskew, Glenn T. "Demagoguery in Birmingham and the Building of Vestavia." *Alabama Review* 42 (1989): 192–217.

Esman, Aaron H. "The Dream Screen in an Adolescent." *The Psychoanalytic Quarterly* 31 (1962): 250–51.

Faber, Mel D. *Culture and Consciousness.* New York: Human Sciences P, 1981.

———. *Objectivity and Human Perception.* Edmonton: U of Alberta P, 1985.

Faust, Beatrice. *Women, Sex, and Pornography.* New York: Macmillan, 1980.

Fenichel, Otto. *The Psychoanalytic Theory of Neurosis.* New York: Norton, 1972.

Ferenczi, Sandor. *Final Contributions to the Problems & Methods of Psycho-*

Analysis. Ed. Michael Balint. Trans. Eric Mosbacher et al. New York: Brunner/Mazel, 1980.

———. *Thalassa.* Albany: The Psychoanalytic Quarterly, 1938.

Firestone, Robert W. *The Fantasy Bond.* New York: Human Sciences P, 1985.

Fisch, Max. *Peirce, Semiotic, and Pragmatism.* Eds. Kenneth Laine Ketner and Christian J. W. Kloesel. Bloomington: Indian UP, 1986.

Fliess, Robert. *Symbol, Dream, and Psychosis.* New York: International UP, 1973.

Flugel, J. C. *The Psycho-Analytic Study of the Family.* London: Hogarth, 1960.

Freud, Sigmund. "A Disturbance of Memory on the Acropolis: An Open Letter to Romain Rolland on the Occasion of his Seventieth Birthday." *The Standard Edition of the Complete Psychological Works of Sigmund Freud.* Trans. and Ed. James Strachey. Vol. 22. London: Hogarth, 1964.

———. "Dostoevsky and Parricide." *SE* 21.

———. *The Interpretation of Dreams SE,* 4, 5.

———. *The Psychopathology of Everyday Life SE* 6.

Friedrich, Paul. *The Meaning of Aphrodite.* Chicago: U of Chicago P, 1978.

Fromm, Erich. *The Greatness and Limitations of Freud's Thought.* New York: Harper and Row, 1980.

Gaylin, Willard. *Rediscovering Love.* New York: Viking, 1986.

Gedo, John E. "Freud's Self-Analysis and His Scientific Ideas." *American Imago* 25 (1968): 99–118.

Graves, Robert. *The White Goddess.* New York: Farrar, 1966.

Greenberg, Harvey. *The Movies on Your Mind.* New York: Saturday Review P, 1975.

Guntrip, Harry. *Personality Structure and Human Interaction.* New York: International UP, 1961.

Harding, M. Esther. *The "I" and the "Not-I."* Princeton: Princeton UP, 1965.

Harris, J. Rendel. *The Ascent of Olympus.* Manchester, England: UP, 1917.

Harrison, Irving B. "On Freud's View of the Infant-Mother Relationship and of the Oceanic Feeling—Some Subjective Influences." *Journal of the American Psychoanalytic Association* 27 (1979): 399–421.

———. "On the Maternal Origins of Awe." *The Psychoanalytic Study of the Child* 30 (1975): 181–95.

———. "A Reconsideration of Freud's 'A Disturbance of Memory on the Acropolis' in Relation to Identity Disturbance." *Journal of the American Psychoanalytic Association* 14 (1966): 518–27.

Heidegger, Martin. *Being and Time.* Trans. John Macquarrie and Edward Robinson. New York: Harper & Row, 1962.

Works Cited

Hillman, James. *Re-Visioning Psychology*. New York: Harper and Row, 1975.

Hunt, Morton. *The Natural History of Love*. New York: Knopf, 1959.

Jacoby, Mario. *The Longing for Paradise*. Trans. Myron B. Gubitz. Boston: Sigo P, 1985.

James, E. O. *The Cult of the Mother Goddess*. New York: Barnes and Noble, 1959.

James, William. *The Varieties of Religious Experience*. New York: MacMillan, 1961.

Johnson, Timothy W. "Holiday." *Magill's Survey of Cinema*. First Series, II. Ed. Frank N. Magill. Englewood Cliffs, NJ: Salem House, 1980. 758–61.

Jones, Ernest. "The Psychology of Religion." *Psychoanalysis Today*. Ed. Sandor Lorand. New York: International UP, 1944.

Jordan, Ted. *Norma Jean*. New York: Morrow, 1989.

Kanzer, Mark. "Observations on Blank Dreams with Orgasms." *The Psychoanalytic Quarterly* 23 (1954): 511–20.

Kauffman, Stanley. "Album of Marilyn Monroe." *American Scholar* 60 (Autumn 1991): 563–69.

Kepecs, Joseph. "A Waking Screen Analogous to the Dream Screen." *The Psychoanalytic Quarterly* 21 (1952): 167–71.

Kerenyi, Karoly. *The Gods of the Greeks*. London: Thames and Hudson, 1951.

Kierkegaard, Søren. *Fear and Trembling*. Trans. and int. Walter Lowrie. Princeton: Princeton UP, 1941.

———. "The Immediate Stages of the Erotic or the Musical Erotic," *Either/Or*, I. Trans. David F. Swenson and Lillian Marvin Swenson. New York: Anchor, 1959.

Koestler, Arthur. *The Act of Creation*. London: Hutchinson, 1964.

Kretschmer, Ernst. *Textbook of Medical Psychology*. London: Humphrey Milford, 1934.

Landow, George P. *Images of Crisis*. London: Routledge & Kegan Paul, 1982.

Langer, Susanne. *Feeling and Form*. New York: Scribners, 1953.

Lawson, Lewis A. "The Cross and the Delta: Walker Percy's Anthropology." *Walker Percy: Novelist and Philosopher*.

———. *Following Percy*. Troy, NY: Whitston, 1988.

———. "'Spiritually in Los Angeles': California Noir in *Lancelot*." *Southern Review* 24 (1988): 744–64.

———. "Tom More and Sigmund Freud." *New Orleans Review* 16 (1989): 27–31.

———. "Tom More: Cartesian Physician." *Delta* 13 (1981): 67–81.

———. "Walker Percy's *The Moviegoer:* the Cinema as Cave." *Following Percy*.

———, and Victor A. Kramer. Eds. *Conversations with Walker Percy*. Jackson: UP of Mississippi, 1985.

246

Works Cited

————, and Victor A. Kramer. Eds. *More Conversations with Walker Percy.* Jackson: UP of Mississippi, 1993.

Leighton, George Ross. *Five Cities: The Story of Their Development.* New York: Harper, 1939.

Lempriere's Classical Dictionary. London: Routledge, 1984.

Lesser, Wendy. *His Other Half.* Cambridge: Harvard UP, 1991.

Lewin, Bertram D. *The Image and the Past.* New York: International UP, 1968.

————. "Inferences from the Dream Screen." *International Journal of Psycho-Analysis* 29 (1948): 224–30.

————. "Reconsideration of the Dream Screen." *The Psychoanalytic Quarterly* 22 (1953): 174–99.

————. "Sleep, and Mouth, and the Dream Screen." *The Psychoanalytic Quarterly* 15 (1946): 419–34.

————. "The Train Ride: A Study of One of Freud's Figures of Speech." *The Psychoanalytic Quarterly* 39 (1970): 71–89.

Licht, Hans. *Sexual Life in Ancient Greece.* London: Abbey L, 1932.

Little, Margaret I. *Transference Neurosis and Transference Psychosis.* New York: Jason Aronson, 1981.

Luschei, Martin. *The Sovereign Wayfarer.* Baton Rouge: Louisiana State U P, 1972.

Manuel, Frank E. *A Portrait of Isaac Newton.* Cambridge: Harvard UP, 1968.

Mathews, Mitford M. *A Dictionary of Americanisms on Historical Principles.* Chicago: U of Chicago P, 1951.

Mayne, Judith. *Private Novels, Public Films.* Athens: U of Georgia P, 1988.

Metz, Christian. *Film Language.* Trans. Michael Taylor. New York: Oxford UP, 1974.

Morris, Desmond. *Intimate Behaviour.* New York: Random, 1971.

Muensterberger, Werner. "Between Reality and Fantasy." *Between Reality and Fantasy.* Eds. Simon A. Grolnick and Leonard Barkin. New York: Aronson, 1978.

Neiderland, William G. "Freud's 'Déjà Vu' on the Acropolis." *American Imago* 26 (1969): 373–78.

Neumann, Erich. *The Origins and History of Consciousness.* Princeton: Princeton UP, 1954.

O'Connor, Flannery. "Some Aspects of the Grotesque in Southern Literature." *The Added Dimension: The Art and Mind of Flannery O'Connor.* Eds. Melvin J. Friedman and Lewis A. Lawson. New York: Fordham UP, 1966.

Ortega y Gasset, Jose. *The Revolt of the Masses.* New York: New American L, 1950.

Otto, Walter. *The Homeric Gods.* Trans. Moses Hadas. Boston: Beacon, 1954.

Works Cited

Pacella, Bernard L. "Early Ego Development and the *Déjà Vu.*" *Journal of the American Psychoanalytical Association* 23 (1975): 300–26.

Pach, Walter. *Renoir.* New York: Abrams, 1983.

Pepitone, Lena, and William Stadiem. *Marilyn Monroe Confidential.* New York: Simon, 1979.

Percy, Walker. "From Facts to Fiction." *Signposts in a Strange Land.* Ed. Patrick Samway. New York: Farrar, 1991.

———. "The Man on the Train." *The Message in the Bottle.* New York: Farrar, 1975.

———. "Questions They Never Asked Me." *Signposts in a Strange Land.*

———. "Symbol as Need." *The Message in the Bottle.*

———. "Symbol, Consciousness and Intersubjectivity." *The Message in the Bottle.*

Percy, William Alexander. *Lanterns on the Levee.* Intro. Walker Percy. Baton Rouge: Louisiana State UP, 1973.

"Perpetual Calendar." *The World Almanac and Book of Facts 1957.* New York: World-Telegram, 1957.

Person, Ethel Spector. *Dreams of Love and Fateful Encounters.* New York: Norton, 1988.

Powers, Charles H. *Vilfredo Pareto.* Newbury Park, CA: Sage, 1987.

Presson, Rebekah. "Southern Semiotics: An Interview with Walker Percy." *More Conversations with Walker Percy.*

Rado, Sandor. "The Problem of Melancholia." *International Journal of Psycho-Analysis* 9 (1928): 420–38.

Reiss, Timothy J. *The Discourse of Modernism.* Ithaca: Cornell UP, 1982.

Rinsley, Donald B. *Developmental Pathogenesis and Treatment of Borderline and Narcissistic Personalities.* Northvale, NJ: Aronson, 1989.

Rochlin, Gregory. *Griefs and Discontents.* London: Churchill, 1965.

Romanyshyn, Robert. *Psychological Life.* Austin: U of Texas P, 1982.

Rose, H. J. *A Handbook of Greek Mythology.* New York: Dutton, 1959.

Rosen, George. "Percussion and Nostalgia." *Journal of the History of Medicine and Allied Sciences* 27 (1972): 448–50.

Sacks, Oliver. *The Man Who Mistook his Wife for a Hat.* London: Duckworth, 1985.

Sartre, Jean-Paul. *Being and Nothingness.* Trans. Hazel E. Barnes. New York: Philosophical L, 1956.

Schricke, Gilbert. "A Frenchman's Visit to Walker Percy." *Conversations with Walker Percy.*

Schumacher, Stephen, and Gert Woerner. Eds. *The Encyclopedia of Eastern Philosophy and Religion.* Boston: Shambhala, 1989.

Smith, Marcus. "Talking about Talking: An Interview with Walker Percy." *Conversations with Walker Percy.*

Smith, Sidney. "The Golden Fantasy: A Regressive Reaction to Separation Anxiety." *International Journal of Psycho-Analysis* 58 (1977): 311–24.

Sno, Herman N., and Don H. Linszen. "The Déjà Vu Experience: Remembrance of Things Past?" *The American Journal of Psychiatry* 147 (1990): 1587–95.

Spengler, Oswald. *The Decline of the West.* Trans. Charles Francis Atkinson. New York: Knopf, 1932.

Sperber, Michael A. "Freud, Tausk, and the Nobel Prize Complex." *Psychoanalytic Review* 59 (1972): 283–93.

———. "Symbiotic Psychosis and the Need for Fame." *Psychoanalytic Review* 61 (1974): 517–34.

Spivey, Ted R. "Walker Percy and the Archetypes." *The Art of Walker Percy.* Ed. Panthea Reid Broughton. Baton Rouge: Louisiana State UP, 1979.

Sterba, Richard. "Psychoanalysis and Music." *American Imago* 6 (1949): 96–111.

Stern, Karl. *The Flight from Woman.* London: Allen & Unwin, 1966.

Storr, Anthony. *Churchill's Black Dog, Kafka's Mice & Other Phenomena of the Human Mind.* New York: Grove P, 1988.

Sulloway, Frank J. *Freud, Biologist of the Mind.* New York: Basic Books, 1979.

Suttie, Ian D. *The Origins of Love and Hate.* New York: Julian P, 1952.

Swenson, David F., and Lillian Marvin Swenson. Trans. *Either/Or.* Garden City, NY: Doubleday, 1959.

Tartakoff, Helen H. "The Normal Personality in Our Culture and the Nobel Prize Complex." *Psychoanalysis—A General Psychology.* Ed. Rudolph M. Loewenstein. New York: International UP, 1966.

Tausk, Victor. "On the Origin of the 'Influencing Machine' in Schizophrenia." Trans. Dorian Feigenbaum. *The Psychoanalytic Quarterly* 2 (1933): 519–56.

"To Aristophanes and Back." *Time* 14 May 1956: 74.

Tolson, Jay. *Pilgrim in the Ruins.* New York: Simon and Schuster, 1992.

Trilling, Lionel. *Sincerity and Authenticity.* Cambridge: Harvard UP, 1972.

Vauthier, Simone. "Narrative Triangle and Triple Alliance: A Look at *The Moviegoer.*" *Les Américanistes: New French Criticism on Modern American Fiction.* Eds. Ira D. and Christiane Johnson. Port Washington, NY: Kennikat P, 1978.

———. "Narrative Triangulation in *The Last Gentleman,*" *The Art of Walker Percy.*

Vernon, John. *The Garden and the Map.* Urbana: U of Illinois P, 1973.

249

Works Cited

Warner, Marina. *Alone of All Her Sex*. New York: Knopf, 1976.

Washburn, Michael. *The Ego and the Dynamic Ground*. Albany: SU of New York P, 1988.

Webster's New World Dictionary. Cleveland: World, 1960.

Whitmont, Edward C. *The Symbolic Quest*. Princeton: Princeton UP, 1969.

Winnicott, D. W. "Mirror-Role of Mother and Family in Child Development." *Playing and Reality*. London: Tavistock P 1971.

Wolfenstein, Martha. "The Image of the Lost Parent." *The Psychoanalytic Study of the Child* 28 (1973): 433–56.

Wyatt-Brown, Bertram. *The House of Percy*. New York: Oxford UP, 1994.

Zolar. *The Encyclopedia of Ancient and Forbidden Knowledge*. New York: Popular L, 1970.

INDEX

Index

Index

Freud, Anna, 8
Freud, Sigmund, 24, 26, 27, 33, 113, 125, 126, 128, 141, 144, 186, 192, 232n1, 233n1; *Civilization and Its Discontents*, 237n7; "A Disturbance of Memory on the Acropolis," 171, 238n13; "Dostoevsky and Parricide," 114–15; *The Interpretation of Dreams*, 20, 30, 31, 47, 48, 113, 114, 115, 147, 165–66, 170–72, 187–88, 240n2; *The Psychopathology of Everyday Life*, 116
Friedrich, Paul, *The Meaning of Aphrodite*, 54, 61
Fromm, Erich, *The Greatness and Limitations of Freud's Thought*, 219, 233n2

Gardner, Erle Stanley, 44
Garma, Angel, 48
Gaylin, Willard, *Rediscovering Love*, 234n4
Gedo, John E., "Freud's Self-Analysis and His Scientific Ideas," 238n13
Genesis, The Book of, 17, 103
Graves, Robert, *The White Goddess*, 58, 232n12
Greenacre, Phyllis, 167
Greenberg, Harvey, *The Movies on Your Mind*, 30
Griffith, Robert, 231n1
Guntrip, Harry, *Personality Structure and Human Interaction*, 237n6

Hamlet, 78, 106, 125
Harding, M. Esther, *The "I" and the "Not-I,"* 170, 237n6
Harris, Gentry, 239n3

Harris, J. Rendel, *The Ascent of Olympus*, 66
Harrison, Irving B. "On Freud's View of the Infant-Mother Relationship and of the Oceanic Feeling—Some Subjective Influences," 170, 187, 238n14; "On the Maternal Origins of Awe," 167; "A Reconsideration of Freud's 'A Disturbance of Memory on the Acropolis' in Relation to Identity Disturbance," 173
Hegel, Georg W. F., 234n7
Heidegger, Martin, *Being and Time*, 5, 16, 232n1
Heilbrun, Gert, 48
Hillman, James, *Re-Visioning Psychology*, 4, 10
Hobbes, Thomas, 234n7
Housman, A. E., *A Shropshire Lad*, 44
Hume, David, 234n7
Hunt, Morton, *The Natural History of Love*, 197
Husserl, Edmund, 232n1, 234n7

Ibsen, Henrik, *A Doll's House*, 206

Jacoby, Mario, *The Longing for Paradise*, 18, 233n2, 236n17
James, E. O., *The Cult of the Mother Goddess*, 67
James, William, *The Varieties of Religious Experience*, 5, 6, 132, 153
Jaspers, Karl, 5
John, The Book of, 153
Johnson, Elizabeth, 241n8
Johnson, Timothy W., "Holiday," 38
Jones, "Bobby," 237n8

253

Index

Index

255

Index

Index

Spivey, Ted R., "Walker Percy and the Archetypes," 232n10

Sterba, Richard, "Psychoanalysis and Music," 67

Stern, Karl, *The Flight from Woman*, 21, 155, 197

Storr, Anthony, *Churchill's Black Dog, Kafka's Mice & Other Phenomena of the Human Mind*, 234n7

Sullivan, Annie, 153

Sulloway, Frank J., *Freud, Biologist of the Mind*, 233n7

Suttie, Ian D., *The Origins of Love and Hate*, 9, 54, 80, 229n4

Swenson, David F., and Lillian Marvin Swenson, 231n7, 240n4

Tagore, Rabindranath, 40

Taming of the Shrew, The, 107

Tartakoff, Helen H., "The Normal Personality in Our Culture and the Nobel Prize Complex," 198

Tausk, Victor, "On the Origin of the 'Influencing Machine' in Schizophrenia," 197, 239n2

"To Aristophanes and Back," 59

Tolson, Jay, *Pilgrim in the Ruins*, 7, 121, 161, 162, 168, 230n9, 231n5, 234n9, 236n2, 237n7, 238n12, 239n2

Toynbee, Arnold, *A Study of History*, 88, 122

Trilling, Lionel, *Sincerity and Authenticity*, 3–4

Van der Heide, Carel, 48

Vauthier, Simone, "Narrative Triangle and Triple Alliance: A Look at *The Moviegoer*," 227n1; "Narrative Triangulation in *The Last Gentleman*," 227n1

Venus, 61, 197, 240n3

Vernon, John, *The Garden and the Map*, 219, 241n6

War and Peace, 78, 88

Ward, George B., 161, 162, 170, 236n3

Warner, Marina, *Alone of All Her Sex*, 46

Washburn, Michael, *The Ego and the Dynamic Ground*, 81–111, 233n3, 234n9, 238n15

Webster's New World Dictionary, 58, 72

Whitmont, Edward C., *The Symbolic Quest*, 59–60

Winnicott, D. W., 40, 188; "Mirror-Role of Mother and Family in Child Development," 225

Wittgenstein, Ludwig, 234n7

Wolfe, Thomas, 37; *Look Homeward, Angel*, 38

Wolfenstein, Martha, "The Image of the Lost Parent," 44

Wyatt-Brown, Bertram, *The House of Percy*, 5

Yeats, William Butler, 122

Young, Stephen, 231n1

Zolar, *The Encyclopedia of Ancient and Forbidden Knowledge*, 175

257